TRANSFORMING CITIZENSHIPS

SEXUAL CULTURES

General Editors: José Esteban Muñoz and Ann Pellegrini

Times Square Red, Times Square Blue
Samuel R. Delany

*Private Affairs: Critical Ventures in
the Culture of Social Relations*
Phillip Brian Harper

In Your Face: 9 Sexual Studies
Mandy Merck

*Tropics of Desire: Interventions
from Queer Latino America*
José Quiroga

*Murdering Masculinities: Fantasies of Gender
and Violence in the American Crime Novel*
Greg Forter

*Our Monica, Ourselves: The Clinton
Affair and the National Interest*
Edited by Lauren Berlant and Lisa Duggan

Black Gay Man: Essays
Robert Reid Pharr

*Passing: Identity and Interpretation
in Sexuality, Race, and Religion*
Edited by María Carla Sánchez
and Linda Schlossberg

*The Explanation for Everything:
Essays on Sexual Subjectivity*
Paul Morrison

*The Queerest Art: Essays on
Lesbian and Gay Theater*
Edited by Alisa Solomon and Framji Minwalla

*Queer Globalizations: Citizenship
and the Afterlife of Colonialism*
Edited by Arnaldo Cruz Malavé
and Martin F. Manalansan IV

*Queer Latinidad: Identity
Practices, Discursive Spaces*
Juana María Rodríguez

*Love the Sin: Sexual Regulation and
the Limits of Religious Tolerance*
Janet R. Jakobsen and Ann Pellegrini

*Boricua Pop: Puerto Ricans and the
Latinization of American Culture*
Frances Négron-Muntaner

*Manning the Race: Reforming Black
Men in the Jim Crow Era*
Marlon Ross

*In a Queer Time and Place: Transgender
Bodies, Subcultural Lives*
Judith Halberstam

*Why I Hate Abercrombie and Fitch:
Essays on Race and Sexuality*
Dwight A. McBride

*God Hates Fags: The Rhetorics
of Religious Violence*
Michael Cobb

*Once You Go Black: Choice, Desire, and
the Black American Intellectual*
Robert Reid-Pharr

*The Latino Body: Crisis Identities in
American Literary and Cultural Memory*
Lázaro Lima

*Arranging Grief: Sacred Time and the
Body in Nineteenth-Century America*
Dana Luciano

*Cruising Utopia: The Then and
There of Queer Futurity*
José Esteban Muñoz

Another Country: Queer Anti-Urbanism
Scott Herring

*Extravagant Abjection: Blackness,
Power, and Sexuality in the African
American Literary Imagination*
Darieck Scott

Relocations: Queer Suburban Imaginaries
Karen Tongson

*Beyond the Nation: Diasporic Filipino
Literature and Queer Reading*
Martin Joseph Ponce

Single: Arguments for the Uncoupled
Michael Cobb

*Brown Boys and Rice Queens: Spellbinding
Performance in the Asias*
Eng-Beng Lim

*Transforming Citizenships: Transgender
Articulations of the Law*
Isaac West

Transforming Citizenships

Transgender Articulations of the Law

Isaac West

NEW YORK UNIVERSITY PRESS
New York and London

NEW YORK UNIVERSITY PRESS
New York and London
www.nyupress.org

References to Internet websites (URLs) were accurate at the time of writing.
Neither the author nor New York University Press is responsible for URLs that
may have expired or changed since the manuscript was prepared.

LIBRARY OF CONGRESS CATALOGING-IN-PUBLICATION DATA
West, Isaac.
Transforming citizenships : transgender articulations of the law / Isaac West.
pages cm
Includes bibliographical references and index.
ISBN 978-1-4798-3214-9 (hardback) — ISBN 978-1-4798-1892-1 (pbk)
1. Transgender people—Identity. 2. Transgender people—Civil rights. 3. Transgender
people—Political activity. 4. Transsexuals—Civil rights. 5. Transsexuals—Political activity. I.
Title.
HQ77.9.W47 2013
306.76'8—dc23

2013023684

New York University Press books are printed on acid-free paper,
and their binding materials are chosen for strength and durability.
We strive to use environmentally responsible suppliers and materials
to the greatest extent possible in publishing our books.

Manufactured in the United States of America

10 9 8 7 6 5 4 3 2 1

Also available as an ebook

For Jeff

Our lives and our bodies are made up of more than gender and identity, more than a theory that justifies our very existence, more than mere performance, more than the interesting remark that we expose how gender works. Our lives and our bodies are much more complicated, and much less glamorous, than all that. They are forged in details of everyday life. . . . Our lives and bodies are constituted in the mundane and the uneventful.
—Viviane Namaste, *Invisible Lives*

Everyday knowledge is the stuff we live our lives by, but it is not the foundation of great academies. Is this the problem with the great academies?
—Tom Nakayama and Fred Corey, "Nextext"

The vocabulary for articulating any reader's reparative motive toward a text or a culture has long been so sappy, aestheticizing, defensive, anti-intellectual, or reactionary that it's no wonder few critics are willing to describe their acquaintance with such motives. The prohibitive problem, however, has been in the limitations of present theoretical vocabularies rather than in the reparative motive itself. No less acute than a paranoid position, no less realistic, no less attached to a project of survival, and neither less nor more delusional or fantasmatic, the reparative reading position undertakes a different range of affects, ambitions, and risks. What we can best learn from such practices are, perhaps, the many ways selves and communities succeed in extracting sustenance from the objects of a culture—even of a culture whose avowed desire has often been not to sustain them.
—Eve Kosofsky Sedgwick, *Touching Feeling*

CONTENTS

ACKNOWLEDGMENTS

I find it odd when authors thank their partners at the end of their acknowledgements because they are the ones who must live through the writing of a book. In my case, this convention would read especially strangely since our lives are so intimately intertwined as partners and colleagues. Somehow, we have found a way to make it all work. Jeff Bennett's unyielding generosity, tireless work ethic, and unconditional compassion never ceases to amaze me. I count myself as one of the luckiest people in the world because I get to share both my personal and professional life with him, and I am better for it. Whether it is late night drinks on the deck decompressing after long days, sharing meals, enjoying conversations during long drives to visit our friends and families, or watching guilty pleasure television together, he fills my life with laughter and love. His willingness to read my writing at a moment's notice is only one of the ways in which I benefit from his presence in my life. Without his companionship and encouragement, I could not have completed this project. I consider it, at least the good parts, as much his as it is mine.

Second, my two closest friends, Sue Stanfield and Claire Sisco King, inspire me to be a better writer and human being. Sue has been in my life for more than half of it now, and I cannot count the number of times that her counsel has saved me from myself. In an odd twist of fate, we both landed in Iowa City, which means that she, too, had to endure the ups and downs associated with this book. Like Jeff, Sue read every word multiple times, even when it traded off with her own work. Her insightful feedback helped to reshape and clarify my arguments—although she won't agree, I am still her student, and I look forward to learning from her for many years to come. Claire is one of my most trusted confidants, and she always seems to call at just the right time to provide support and advice. I cannot possibly hope to live up to her example, as a scholar and a person, but I am going to keep trying anyway.

A number of mentors have nourished me with intellectual engagement, sage advice, and thoughtful critiques throughout the drafting of these arguments, none more than John Lucaites. John embraced this project from the start despite its distance from his own research at the time. John saw the potential in my arguments when I did not and steered me in the right direction on more than one occasion. Although it may not be obvious to all readers, I know that his influence can be found on every page. Phaedra Pezzullo's course on everyday life changed mine. She has an unparalleled ability to resituate my claims and sort out the stakes of a position. When I am lost in the weeds of my own thoughts, Phaedra helps me to remember that our work is valuable and necessary—her narration of the importance of my work gives me the courage to keep writing. Bob Ivie's perspectives on rhetorical criticism led me to revisit the importance of reparative readings as a strategy for approaching this project. Additionally, Bob's demand that we attend to discourses as a mode of bridging human divides is where I begin all of my work, and this book is no exception. Finally, I suspect John Sloop reviews my work more than I know. I am fortunate to have found such a reasonable and giving interlocutor. His humor and honesty are surpassed only by his charity and kindness.

My colleagues and students at the University of Iowa provided encouragement, support, and occasions for laughter, both in spite and because of it all. In the most unthreatening ways possible, Kembrew McLeod kept me honest when he checked in on the progress of my manuscript. Leslie Baxter, Leslie Schwalm, Ellen Lewin, John Peters, Tim Havens, and Dave Hingstman have been and continue to be sources of valuable advice about the writing of a book and navigating my way as a junior faculty member. Rachel McLaren, Rita Zajacz, Keli Steuber, Jiyeon Kang, Darrel Wanzer, Natalie Fixmer-Oraiz, Andy High, Mary High, and Naomi Greyser make being a junior faculty member fun, and I very much look forward to our futures together as co-workers and friends. As for my students, I honestly could not have written this book if Brook Irving were not the best teaching assistant ever. Her independence and intelligence removed the distractions of instruction from my life to give me the space to think and write, and I am eternally in her debt for it. Despite being one of my advisees, Michaela Frischherz exchanged ideas with me without hesitating to engage me as an equal or challenge my ideas. She also indexed the book at a time when I needed time the most. Conversations with Lisa Silvestri, Paul Johnson, Sarah Spring, Rebecca Robinson, Dana Gravesen, and Bryan Asbury also informed my thinking about issues large and small. The often invisible labor of my department's support staff, especially Troy Fitzpatrick, must be acknowledged as an essential part of our daily lives as writers and teachers.

My families have always supported me unconditionally, without reservation or judgment, although they have had ample reason to do otherwise. My parents and brother, along with his family now, have been a source of strength for me throughout my life, especially over the last few years. The following pages are a small repayment for the joy they have given me. I lucked out in the in-law department as well. They welcomed me into their lives right from the start. My kin of choice may be the best choice I have ever made. Cara Buckley, Suzanne Enck, Claire Sisco King, David and Leigh Moscowitz, Jeff Motter, Jaime Skerski, and Darrel Wanzer are simply the best friends in the world. Everyone should have a fairy godfather like Chuck Morris to champion their work. Chuck also brought Rob Asen, Dan Brouwer, Karma R. Chávez, and Sara MacKinnon into my life, and I look forward to celebrating this accomplishment with all of them. Last, but not least, Shane Grant, Bill and Pam Newberry, and the rest of my Atlanta family made the formative years of this project some of the best in my life.

The folks at NYU Press made my dream come true. Ciara McLaughlin took an interest in this project before I even knew what it would become, and she shepherded this book through its early stages. After Ciara's departure, Alicia Nadkarni saw the book through to its completion with equal care. The series editors, José Esteban Muñoz and Ann Pellegrini, and the manuscript reviewers' careful readings and generous suggestions made this a better book. Similarly, the copyeditors' attention to detail improved the prose. Eric Zinner's guidance, including the selection of the cover art, made the whole process a smooth one.

Because of the insane copyright regimes we subject ourselves to, I must acknowledge that Taylor and Francis graciously allowed me to reproduce the fruits of my own labor in this book. Previous iterations of the first and second chapters, respectively, can be found in "Debbie Mayne's Trans/scripts: Performative Repertoires in Law and Everyday Life," *Communication and Critical/Cultural Studies* 5 (2008): 245–63; and "PISSAR's Critically Queer and Disabled Politics," *Communication and Critical/Cultural Studies* 7 (2010): 156–75.

Finally, and again, no words can convey the immense gratitude I feel for Jeff's patience, comfort, and love. When I first met him in the summer of 2002, I knew we would be friends—that we continue to be the best of friends years later is more than I deserve. Above all else, I am grateful that he makes the quotidian oh-so-queer!

Introduction

Transgender Citizenships

In 2006, during my first summer in Atlanta, Georgia, sex-panicked residents in the gayborhood around Piedmont Park took it upon themselves to intensify their policing efforts and crack down on suspected criminal activities. At just under two hundred acres, Piedmont Park is a stunning green space in a pink haven in a blue city in the red South. The crown jewel of Midtown, it has long been a gathering place for any number of activities, including public sex. Undoubtedly, more than a few of Midtown's current residents have firsthand knowledge of this history even if they have conveniently forgotten their own participation in it.[1] Therefore, the communal outrage directed at those whom they had termed "transvestitutes" was not animated by surprise or shock as much as it was by naked financial self-interest and the judgment that sex work is somehow more threatening and shameful than the free exchange of pleasures. In addition, racial prejudices played no small part in these confrontations between the primarily white residents and the presumed non-residents who were often people of color.

Like so many gayborhoods around the United States, Midtown has experienced a renaissance if measured by the metrics of gentrification. The demolition of older properties to make way for the construction of pricey, high-density housing, restaurants, and other amenities associated with middle- to upper-class American life is often trumpeted as a successful revival of a supposedly once-dead urban core. The steady increase in property values and taxes, along with revised zoning laws, slowly and unevenly squeezed out many of Midtown's previous residents and lesbian, gay, bisexual, and transgender (LGBT)[2] businesses, including the iconic, twenty-four hour bar, Backstreet. As is so often the case with gentrification, race and class conflicts have complicated

Midtown's evolution, and they continue to generate anxiety and distrust, especially in and around Piedmont Park, where distressed property owners understand their financial investments as inversely related to perceived criminal activity.

As the summer turned to fall, the Midtown Ponce Security Alliance (MPSA), a community funded and staffed safety patrol, escalated its surveillance of those it deemed to be non-residents of the area to prod the Atlanta Police Department (APD) to take action. With increasing vigor, the MPSA singled out transgender sex workers as particularly troublesome inhabitants of the gayborhood, and the APD proceeded to arrest scores of people for sex work. A significant number of the arrestees self-identified or were identified as transgender, and many of the accused were people of color. After the first wave of arrests, Orrick Curry, a vice squad investigator, publicly stated his mission as the apprehension of "transgender individuals and the hustlers, the male prostitutes."[3] When trans and other community activists pressed the APD to justify their actions—that is, to explain the disproportionate arrest rate of trans people and the choice to use public resources to prosecute individuals as opposed to giving them the resources to transition out of sex work—Darlene Harris, the APD's LGBT liaison, denied any prejudice directed toward trans people: "We're actually targeting the crime itself. It doesn't mean that we are specifically targeting these people."[4] Even though the sting operation led to a dialogue between the APD and trans activists and allies, unsurprisingly, the call for social support and services went unanswered. All the while, the cooperation between the MPSA and the APD led to more arrests.

The community policing efforts went largely unnoticed to the broader public until the following summer when two events converged and redirected the spotlight onto the MPSA's attitudes and actions. First, the security personnel augmented their surveillance techniques with digital media while photographing and then videotaping persons suspected of participating in illegal activities. The MPSA then published these photographs on their website and passed them along to law enforcement, while also posting the videos on YouTube in an effort to shame the targets of their surveillance. Needless to say, the videos failed to deter these activities. If anything, for many viewers, the videos documented the vitriol and scorn that MPSA personnel directed at the camera's targets and further strengthened public opposition to the MPSA's tactics. Meanwhile, the circulation of the YouTube videos forced the APD's hand, leading to another round of sting operations and "the arrest of 32 people, all but one of whom were black."[5] Having achieved a short-term goal, the MPSA deleted the videos from YouTube after media investigations into their antagonizing activities raised considerable objections on the part of LGBT community leaders.

Around the same time, an incendiary newsletter attributed to Steve Gower, a self-identified gay man and vice president of the MPSA's Board of Directors, found its way into the local press.[6] Gower asserted that there was an escalation of violence associated with Sunday gatherings of LGBT youth in Piedmont Park—which would be understood as youth of color by residents of the area—claiming it to be "probably the most dangerous ongoing situation we have encountered so far."[7] Teens and young adults of color have long come together in this relatively safe space to be out in public without the surveillance of their families and neighbors, and violent incidents are the exception, not the rule. Gower recounted a few isolated acts of violence, over an indeterminate period of time, to justify a swift and firm response, and even went so far as to write, "The problem continues to escalate weekly and we fear that if some concrete solutions are not found, someone will be seriously injured or even killed." According to Gower, the troubles stemmed from large, disorderly crowds dancing in the park: "This is somehow tied in with a group that has been meeting there for several years—they are organized to some degree into groups known as 'houses,' and into something known as 'vogue dancing.'" Describing the groups as "apparently somewhere between a fraternity and a sub-culture of mostly African-American gay men and transgenders," Gower assured his readers that much could be learned from an iconic documentary: "We are told the movie 'Paris is Burning' would shed more light on them." (In response to these stunning statements, a *Queerty* blogger quipped, "You may want to go back a little and start with Roots."[8]) In what can be read as a preemptive qualifier to insulate himself from accusations of racism, Gower concluded, "We don't fully understand what this group is, but we do not think there is anything problematic about the group's intention or philosophy—and certainly nothing problematic about vogue dancing—but some bad elements are definitely coming into their midst." Although we might generously read this last statement as Gower's acknowledgment of the tenuous linkages between LGBT youth of color and random acts of violence, in its totality, the alarmist rhetoric of the rest of the report drowns out this differentiation.

Whatever Gower's intentions or motives, the combination of the YouTube videos and the newsletter triggered intense scrutiny of the MPSA's actions, including community-wide discussions about the affinities uniting LGBTs and the ethics of intracommunity scapegoating and violence. Of course, some Atlantans sided with the MPSA. Take, for example, two anonymous comments printed in *Southern Voice*, a local LGBT newspaper: "Whether you call them sex workers, transvestitutes, tranny ho's [*sic*] or just plain old hookers, they are breaking the law and making life all the harder for law abiding gay residents of Midtown";[9] and "Get out there with searchlights, cameras, and big dogs—and maybe shotguns too—to run off this vermin."[10] The us/them juxtaposition in these preceding statements initiates its own immanent logic of justified ridicule and brutality, pitting lawful citizens against transgender criminals. By and large, however, community leaders, at least in print and digital media, directed their horror at the MPSA. For instance, in a *Southern Voice* editorial, Laura Douglas-Brown took the MPSA to task for its historical ignorance and blatant racism when she wrote, "Vogue isn't new, house culture isn't new, and black gay people enjoying the amenities of Piedmont Park aren't new. What is new, and telling, is the MPSA's fearful reaction to what amounts to a large group of black gay people."[11] Others used this controversy as a teachable moment to argue for LGB support for transgender-inclusive anti-discrimination legislation, more and better forms of comprehensive social services, and overall acceptance of LGBT diversity.[12] I wish I could write a happier ending wherein these events led to some greater understanding between Midtown residents and the assumed to be non-resident trans people. Unfortunately, even with all of the negative press directed their way, the MPSA refused to engage their critics, and they continue to target trans people with vigor and pride. In fact, as I finished writing this book, two local news stations, with the full cooperation of the MPSA, aired sensationalistic reports purporting a spike in violence perpetrated on Midtown residents by transgender sex workers. While APD officials summarily dismissed the validity of the reports, the commander of the

APD's vice unit blamed overzealous vigilantes for the violence: "[T]he only violence I see is when citizens approach the prostitutes and are trying to challenge them. I don't see it [violence] any other way."[13] As heartening as the officer's comments may be in shifting the cause and blame of the violence to the MPSA, the subtle, yet telling, distinction between citizens and sex workers is instructive about how citizenship is imagined and who counts as a citizen. In this instance, suspected sex workers are not citizens even if they are harassed by one.

The opening anecdotes influenced the development of this book in a number of ways, some autobiographical, others theoretical. As a white, gay, middle-class man, who did not identify as transgender, I was ashamed of the MPSA's actions, but, sadly, not surprised. LGB repudiation and demonization of trans people is a regrettably common occurrence. Even so, rather than get caught up in divisive narratives, I wanted to write against this tendency in the hope of encouraging other futures. For me, the motivation is not so much contrition as it is a desire to start to understand LGBT community formations, to culti-vate points of identification within and outside of these communities, and thus to work against the tendency toward othering operative in many forms of LGBT identity politics. Rather than reinforcing the dif-ferences between these subject positions, I would prefer to emphasize those moments when individuals and groups offer a different model of identification, one premised on the logics of "not not me." Accordingly, others are not figured as threats to one's sense of self, but as implicated in one's sense of self, and as humans worthy of acceptance, compassion, and justice.[14] At the same time, given its general omission from discus-sions of LGBT politics, I wanted to privilege transgender activism as the basis for this inquiry. Throughout the coverage of the controver-sies in Piedmont Park, I noticed a distinct lack of voices from trans communities as trans people were treated as objects of the law instead of as equal citizens worthy of being addressed as such. Even sympa-thetic coverage approached the situations from the vantage point of what LGBs could or should do for trans people. This realization set me down a path guided by another possibility—one committed to theoriz-ing community and politics from the perspective of trans people. This need not be an essentialist endeavor if we take contingency and context as operative qualifiers for political action and our judgments of these actions. Therefore, I wanted to investigate further how legal discourses participate in the figuration of citizens, publics, and politics, the uniting characteristics and boundaries of LGBT communities, the anxieties associated with sharing spaces with strangers, and transgender and queer world-making responses to these problematics.

These aims involve raising a number of questions. What are the stakes in understanding trans people as legal subjects imbued with agencies beyond those associated with criminality? How is the law performatively reproduced and undone in everyday life? Are transgender demands for equality and recognition as citizens incompatible with the queering of public cultures? What obligations do strangers owe each other, and how do legal discourses allow for multiple configurations of these relations? How do transgender embodiments of citizenship negotiate the logics of visibility and to what ends? What forms of affiliation are available when sexuality is not the unifying basis for political action? And, finally, what forms of coalitional politics are available to us when transgender identities and practices are treated as a resource, not as a hindrance, for negotiating the limits of identification?

Guided by such questions, *Transforming Citizenships* takes as its purpose the exploration of citizenship, broadly conceived in this work to be the communicative negotiation of the actual or perceived rights, obligations, and privileges among members of a collective. Focusing on persons who self-identify as, or can be understood to be transgender, the book's goal involves mapping the complex and productive intersections of bodies, genders, sexualities, and politics. In contrast to theorizing citizenship as a state-centered form of recognition (e.g., in terms of the rights and privileges afforded to someone through statutory means), a discursive approach to citizenship proposes and answers a different question, formulated succinctly by Robert Asen: "[H]ow do people enact citizenship?" "Reorienting our framework from a question of *what*" citizenship is and is not "to a question of *how*" citizenship is communicatively practiced, Asen suggests, "usefully redirects our attention from acts to action," thus enabling us to "recognize citizenship as a process" and not just a legal status.[15] Approaching citizenship from this discursive perspective is not to deny its material manifestations. To the contrary, attending to discursive practices of citizenship requires not only consideration of material communicative acts, including speech, writing, and other modalities of moving through time and space with others, but also attention to the ways in which these actions recursively reconfigure the "effectivities" of materiality as dynamic pieces of the discursive whole.[16] Without question, official forms of citizenship such as the right to vote or work legally are conferred onto certain bodies and not others, but categories of state recognition are not materialized in a self-executing manner; instead, they are articulated unities generated by a practice of citationality that may appear to be extradiscursive when in fact they are materialized in and through their rhetorical recirculation and rehearsal of previous iterations of these symbols and signs.

At this point, the use of *articulation* in the subtitle indicates a specific investment in an ongoing conversation about the practice and politics of meaning-making. While this book is much more than just the exposition of one single concept, and while articulation operates more implicitly than explicitly as an orienting perspective throughout, it is worth examining the concept briefly.[17] As defined by Stuart Hall, articulation involves both its usual reference to the medium enabling the communication of messages (e.g., to articulate an argument through written or spoken prose) and its more specialized reference to the process and product of linking together distinct discursive elements to create meaning. The crucial point in this seemingly simple theory of meaning-making, according to Hall, is that an articulation is "the form of the connection that *can* make a unity of two different elements, under certain conditions," and that this linkage is not "necessary, determined, absolute and essential for all time."[18] Articulation, so goes the common refrain, underscores that there are "no necessary relations" between any two discursive fragments—a situation that gives us the opportunity to continually contest our rhetorical relations with objects, ideas, and each other.[19]

In the context of this book, this means that when a trans person lays claim to citizenship and demands to be treated equally, say as a citizen guaranteed equal protection under the Fourteenth Amendment, the fusing together of a trans identification and a constitutional principle into a temporary unity can be a useful articulation in a given context. Whether or not this articulation would withstand judicial scrutiny as a faithful recitation of the law may not be as important as the potential leverage gained by this unity of distinct elements in response to someone who would otherwise deny its value as a truth claim. Once articulated in unexpected or novel ways, these dynamic pieces in the networks of larger discursive formations transform the meaning of the elements themselves. Thus, in contrast to those who envision the symbolic field as one structurally determined in advance, for Hall, the logics of articulation allow us to understand how "an ideology empowers people, enabling them to begin to make some sense or intelligibility of their historical situation, without reducing those forms of intelligibility to their socio-economic or class location or social position."[20] A more agentic version of semiotics, articulation is meaning-making without guarantees with regard to intention, reception, and recirculation of the momentary unities created by any particular articulation. For our purposes, attending to citizenship practices as articulations enables us to read demands for equality and freedom as claims for recognition that are much more complex than any unreflecting adoptions of assimilationist attitudes. If there are no necessary relations involved in, before, or after an articulation, we cannot make any judgments about their normative force without the proper contextualization of these claims. A demand for trans equality can reverberate throughout the discursive field, altering not only the meaning of equality, but also the elements involved in the articulation itself (e.g., the meanings of sex, gender, sexuality, bodies, public propriety, fairness, etc.). Consequently, the critical predisposition to dismiss the exercise of citizenship as necessarily normative needs to be revisited.

Admittedly, we cannot fully chart out all of the possible articulations available for transgender claims to citizenship. This mapping would be an impossible task if we accept the proposition that citizenship is performatively reproduced from innumerable points in contingent situations by individuals with unique motivations and understandings of what being and acting like a citizen means. From the outset, then, this book adopts a number of constraints, including a focus on the United States and the selection of certain topics over others, and therefore does not develop a universalizable thesis about transgender citizenship.[21] Instead, it is concerned with contextualized investigations of specific acts, advocacy campaigns, and deliberations about the inclusion of transgender individuals as equal members of polities, while also pursuing the related goal of complicating and troubling the concept of citizenship itself. The choice to operate from the particular is an act of critical humility intended to avoid presumptive pieties associated with dogmatic renderings of the inescapability of normalizing pressures of genders, sexualities, and citizenships, those unfortunate coin of the realm in many corners of queer studies, which relies on a guaranteed set of relations inimical to the perspective of articulation.

At the same time, I also approach these citizenship practices with an eye toward interrogating the prevailing cultural assumptions associated with trans people. In contradistinction to pathologized and medicalized depictions of trans people, wherein they are robbed of agency and presumed to be less than equal citizens in a community, I take a more affirming perspective, emphasizing how trans people make their way through the world and live meaningful lives. To explore trans people and trans lives as valuable in and of themselves, not as a means to another theoretical end, it is important to avoid treating them as an exceptional case to shore up the boundaries of other categories of identity and action.[22] Vivian Namaste's indictment of the academic tendency to introduce trans individuals as a "mere tropological figure" or "a textual and rhetorical device that points to the crisis of category and the category of crisis" serves as a useful warning about the limits and politics of extrapolation.[23] Before pursuing these lines of inquiry, however, I want to examine the genealogies of *transgender* and *citizenship*, the central terms of this study, and expose some of their productive (dis) junctures.

Trans-

Although all identity categories are contingent and protean, as well as intersectionally informed by other identity markers and riven with contradictions, few are as slippery as transgender.[24] Both transgender and the increasingly popular shorthand *trans*, commonly referred to as umbrella terms marking resistance to the assumed stability of sex, gender, and sexuality generated by "compulsory heterosexuality," evade easy or succinct definition.[25] One of the inherent problems associated with defining transgender is that in naming it we risk assigning a normative telos to an identity category that is often employed to oppose this modernist, binary logic.[26] Transgender encompasses such a wide variety of practices and identities that its center of gravity is not a stable referent. Instead, it may be more accurately thought of as a constellation of practices and identities variably implicated in sexual and gender normativities. If we radically defer any ontological and/or epistemic closure on the term, all the while remaining aware of the exclusions engendered by the imposition of definitional boundaries, transgender serves a provisional purpose, open to contestation and revision. As should be clear, this does not mean transgender is an empty signifier. Rather, transgender, at least when I use the term, is always already an unstable identity marker that defines related yet disparate, if not infinitely variable, gender projects. As with all identities, transgender is not fixed, but invokes instead a "necessary error of identity" to mark commonalities and sites of affinity among individuals even as those laboring under this sign experience themselves and the worlds they inhabit in unique ways.[27]

Susan Stryker's definition of transgender best captures the performative, or non-essential, nature of identity that I advance here. For Stryker, transgender refers to

> people who move away from the gender they were assigned at birth, people who cross over (*trans-*) the boundaries constructed by their culture to define and contain that gender. Some people move away from their birth-assigned gender because they feel strongly that they properly belong to another gender in which it would be better for them to live; others want to strike out toward some new location, some space not yet clearly defined or concretely occupied; still others simply feel the need to get away from the conventional expectations bound up with gender that was [*sic*] initially put upon them. In any case, it is *the movement across a socially imposed boundary away from an unchosen starting place*—rather than any particular destination or mode of transition—that best characterizes the concept of "transgender."[28]

Thus, as opposed to medical and/or psychological diagnosis, Stryker's conception of transgender emphasizes self-identification, the malleability and mobility of gender identifications, and the agentic navigation of discursive networks. Consequently, transgender subjectivities are constrained and enabled by the cultural normativities they operate within and against, and thus, in Gayle Salamon's words, laying claim to trans, like any identity, is "something akin to an act, but also as something that is not reducible to a question of choice."[29] Employed here as an imprecise yet necessary marker, transgender is an abstract term given meaning through a set of more concrete practices.

Transgender is a relatively new identity category, even though the subjectivities and gender-variant practices articulated by and through this sign may be recognizable throughout human history. While gene-alogies of the category trace its roots to a number of sources and loca-tions, all share a common history as a vernacular discourse developed by and in gender-variant subcultures.[30] In the most comprehensive conceptual history of transgender identity, David Valentine locates the first widespread usage of this term by activists and advocates in the early 1990s as a way to capture various forms of gender variance in one expression. More than just another identity politic carving out its own distinct space from other sexual and gender minorities, transgen-der equipped individuals with a vocabulary to "[wrest] control over the meanings and definitions of gender variance from medical and men-tal health professionals to replace an assumption of individual pathol-ogy with a series of claims about citizenship, self-determination, and freedom from violence and discrimination."[31] For some, transgender provided a discursive space completely divorced from the meaning of transsexual.[32] For others, transsexuality was included within the pur-view of this neologism. As a result, even from its earliest uses, trans-gender was a contested, politicized, and agential term that many found useful in forging coalitional politics between and among gender-variant and gender-nonconforming individuals.[33] In the absence of any stable ground for its meaning, transgender might be thought of as a linguistic placeholder giving an individual a foothold within the discursive cir-cuitries of subjective recognition. In Jack Halberstam's words, "trans-gender may indeed be considered a term of relationality; it describes not simply an identity but a relation between people, within a com-munity, or within intimate bonds."[34] What I want to stress here, above all else, is the ways in which the fluidity of transgender affords gender-variant individuals a potentially productive articulation of identity.[35]

Transgender is not synonymous with transsexual, although some-one who self-identifies as transsexual may also use transgender as a way to describe his or her identity. Unlike transgender, which developed in vernacular discourses in the last two decades of the twentieth century, transsexual has a medicalized past. Coined by medical and psychological professionals to describe those individuals who expressed desires to hormonally and/or surgically alter the physical markers of their sex, the term *transsexual* first appeared in the middle of the twentieth century in the work of David Cauldwell and Harry Benjamin.[36] Of course, the conception of this medical and psychological category did not inaugurate these subjectivities. Cauldwell and Benjamin crafted the category in response to the narratives provided by patients who desired varying forms of bodily modification. Whether in response to medical and psychological expectations or because it was the best available metaphor for such an intimate feeling, or maybe on account of both, many transsexuals started to use phrases such as "trapped in the wrong body" to describe their sense of self. As the media and interested individuals latched onto the "wrong body" metaphor, many interpreted transsexuality as a border crossing from one sex to the other. Again, transsexuals themselves may not have always understood themselves or their genders and bodies in this manner, but hegemonic sexual and gender codes encouraged and privileged such articulations to shore up the borders ruptured by those who refused identification with the sex assigned to them at birth.[37]

Over time, transsexuals increasingly challenged the necessary connection between transsexuality and surgical/hormonal intervention as well as the presumption that transsexuality trades in one stable sexual category for the other (e.g., male-to-female or female-to-male). Thus, in spite of the medicalized past of *transsexual*, today those who self-identify as a transsexual may not ever desire medical interventions of any kind, especially when the medical, emotional, and physical costs may outweigh the potential benefits of these procedures and regimens. The difference between transsexual and transgender is, then, not a normative/non-normative dichotomy; transsexual is not to transgender as gay or lesbian is to queer (the false choice presented by these dichotomies is a recurring theme throughout this book).[38] Instead, like transgender, transsexual is a contested term indexing a wide range of corporeal and gender practices.

However, the distinction between transsexual and transgender should not be understood to rely on a strict separation between sex and gender. In other words, transsexual does not simply refer to one's sexual identification, nor is transgender reducible only to gender performance. Sex and gender are not so easily parsed, even in the distinction between transsexual and transgender. If we return to Stryker's definition, notice that the word "sex" is never employed and that "gender" is used in places where we might expect "sex." This choice of terminology is not an accident as Stryker means to call attention to the slippages between sex and gender. The commonplace understanding of gender as the cultural construction of sexual difference has served an important pedagogical purpose in that it allows us to draw attention to the fallacies of gender essentialism. At the same time, one of the unintended consequences of this framing of nature (sex) versus culture (gender) is that gender is relegated to the realm of epistemology while sex is incorrectly assigned an ontological stability. Thus, questioning the "truth" of sex is translated into the denial of materiality itself. But interrogating the ontological stability of sex does not negate the material existence of bodies. Matter that we label bodies and further classify into sexes does exist. Yet, we must recognize the ways in which both sex and gender are rhetorically materialized in and through their articulations. Sexual attributions and self-identifications, especially those reliant upon a binary scheme, are not simple reflections of a self-evident truth. Instead, as Judith Butler suggests, the "production of sex as the prediscursive ought to be understood as the effect of the apparatus of cultural construction designated by *gender*."[39] Butler continues, "gender is the discursive/cultural means by which 'sexed nature' or 'a natural sex' is produced and established as 'prediscursive,' prior to culture, a politically neutral surface *on which* culture acts." As a result, Butler concludes, "if the immutable characteristic of sex is contested, perhaps this construct called 'sex' is as culturally constructed as gender; indeed, perhaps it was always already gender, with the consequence that the distinction between sex and gender turns out to be no distinction at all."[40] In this move, Butler is not fully collapsing sex into gender. Rather, she is reminding us of the conceptual cloudiness of these terms and asking us to interrogate our investments in the stability of sexual categories. In effect, Butler's insight highlights how transsexual and transgender are not defined solely and respectively by sex or gender, but instead involve both at the same time and in unstable and unpredictable ways.

The very elasticity of transgender makes it difficult to compile reliable statistics about the number of self-identified trans people living in the United States. The National Center for Transgender Equality suggests one-quarter of 1 percent to 1 percent of Americans could be identified as transgender.[41] The Transgender Law and Policy Institute (TLPI) estimates a slightly higher percentage of the population could be considered transgender. Employing a medicalized definition in their literature, the TLPI claims that 2 to 5 percent of the American population "experiences some degree of gender dysphoria."[42] As these numbers demonstrate, trans people are not an insignificant minority. Placing the numbers in the context popular culture, there are about as many trans people as there are viewers of *The Daily Show* on any given night—and that is only if we think of trans as a persistent self-identification and not as temporary, contextualized experiences, arising when someone unintentionally troubles sexual and gender normativities.

Whatever the actual number may be, trans people are increasingly visible and vocal— so much so that one *New York Times* columnist predicted that 2010 would "be remembered as the year of the transsexual."[43] It might have been, but, I am not sure how we would measure the accuracy of this claim. Yet, in this second decade of the twenty-first century, the uptick in the public circulation of positive transgender representations provides some hope that we may be nearing such a watershed moment. More than just the subjects of exploitative documentaries and talk shows, trans people are more respectfully and affirmatively represented in popular culture. Whether these representations enable trans people to live their lives more openly or whether greater numbers of visible trans people generates increased media interest, trans people are less and less an invisible gender minority in public cultures.

Of course, visibility cannot command equality, safety, or acceptance. Trans people continue to face discrimination in the workplace, housing, and education. In a recent survey of trans people in California, which is notable for its urban centers and sizable trans populations, the Transgender Law Center found that transgender individuals are twice as likely to live below the poverty line despite being twice as likely to have undergraduate degrees as their cisgender counterparts. (Here and throughout, *cisgender* or *cissexual* "names the usually unstated assumption of nontransgender status contained in the words 'man' and 'woman.'")[44] Trans people are also harassed, threatened, and murdered at alarming rates. Some estimates place the murder rate of trans people in the United States at one homicide every fourteen days.[45] Shocking enough on its own, what makes this statistic all the more tragic is that the number of murders may be much higher as law enforcement officials underreport the murders of trans people.[46] In light of these facts, we must acknowledge how trans demands for recognition carry substantial risks.

As of this writing, approximately 40 percent of Americans live in cities, counties, and/or states with some form of legal protections against gender identity discrimination.[47] Rather than look at this glass as three-fifths empty, the expansion of these measures is relatively exponential: in 2002, only 13 percent of Americans resided in a jurisdiction with trans legal protections.[48] The rapid spread of antidiscrimination laws speaks to the political learning curve of trans advocates and evolving attitudes about trans people. Especially noteworthy are the vote totals at the local level when these measures are put to a vote. Of the 61 cities and towns incorporating trans people into their antidiscrimination regimes between 2002 and 2009, city officials registered 558 votes in favor of the measures, 64 votes against them, and 2 abstentions.[49] That the city commissioners in my hometown of Manhattan, Kansas, with a population of just over 50,000, recently recognized the need to protect its citizens from this form of discrimination speaks loudly about the progress made by transgender advocates even in locations that may seem otherwise hostile to them.

The scope of these ordinances and statutes, as well as the avenues of remedy, varies greatly.[50] Some states, such as Minnesota and Iowa, have enacted statutes allowing individuals who have experienced gender identity discrimination full and equal access to the state's anti-discrimination apparatuses. In contrast, most municipal protections afford only symbolic protection and voluntary mediation because the local law creates a protected class not recognized by or in state law. When the two conflict—that is, when the local law exceeds the scope of state-sanctioned protections—courts tend to defer to state law and nullify locally-based codes.[51] Because of this legal patchwork, it is difficult to discuss the status of trans people in any unified way. Thus, while we may discern a general trend toward legal recognition, we must be careful not to assume that the course of history runs only in an inclusive direction, especially since many of these protections are but a pen stroke away from invalidation. To return to my hometown, when the city commissioners included gender identity within the protective purview of the city's human rights ordinance, the decision ignited a citywide debate, and it became a central topic in an upcoming election. The transphobic candidates prevailed and removed gender identity from Manhattan's protected categories a mere two months after its passage.

In contexts where rights carry significant force, legal recognition and protection are only limited measures of citizenship, albeit incredibly consequential ones. Kylar Broadus, a trans attorney and activist, explains the importance of legal protection in the following manner: "Rights both empower transgender people to contest discrimination and allow us to envision ourselves, and to be seen by others, as fully human."[52] Self-described queer sex radical Patrick Califia Rice associates formal equality with the ability of trans people to freely move about and live in the world: "Transgendered people's ability to legally marry, retain custody of children, and even simply use the restrooms in the workplace and in venues like shops, parks, movie theaters, or stadiums is fraught with difficulty until we become full citizens in the eyes of the law."[53] Paisley Currah, Richard Juang, and Shannon Minter, three of the leading trans legal theorists, similarly situate rights assertion as "a familiar, and thus quietly powerful, lexicon through which to challenge injustice," especially when "violence and exclusion are clearly targeted at particular *kinds* of persons."[54] At the same time, Currah, Juang, and Minter concede the limited effectivities of legal protection. Noting the need for transforming cultural perceptions about trans people and for their official inclusion in legal regimes, they conclude that "the success of rights-based arguments depends on creating a culture in which trans people are not just a curiosity or a perversion of nature."[55] Consequently, the realm of the political must be expanded to include more than just campaigns designed to gain formal equality. Citizenship cannot be guaranteed through the printed or spoken word. Rather, as Stryker succinctly states, the struggle for and about citizenship is one that includes not only politics as it is traditionally defined (efforts such as lobbying, litigation, voting, and protesting), but also cultural contestations over "the very configurations of body, sense of self, practices of desire, modes of comportment, and forms of social relationships that qualify one in the first place as a fit subject for citizenship."[56] To fully understand these articulations of citizenship, we have to focus our attention on political spaces within and beyond the familiar confines of the properly legal. We also need a richer theory of subject formation and rights assertion to avoid equating the demand to be recognized as a citizen with an uncritical adoption of norms.

Citizenships, Queer and Otherwise

Citizenship, when calibrated textually by reading statutes and case law, is reduced to the rights and privileges afforded to citizens. This narrowly tailored reading practice aligns citizenship with explicitly codified recognition by the state and, often in the case of queer theorists interested in the possibilities of queer citizenships, the adoption of homo- and heteronormativities. The corresponding equivocation of legal recognition with normativities relies on an instrumentalist understanding of discourse and an assumption that language has a plain and clear, if not true, meaning. It also labors under the notion that citizens faithfully adopt and follow the state's mandates when they act as citizens. Consequently, this framework obscures the ways in which citizenship is actually practiced and lived in our movements through space and time.

Academic critique that is limited to official state texts, including legislative debates, statutes, and court opinions, embraces an impoverished sense of the rhetoricity of citizenship and its corresponding agencies. The preoccupation with official legal texts neutralizes the radical potential of rhetoric per se in its treatment of rhetoric either as an instrumentalist tool in a reformist legal project, guided by the principle that better or different legalese would result in more equitable distributions of justice, or, alternatively, as legal discourses that avail themselves only as ideologically determined discursive traps.[57] Either way, the evacuation of human agency in these scenarios fails to reflect the lived experiences of how people negotiate these limits and opportunities in everyday life. In the case of trans people, these approaches fail to provide useful cultural interventions for a number of reasons, not the least of which is that trans people engage "a complex or unacknowledged relationship to the state and civil society" beyond the moments

where officials define sex and gender.[58] Moreover, when this genre of
scholarship calls attention to trans people, it is often to make them logical foils for demonstrating legal inconsistencies created by definitions
of sex and/or gender. However well-intentioned this may be, Currah
reminds us that "merely pointing out the definitional chaos resulting
from attempts to define objective criteria for legal sex will not necessarily entail the collapse of the entire edifice of legal sex classification"
because "state policies can accommodate any number of logical contradictions."[59] Refusing incoherence as the sole provenance of the queer,
Janet Halley goes even further to posit that "definitional incoherence is
the very mechanism of material dominance."[60] Currah therefore advises
us that "it is not enough for transgender advocates merely to describe
these inconsistencies"; instead, advocates of trans self-determination
must engage the state's ability to assign and confine individuals to sexual categories as well as develop strategies to undermine the cultural
assumptions authorizing the government's regulation of sex.[61] As a
result, legal reform and litigation must be complemented with concur-
rent commitments to engaging one's fellow citizens about these matters;
if measured only in narrow legal terms, the importance of these over-
lapping enactments of citizenship will be overlooked.

In other words, the reading of a weak relationship between rhetoric
and legal discourses of citizenship—that is, one that restricts the law to
a state-based practice of meaning-making—should concern us insofar
as it fails to enrich our repertoire to resist the law's hegemonic enticements. Such readings of articulations of citizenship may assist us in
gaining a fuller understanding of how hegemonic institutions narrate
the law, but they do not help us to engage the ways in which forms of
legal recognition circulate within and among its citizenry. Here, legal
scholar Robert Cover's appeal to "stop circumscribing the *nomos*" and
instead "invite new worlds" is instructive.[62] We should engage in more
than negative critique given that discursive formations are a site of
judgment *and* invention.[63] The task for those of us interested in engaged
criticism is to move beyond the critique of official legal texts and instead
interrogate actually existing mobilizations of legal discourses in everyday life.

We might think of this project as cultural studies of the law, to use
Paul Kahn's terminology, or as legal cultural studies or cultural studies

without any modifier. I would prefer the last option because it does not hint at any separation between autonomous spheres of law and culture, but the proper name of this approach concerns me less than the habits of mind of these projects.[64] The perspectives associated with cultural studies afford us the freedom to interrogate the law as a lived set of imagined and actualized relationalities apart from their strict legality; this means that we need not concern ourselves first and foremost with proposing legal reforms. Unlike law and society research, which is a branch of legal studies interested in the mapping of empirically verifiable effects of the law, or the legal pragmatism found in a typical note in a law review, the injunction against a law-first perspective is valuable, according to Kahn, "not because [we are] satisfied with things as they are, but because [we want] to better understand who and what we are."[65] This critical posture is not a recusal from political commitments, nor need we be neutral or objective, for none of these reading positions is ever actually available to us. Instead, cultural studies, as an academic endeavor, marshal, "the intellectual resources available to gain a better understanding of the state of play of power as a balance in the field of forces constitutive of a particular context, believing that such knowledge will better enable people to change the context and hence the relations of power."[66] Although this approach is not a method or theory in the mode of social scientific research, cultural studies is also not a polemic restricted to rehashing leftist platitudes about social justice for this orientation would contravene the logics of articulation and radical contextualization. Cultural studies, Lawrence Grossberg argues, "investigates how people are empowered and disempowered by the particular structures and forces that organize their everyday lives in contradictory ways, and how their (everyday) lives are themselves articulated to and by the trajectories of economic, social, cultural, and political power"; cultural studies thus also pays particular attention to "the construction of the contexts of life as matrices of power, understanding that discursive practices are inextricably involved in the organization of relations of power."[67] To be clear, cultural studies does not entail a purely descriptive exercise; instead, we will be interested in contextualized discursive practices so that we can gain a firmer grasp of how cultural formations are made and unmade in and through their circulation, and in the process, refrain from presuming we know ahead of time how the law functions in everyday life.

This conceptualization of cultural studies directs us to shake off queer studies' predilection for paranoid readings wherein the specter of normativity haunts everything within its gaze and determines the value of any and all practices. The impulse is understandable when institutions and other cultural forms are often inhospitable to queer practices. Yet, as Eve Kosofsky Sedgwick opines, we are poorer for it, especially when sedimented knowledge production practices make "it less rather than more possible to unpack the local, contingent relations between any give piece of knowledge and its narrative/epistemological entailments for the seeker, knower, or teller."[68] In place of this critical determinism, Sedgwick proposes reparative readings as an alternative strategy for mining affective tactics not fully captured by recourse to judgments of normativity.[69] A reparative reading is not the trading in of unhappy endings for happier ones or wishing away the contamination of practices with complex power relations. Rather, this approach asks us to attend to cultural practices as implicated in complementary and conflicting flows of exercises of power, wherein the imposition of one true meaning of an action is refused for multiplicitous affective attachments. At this point we can further refine the goals of reparative readings by renouncing the disjunctive rhetorical form of either-or, to borrow Grossberg's terminology, for the embrace of the conjunctive rhetorical form "'yes (that is true), but so is . . . (and so is . . . and so is . . .),' a logic of 'yes and . . . and . . . and,' where each additional clause transforms the meanings and effects of all the previous ones."[70] In the process, we will be answering John Erni's challenge and endeavoring to "remap the ethico-political commitments of cultural studies" and queer studies "from within a 'rights imaginary'" to make each accountable to the other.[71]

Accordingly, one contribution of *Transforming Citizenships* is a critical attitude that focuses on law's materiality across and through a number of discursive practices while also offering suggestions about alternative world-making projects capable of resisting these norms. In the case of trans people, an exclusive focus on litigation does not provide an accurate picture of legal subjectivities. First, litigation is a costly endeavor few trans people can afford.[72] Second, due to judicial ignorance and statutory impediments, "litigation alone has proved to be a singularly unsuccessful route to winning basic civil rights protections for transgender people."[73] If we direct our attention solely to court decisions or legislation to understand trans legal subjectivities, we find, with only a few exceptions, an archive of failure. Thus, in the following chapters, I suggest that contextualized critiques of articulations of citizenship are necessary correctives for conceptualizing the law not as an external force acting on culture, but rather as an actually existing set of cultural effectivities, for while legal cultures undoubtedly depend on coercion and violence for their legitimacy, nevertheless, even with all of the resources available for its maintenance, the law's hegemony remains incomplete. As it overreaches, the imperial aspirations of the law leave it open to rupture, resistance, and rearticulation. Therefore, to get at the particular ways in which trans people negotiate citizenship, we will engage a wide range of textual sites including advocacy campaigns, city council meetings, coalitional politics of trans and disabled activists, and archival research to get past the one-dimensional flattening of subjectivity offered by scholarship based solely on official legal texts.

What this perspective offers us is a greater understanding of how seemingly legal categories such as citizen and its legal effectivities circulate in the articulations of interested parties. We move from the courtroom to the spaces of everyday life, allowing us the space to recognize the ways in which the everyday is "a domain of action as well as events, and of production as well as consumption," and therefore to gain an appreciation for how "law is reenacted and remade far from its well-recognized, well-marked official sites."[74] In this endeavor, Rosemary Coombe's approach to law and culture as an "ongoing and mutual rupturing—the undoing of one term by the other," serves our purposes for recognizing the productive instabilities of transgender articulations of the law.[75] Coombe's distinction directs our attention away from constitutive moments of communal compromise and toward the radical indeterminacy of legal language, institutions, and cultures, all of which open up the possibility for counterhegemonic articulations. In a manner similar to Coombe, John Louis Lucaites urges us to "look *between* rhetoric and 'the law' to discover the materialized practices of language-in-action which create conditions for the collective experience of power, legitimacy, and social change."[76] Therefore, in order to understand the disciplinary effectivities of legal ideologies and hegemonies, we must engage the law not only in its reified forms, but also as a cultural practice of managing stranger relationalities.

The law, especially in its everyday articulations, is primarily a way to manage stranger relationalities and balance the conflicting, if not competing, agendas of citizens in liberal democratic cultures. If, as Michael Warner suggests, we want to capture a more robust sense of publics as something more than either "*the* public" or a "concrete audience," we must reconceptualize publics as textually based collectivities dependent upon the interpretation, appropriation, and recirculation of their animating texts among strangers.[77] Advocates of smoking bans articulate a right to clean air, while opponents of these measures allude to liberty and freedom as guarantees of their right to smoke. Notions of property rights and contracts can mediate or incite disputes between neighbors about tree branches crossing a property line, obnoxious holiday displays, or restrictive covenants. Equality, in its liberal incarnation as the equality of opportunity or in its more democratic form as the equality of outcome, informs concepts of fairness that even three-year-olds quickly learn to manipulate to their own ends. Of course, all of these scenarios rely on appeals to legal ideals more and less faithful to the letter of the law—the Constitution does not explicitly outline a right to smoke or a right to clean air, but this does not negate the rhetorical force such appeals may have for the negotiation of everyday life in a world of strangers. As these examples demonstrate, publics "cannot be understood apart from the way they make stranger relationalities normative, reshaping the most intimate dimensions of subjectivity around co-membership with indefinite personas in a context of routine action."[78] That is, the law provides rhetorical resources and normative guides for interacting with others, whether interaction occurs in their actual presence or an imagined co-presence. At the same time, we should not overstate the determining force of these norms as they are contested and redefined as they are employed.

In the following chapter, "Performative Repertoires of Citizenship," we will further explore the need to move beyond official legal texts as a measure of legal agencies. Mayne, a male-to-female transsexual who repeatedly provoked her own arrest in Los Angeles in the 1950s, also occasions an opportunity to contextualize the instability of legal and cultural normativities. Inspired by Christine Jorgensen, the first transsexual celebrity in American culture who, according to Joanne Meyerowitz, "made sex change a household term" after her much-publicized return from Denmark in December 1952, Mayne refused to live a quiet and invisible existence.[79] After struggling for years to find a doctor who would take her seriously, Mayne came into contact with Harry Benjamin, one of the first researchers interested in trans medical and psychological issues. Mayne lived in Los Angeles and Benjamin in New York, and, as a result, Benjamin could act only as Mayne's advisor. Through extensive correspondence, Benjamin coached, counseled, and consoled Mayne as she searched for a doctor who would perform her sex-reassignment surgeries. Compassionate, yet also cautious, Benjamin often clashed with Mayne about her choices, including her association with a tabloid that promised to pay her medical bills in exchange for exclusive rights to her story as well as her defiant attitudes toward medical authorities who refused to respect her own sense of self. Frustrated by her inability to find anyone in the United States who would perform her surgeries, Mayne traveled to Mexico in 1955 for a set of medical procedures.

Shortly after her return to the United States, Mayne had her name and sex legally changed. Even with official state recognition of her identity, Mayne wanted to ensure that she would be able to frequent public places without harassment from the police. To force the issue, Mayne taunted and encouraged the police to arrest her as she entered and left bathrooms in Pershing Square, an area under surveillance by vice officers given the task of preventing gay cruising. Newspapers in the Los Angeles area covered the arrest and trial, and it wasn't long before a number of Mayne's acquaintances sent their clippings to Benjamin. Throughout this period, Mayne kept in close contact with Benjamin, denying, at least initially, any complicity in her own arrest—Mayne needed Benjamin to provide an affidavit for her trial, and he disapproved of Mayne's previous attempts at gaining media attention. A close reading of their correspondence, informed by James Scott's conceptualization of hidden and public transcripts, exemplifies how it was that a trans person navigated the complicated territories of medical and legal discourses to create agential articulatory pathways.

To address the aforementioned limited perspectives on legal subjectivity and agency, I offer up the concept "performative repertoires," a concept that also addresses the corporeality of resistance to the legal and medical disciplining of good citizens. Indebted to the work of Judith

Butler, especially her revision of interpellation as a generative, rather than determinative, moment of subjectivity, my treatment of Mayne's case returns us to the archetypal scene of interpellation: the hailing of an ideologically-determined subject by a police officer. In a reversal of roles, Mayne invited the threat of legal discipline to afford herself an opportunity to challenge dominant understandings of sex, gender, and sexuality. In this way, Mayne's actions help to explain how stranger relationalities are a series of articulations and subjective negotiations without any predictable outcome. In the end, Mayne's correspondence demonstrates how the law inaugurates resistant subjectivities capable of challenging its coherence and legitimacy. Legal agency, then, is not necessarily synonymous with official legal recognition—sometimes it emerges in opposition to the intentions of the state.

Although it begins with an examination of an individual and her resistance to legal normativities, the majority of the rest of this book is dedicated to collective politics, moving from local to state to national advocacy efforts to trace how trans advocates and their allies performatively produced citizen subjectivities. When the law is understood as a way to performatively manage stranger relationalities, we are better positioned to see the law less as an activity determined and enforced by the state and more as an everyday practice of making one's way in the world, sometimes to address urgent political needs. Danielle Allen offers a similar perspective on stranger relationality when she states that "political order is secured not only by institutions, but also by 'deep rules' that prescribe specific interactions among citizens."[80] Concerned about the lack of interracial trust and the general unwillingness to sacrifice for another's benefit that poisons American culture (for example, identity groups may see themselves as involved in zero-sum battles for position within cultural hierarchies), Allen locates the effectivities of these "deep rules" in everyday interactions (or in the absence of interaction) and concludes that "ordinary habits *are* the stuff of citizenship."[81] In effect, Allen provides a way out of an intractable framework of cultural division by reorienting us to see ourselves not as "one people," a move that suppresses difference, but instead as a "whole people," where difference is accepted as a generative resource for renewing our civic bonds to one another.[82] In her words, "an effort to make the people 'whole' might cultivate an aspiration to the coherence and integrity of a consolidated but complex, intricate, and differentiated body."[83] Allen elaborates further: "To be the people as 'whole,' citizens do not need to spend more time in the public sphere attending to politics than they presently do, but they must learn to see and hear what is political in the interactions they already have with fellow citizens."[84] The actions of trans people and their allies explored in this book provide valuable political and cultural lessons about the challenges associated with thinking of ourselves as whole instead of one.

Obviously, we cannot impose the perspective of wholeness onto individuals who do not express these motives. Nonetheless, I do want to suggest that the mode of reparative reading can help us understand how practices of citizenship can be productive sites for engaging others and queering public cultures. Upon first impressions, much of what we will explore appears to be outside of the expected range of queer practices due to their failure to resist or reject the state and its authority to regulate gender. In this regard, though, the failure may be located in our own biases more than in the actions of transgender advocates and allies. Even though resistance circulates prominently in queer studies as its preferred modality of agency, it is all too often figured as an oppositional occupation somewhere visibly outside of normativities, rather than as a dialectical negotiation within and between them; the result is a repudiation of the most basic of Foucaultian insights about the inescapability of power relations because it installs agency as a possibility if, and only if, one refuses all modes of recognition and legibility.[85] For, if we are always already legible as subjects due to our interimplication with power relations, there is no outside from which one can function as power's opposite, as its pure negative or refusal. Additionally, not all norms and normativities function in the same manner, and therefore not all oppositions to them are equally valuable to sustaining cultures amenable to tolerating or accepting non-normative practices and identities. Resistance thus requires further refinement as an analytic, not in the service of a more orthodox definition of queer, but rather to recognize resistance as a relational and contextual troubling of mythic norms in the employ of vital world-making practices in particular spaces and temporalities. Without this awareness of contingency, the anti-essentialist qualities of queerness are lost to a predetermined and fixed sense of radical anti-normativity incapable of accommodating anything other

than facially recognizable acts of being against something, most nota-
bly, *the* norm.

Another unfortunate consequence of this mode of theorizing queer
resistance as oppositional is how it prefigures a norm and its subsequent
hegemonic solidification into the normal as an isolated node of meaning rather than as part of a reticulated relay between and among norms.
From this perspective, the moment of queer judgment involves a comparison between an action and the norm to discern its incongruency
with the norm. The greater the gap between them, the more queer it is.
Intentionally or not, this approach attitudinally orients us toward the
noun and adjectival forms of queer, assigning fixed qualities to a person or action, rather than mobilizing queer as a verb and asking how
someone or something is queering the interdependent norms within
the normativities operative in a given situation. The singular attention
to a norm, rather than the norm's situation in a network of norms, as
Janet Jakobsen argues, "can be (misleadingly) appropriated as if resistance to normalization undid the question of normativity rather than
moved us into another normativity."[86] If culture cannot be queered in
the final instance, both because normativities are necessary conventions
of interpersonal relationships and resistance is dialectically enjoined to
the exercise of power, we need to be sensitive to the particular ways in
which resistance participates in both the undoing and doing of norms
and normativities. When we do this, Jakobsen concludes, we can appreciate how it is that "agency can be constituted not just from different
iterations of the norm and the ambivalence within the subject but also
from various norms played off against each other within the network,"
all while the network is recursively transformed as it is performatively
reproduced.[87]

When we refrain from immediately trying to position demands for
recognition within a framework of assimilation (the perspective of oneness), we start to hear how individuals may be making more robust
claims on the body politic. More often than not, these demands argue
for the acceptance and accommodation of difference, not its denial or
erasure. Thus, the expression of one's desire to be treated with dignity
and respect must not be equated with conformity or false consciousness. To the contrary, rights claims and demands for recognition, as
we have already established, are articulations that can performatively

produce subjective opportunities for challenging the pressures of oneness. Karen Zivi accurately describes these discursive formations as "a
performative politics" that is "neither perfectly subversive in its effects
nor an exact replication of existing regulatory norms." Such claims are
not perfectly mimetic and hence normalizing for they require "two
moves: invocation and critique."[88] Butler names this practice a "performative contradiction" to explain how individuals can articulate themselves into symbolic economies to expose the failures of the promises
of equality and freedom for all citizens. The demand for equality and
freedom, Butler contends, "starts to take what it asks for," because "to
make the demand on freedom is already to begin its exercise and then
to ask for its legitimation is to also announce the gap between its exercise and its realization and to put both into public discourse in a way so
that that gap is seen, so that that gap can mobilize."[89] The demand alone
cannot materialize its desired effect—it is, after all, an articulation available for multiple interpretations and effectivities. Yet, an articulation of
citizenship works within the performative contradiction's invocation of
already established norms and its linkage to its own constitutive exclusions to initiate a critique of the universality of freedom and equality.
Therefore, the outright dismissal of citizenship as inherently normative and normalizing must be resisted as a critical impulse and deferred
until the articulation is properly contextualized.

With this theoretical framework in play, we must be mindful of
the fact that the use of rhetorics of normalcy employed in citizenship
claims, as in "I'm a citizen just like you," does not carry the same connotations for all people in all situations. We can take this seemingly
simple phrase at face value and strip it of its nuance, but its complete
and complex articulation may be lost when we assume this claim is tied
to an intention of denying one's differences from others. Michael Cobb's
study of queer articulations of religious and national identities underscores this point in suggesting that "perhaps the 'normal' is the desire
for legibility, a desire for community, and a desire for another route into
social resistance and minority complaint that need not be so 'counter'
public in order to be innovative and queer." The publicity attached to
and enabled by articulations of normalcy and equality, Cobb concludes,
"does not always imply that one has uncritically submitted to, or is even
protected by, the state or even the church. Perhaps this decision is not

so much about ease as it is about protection, about insuring that one's life is still valuable enough not to destroy."[90] It is not always the case that invocations of citizenship rely on an either/or logic of assimilation or radical alterity—sometimes it is a rhetorical move of both/and involving the desire to be a citizen like everyone else even as an individual wants to preserve his or her difference and maintain a critical relationship with the norms authorizing inclusion into a community. Thus, Currah, Juang, and Minter invite us to consider this radical demand in relation to trans people:

> the radical dimensions of the transgender movement arise neither from simply claiming that trans people are "normal," which we certainly are, nor from claiming that we are "exceptional," which we also are, but from arguing that being transgender is eminently compatible with all else that comes with being human, the ordinary as well as the extraordinary.[91]

If we want to work toward cultures underwritten by wholeness, as opposed to oneness, we cannot make sweeping generalizations about the experience of citizenship. Instead, we must look to see how citizenship is a performatively produced set of stranger relationalities that may not be entirely faithful to the intentions of the state or cultural hegemonies. The performativity of citizenship entails a reiteration of discourses already operating in culture, discourses saturated with history and ripe with the potential for appropriation. As spaces of citizenship are performatively reproduced, individuals both do and undo citizenship. They do citizenship as they rely upon certain discursive expectations to gain recognition as subjects. At the same time, they also undo citizenship as subjects articulating unexpected elements into their demands for recognition. Likewise, subjects are constantly done and undone as they struggle to negotiate the contingent discourses working around and through them. It is in this dialectical negotiation that subjective agency is born, which leads us to the second intervention proposed by *Transforming Citizenship*'s more generous judgments about these contextualized performances of citizenship.

By focusing on transgender deployments of citizenship as performatively produced articulations of the law, we do not have to see mundane activities or demands for equality as merely the enactment of unreflective liberal subjectivities. Instead, we can start to see how individuals exercise agency in these interactions and make the worlds around them more inhabitable by queering public cultures. To this point, I have avoided defining *queer*, *queering*, and *queerness* for fear of assigning them essentialized meanings. I recognize, however, my use of these terms is the fulcrum on which disagreements over my readings may rest. In that spirit then, I wish to adopt Sedwick's rendering of queer as "the open mesh of possibilities, gaps, overlaps, dissonances and resonances, lapses and excesses of meaning when the constituent elements of anyone's gender, of anyone's sexuality aren't made (or *can't* be made) to signify monolithically."[92] For what follows, the key phrase is "open mesh" as we want to remain aware of dissident identities that may not always appear queer at first glance. To begin to draw out the implications of this understanding of queering public cultures, stranger relationalities, and the performativity of citizenship, we will return in another chapter, like Mayne herself, to one of the most, if not *the* most, quotidian practices of citizenship: using public bathrooms.

The actions of People in Search of Safe and Accessible Restrooms (PISSAR), a genderqueer and disability coalition committed to improved accommodations in campus bathrooms, give us a chance to elaborate on the possibilities of and obstacles to coalitional politics. In that context, the deep rules Allen alludes to, here contextualized as the fiercely enforced and defended logics of sex-segregated public bathrooms, were challenged by a short-lived coalition on the University of California–Santa Barbara campus. Precisely because of its banality, the use of public bathrooms might not seem like a crucial or serious act of citizenship. Yet, from a very young age, we learn the rules and etiquette of public bathroom usage and generally follow these unwritten codes without much thought. In this way, we learn to share a common space with others in an orderly and hygienic manner. There is, of course, no small amount of privilege in the taken-for-granted assumption that bathrooms are simply functional; on the contrary, the assumption does mask any number of accommodations made for certain bodies to the exclusion of others. Moreover, certain acts of citizenship are tied to one's ability to be in public places and the inability to find a suitable public bathroom can limit, if not prevent, the ability of trans people and people with disabilities to participate in even the most basic of public activities. As should be clear, public bathrooms and the practice and notions of citizenship enjoy a profound, not a trivial, relationship.

In the main, we approach place and space as sites where citizenship is practiced. When we treat place/space as an objective, material constraint, what is lost is a more complex understanding of how place/space, subjectivity, and agency interpenetrate one another. Contextualization is not just a macropolitical consideration, but also one that accounts for micropolitical exercises of power. We must attend more closely to the doing and undoing of place/space, identity, and agency when we discuss acts of citizenship if we want to understand how citizens experience the worlds they inhabit. In this instance, the legal language of accessibility, typically associated with accommodations for people with disabilities, provided PISSAR with a productive discursive site for thinking through the shared obstacles between seemingly disparate identity groups. Once they worked through a preliminary list of shared interests upon which to act and developed a checklist for inspecting the campus bathrooms, PISSAR set out on their patrols. In so doing, the sharing of space with others in public bathrooms enabled PISSAR members to understand better how they were made unsafe and not accounted for in these places. For many of the coalition's members, this sharing of space allowed them the opportunity to interrogate the gendered and able-bodied logics of public bathrooms and draw connections that may have gone otherwise unnoticed.

As PISSAR's activism evinces, public bathrooms can be more than a space of fear and shame; they can also be a generative space of politics. Thus, in the chapter on "PISSAR's Critically Queer and Disabled Politics," I demonstrate how these attitudes can energize political coalitions between strangers. By addressing the shame associated with their bodies and bathroom politics, PISSAR negotiated what I term a "spatially based consubstantially of shame" to mobilize their coalition. In so doing, PISSAR provides an insightful model of how we might theorize and practice critically queer politics outside of the logics of gay white male shame hindering a number of LGBT and queer political groups. To return to Allen's lexicon, PISSAR is an exemplar of the practice of citizenship based on wholeness, not oneness, for individual activists did not try to prioritize their own struggle over that of others in the group; instead, they chose to utilize their differences as a resource for making public bathrooms safer and more accessible for all. The perspective of wholeness, or emphasizing the need to accept others on their own terms without demanding fealty to a belief in essential similarities, informs the rest of this book with regard to the relationships between the regulatory force of norms and claims of citizenship.

If we refocus our attention on how individuals articulate themselves as part of the whole, as opposed to assuming they are making a claim to an essential sameness, we find a way out of stultifying debates about whether or not claims of equality and citizenship are necessarily assimilationist. All too often, scholarship concerned with LGBT and/or queer citizenship dismisses the transformative potential of individuals who articulate themselves as equal citizens. In general, these critics are so squarely focused on public campaigns for equality that they miss how equality is actually demanded and practiced by individuals in their daily lives. For example, Brenda Cossman claims that formal equality efforts find success only when "sexual citizens have been prepared to reconstitute themselves as privatized, depoliticized and de-eroticized subjects."[93] As a result, Cossman argues, LGBT enactments of citizenship adopt neoliberal attitudes by "recoding citizens as consumers, whose political participation is measured by their access to the market."[94] Steven Siedman similarly chastises gay movements for their participation in "gay purification" by distancing themselves from those who do not look and act "normal." Consequently, according to Siedman, "apart from aiming to normalize same sex preference and hence to legitimate the gay citizen, the gay movement has not challenged the meaning of civic inclusion."[95] Warner takes this argument one step further when he characterizes national gay and lesbian organizations as "instrument[s] for normalizing gay men and lesbians" in that they have "increasingly narrowed [their] scope to those issues of sexual orientation that have least to do with sex."[96] Even when Warner concedes the possibility that norms can be challenged by those who articulate themselves as equal citizens, he short-circuits any possibility of transformative politics when he declares "there is a will to naiveté in the implication that false consciousness cannot exist."[97] Following a similar logical path, Amy Brandzel rejects the possibility of queer citizenship due to its inherently normative location of identity and its constitutive exclusions: "A queer citizenry would refuse to participate in the prioritizing of one group or form of intimacy over another; it would refuse to participate in the

differentiation of people, groups, or individuals; it would refuse citizenship altogether."⁹⁸ David Eng concurs about the impossibilities of queer
liberalisms when they are "linked to a politics of good citizenship, the
conjugal marital couple, and the heteronormative family."⁹⁹ All of these
authors are correct in the sense that there are some LGBTs who employ
discourses of normalcy without any reflection on what that means and/
or they want to assimilate into the dominant norms of citizenship. At the
same time, it does not follow that *all* LGBTs necessarily align themselves
with assimilationist attitudes when they invoke their desire to be treated
as respected members of their communities.

Accordingly, the chapter on "INTRAAventions in the Heartland"
engages transgender activism to account for how it is that transgender advocates agitate for legal protections as citizens of states and cities
without necessarily aligning themselves with assimilationist attitudes.
Far away from the expected sites of trans activism such as San Francisco or New York City, a small but dedicated group of trans advocates
in Indiana have organized into a relatively effective advocacy group.
The Indiana Transgender Rights Advocacy Alliance (INTRAA) works
primarily for the adoption of measures intended to prevent discrimination based on one's gender identity or gender expression. Allied
with Indiana Equality (IE), a collective of sexual minority advocacy
groups, INTRAA members must negotiate the complexities of this alliance, including decisions about which goals to prioritize. For example,
although some members of IE strongly support the pursuit of civil
marriage equality, these goals may not be shared by INTRAA members who value the right not to be discriminated against at their job, in
renting or buying a home, or in public accommodations. As a result of
these differing priorities, INTRAA has developed specific strategies for
engaging local and state officials about the need for trans legal protections. To contextualize this discussion, I focus on the struggle to amend
the Human Rights Ordinance of Bloomington, Indiana, and consider
the public debate about the measure in order to demonstrate how non-
metropolitan trans advocates invoke and understand themselves vis-à-
vis the state. When they articulate themselves as ordinary citizens who
do ordinary things, this act need not be read as one in which they align
themselves with regimes of the normal. Instead, as suggested earlier, the
act can be seen as one of making the polity whole instead of one.

INTRAA's actions thus provide an opening for a discussion of the possibilities of queer liberalism, queering citizenship/queer citizenships, and queer politics more generally. As I have just outlined, a number of queer theorists question whether queer identities can survive their integration into the citizenry, and some argue that citizenship must be queered before LGBTs accept its seductive and subjective invitation. Although I am sympathetic to the spirit of this claim, at least in its desire to resist normalization as the only path to citizenship, this privileged position of legal critique must negotiate the reality that the call to reject citizenship until it has been queered is a political stand few, if any, can afford to take. If you recall the rates of discrimination and violence directed at trans people, you can understand that they cannot forego full and equal citizenship for some imagined queer future more accommodating to their identity. INTRAA's advocacy activities exemplify the need to engage the state and simultaneously critique the state's authority to control the definitions and privileges of sex and gender. This two-track strategy is a useful model for thinking about queering citizenship without discarding it.

The scene of coalitional politics transitions to the national stage in the next chapter, "GENDA Trouble," which considers how transgender advocates work in concert with LGB advocates in the area of protecting LGBT workers from unfair employment practices. These groups have long sought a federal legal remedy against employment discrimination, known in its current form as the Employment Non-Discrimination Act (ENDA). Dating back to Bella Abzug's introduction of a federal statute barring employment discrimination against gays and lesbians in 1974, numerous attempts have been made to incorporate LGBTs into employment protection regimes. After a glimmer of hope near the end of the Clinton presidency, ENDA did not enjoy a realistic chance of congressional passage until 2007, when Democrats regained the majorities in both houses of Congress. With champions such as Barney Frank and Tammy Baldwin willing to force Congress's hand, LGBT advocates increasingly devoted their efforts to lobbying for an ENDA that would be inclusive of gender identity. From the outset, all involved understood that President George W. Bush would likely veto the bill, but this did not deter them from pressing forward with the vote to place it on the national agenda in future elections. As a congressional vote loomed,

Frank unexpectedly withdrew his support for a gender identity–inclusive ENDA, asserting that the coupling of gender identity with sexual orientation would doom the bill's prospect. Unwilling to sacrifice what he saw as an opportunity to advance gay, lesbian, and bisexual rights, Frank instead proposed two votes on two separate bills, one without gender identity protections (ENDA) and one with gender identity protections (GENDA). The backlash from the vast majority of LGBT advocacy organizations provides the entry point for our inquiry into how GENDA instigated a revitalization of queer identity politics by forcing LGBTs to examine explicitly their shared interests and the importance of solidarity as a strategy for gaining full and equal citizenship for all LGBTs.

In response to Barney Frank's proposal, almost four hundred LGBT groups, from local to state to national organizations, banded together to form United ENDA and pledged to work against passage of ENDA if it excluded gender identity protections. United ENDA's form of queer identity politics models a productive strategy for harnessing differences as a resource for making the people whole, not one. The complicated and fractious histories of LGBT unity and discord underscore both the difficulties of and the possibilities for imagining communities in common cause. Instead of arguing for an essential sameness in their identities, transgender advocates and allies appealed to a common history of shared struggle and their shared sources of discrimination based on gender to unify them. The public disputes involving ENDA/GENDA illuminate a political trajectory that differs in form and content from many previous articulation of LGBT community and politics as it was grounded in gender, not sexuality. The coalescence around the importance of gender identity protections offers a site for dissecting how transgender advocates and allies can articulate their interests to and with LGBs apart from the logics of sexuality to create useful alliances in the future.

The concluding chapter, "In Defense of an Impure Transgender Politics," is prompted by a recent cover story from the *New Republic* that declared transgender rights to be the next great civil rights issue of our time. A close reading of the cover image and the accompanying story allows us to engage the limits of criticisms of left legalism, which track closely along the lines of queer critique guided by mythic standards of unachievable queerness. Left legalism is understood by its critics as a misguided, if not dangerous, form of politics due to its investment in already established modes of legal thought and practice. In many ways, queer critique relies on a similar pattern of argument, and we can use the texts in question to reach an alternative understanding of the ways in which the law is a more complex network of meaning-making than the simple repetition of hegemonic discourses. If we approach transgender advocacy as a form of impure politics—meaning that politics must always be understood as a tactical navigation of norms and normativities never free from the power relations that authorize them but also not subservient to them—we can imagine futures where different articulations of citizenship will emerge.

In total, these chapters address concepts connected to citizenship, including agency, recognition, and norms. When citizenship is viewed as performatively produced relationalities among families, friends, and strangers, legal recognition is transformed as it is practiced. Therefore, we need to revisit what it means to be recognized. By looking beyond official legal texts and the narratives preferred by the mass media, we can see that the normalized practices of citizenship are often only the public transcript. When we look beneath the public transcript, we find that trans people, as well as other legal subjects, do not necessarily embrace hegemonic subjectivities in their everyday lives. Citizenship, then, is a fluid and dynamic discursive resource available for rearticulation, and, upon closer examination, practices of citizenship may be more complex than complicity with or rejection of normativities.

1

Performative Repertoires of Citizenship

On November 14, 1955, Debbie Mayne, a male-to-female transsexual, started her lunch break with a walk through Los Angeles's Pershing Square, a popular cruising area for gay men.[1] Dressed in men's clothing, she entered the men's bathroom. After exiting the bathroom, Mayne walked across the square and approached G. H. Nelson, a vice officer described in one newspaper account as "an old acquaintance."[2] Mayne informed Nelson that she had undergone gender confirmation surgery and stated her intention to start dressing as a woman. Taking Mayne at her word, the vice officer arrested her for "masquerading as a man."[3] Less than a month later, on December 6, Mayne, dressed in women's clothing, returned to Pershing Square to use the women's bathroom. Upon her exit, Mayne searched out and found Nelson to ask him the following question: "Here I am. How do you like me as a female?" Nelson responded by arresting Mayne for "masquerading as a woman" and "outraging public decency."[4]

Wanting to simplify an already complex situation, the city prosecutor combined the charges and scheduled one hearing. At the hearing, Judge Ben Koenig ordered Mayne to undergo a series of examinations with a county jail physician to help him determine Mayne's sexual status. The physician's report recounted Mayne's medical history, but it stopped short of declaring Mayne a woman: "The examiner feels this defendant has made considerable strides in superficial transformation of secondary sex characteristics. However, surgery, electrolysis, hormones and apparel have not produced a woman but clearly an emasculated male."[5] After reading the physician's findings, along with affidavits from other medical experts, Koenig rendered his decision on February 14, 1956. In an opinion crafted without the use of any pronouns, Koenig sidestepped the issue of Mayne's legal sex, choosing instead to focus on whether or not Mayne "masquerade[d] as a member of the opposite sex for lewd purposes."[6] Failing to find any lewd intentions in Mayne's actions, Koenig acquitted her.[7]

If treated primarily as a jurisprudential matter, Mayne's trial is an interesting yet inconsequential anecdote. Mayne's demand for legal recognition was not the first of its kind in the United States or even in the Los Angeles area.[8] In fact, this was not even the first time Mayne demanded legal recognition as a woman. In mid- to late-November of 1955, Mayne requested and received a legal order to change her name and sex for the purposes of legal identification.[9] Widening the lens from the particular case to the larger legal landscape similarly fails to provide sufficient cause to examine Mayne's case. While reminding us of the harassment and violence trans people face, especially in public bathrooms, Mayne's acquittal did not radically transform the legal status of trans people. Judge Koenig's circumscribed reading of the facts of the case, limited to an interpretation of Mayne's motives and therefore avoiding thornier questions about how sex ought to be legally determined, prevented his decision from having any precedential value. Finally, it is impossible to identify the direct and lasting public effects of Mayne's actions. Therefore, at first glance, Mayne's arrest and trial, a narrative composed exclusively from press reports and court documents, seemingly offers little more than fragmentary evidence of the legal problems of one transsexual at a historically specific moment.

At this point we face the limits of legal critique informed solely by public texts such as judicial decisions or legislative debates about statutes. As John Lucaites contends, confining our attention to state-based discourses "seldom seriously engage[s] the political and ideological implications of the relationship between rhetoric and law for *life-in-society*."[10] Put another way, our histories of legal effectivities rely almost exclusively on "public transcripts," defined by James Scott as "the open interaction between subordinates and those who dominate."[11] Limiting ourselves to the optics of publicity and visibility, Scott suggests, impedes our ability to recognize "the immense political terrain that lies between quiescence and revolt and that, for better or worse, is the political environment of subject classes."[12] In order to gain a more accurate reading of the dynamic operations of power relations, we must seek out "hidden transcripts" or "discourse that takes place 'offstage,' beyond direct observation of powerholders" challenging contextually dependent configurations of cultural conventions.[13] Attention to hidden legal transcripts, the dialectical and "silent partner of a loud form of public resistance," illuminates the radical instability of legal language, institutions, and cultures and the corresponding opportunities for counterhegemonic articulations of legal subjectivities.[14]

In Mayne's case, archival materials present us with a public transcript of her ordeal via press reports and court documents. The public transcript, to varying degrees, flattens the complexity of the situation to a simple matter of a transsexual's arrest for using a public bathroom. However, textual traces allow us access to hidden transcripts that paint a different picture. The hidden transcript, including Mayne's correspondence with and between her friends and acquaintances, reveals a resistant rather than a passive subject, and one who actively sought out a confrontation with the law. Mayne's correspondence provides concrete evidence of the operation of agency in a world of legal constraints, an especially fertile site for reconsidering the capacious flows of discourse and action that may go unnoticed when we assume public actions reflect an implicit agreement with the cultural codes of legibility. Taking this dynamic relationship into account, I suggest that agency must be understood as a "performative repertoire," or as embodied practices enabled by and negotiated through the logics of subjective recognition.[15] When formulated in this manner, in a way similar to Dwight Conquergood's thinking on the subject, we can understand how performative repertoires allow "subordinate people [to] skirt patrols, elude supervisors, pilfer the privileged, and make end runs around occupying authorities."[16] The emphasis of performativity stresses these repertoires as embodied practices that have varying degrees of legibility. Accordingly, agency is not completely born anew in response to a rhetorical act and/or situation but is instead a psychic reservoir constantly and dialectically renewed against the accumulation of one's experiences.

Exploring agency in this way is relevant especially for those of us interested in what it means to articulate one's self as a citizen when legal recognition is not guaranteed or expected and where recognition might require more complex negotiations of one's identity than can be encompassed by critical vocabularies such as passing, assimilation, or homo-/

heteronormativity. Here, what Charles Morris terms an "archival queer" is a useful concept, defined as a critic who "utilize[s] the tools of rhetorical criticism and theory to enhance navigation of archives and produce rhetorical histories of archives that will warrant and arm our queer scholarship, pedagogy, and activism."[17] In this way, I mobilize Mayne's case as an example of one of the means by which trans people negotiate the material conditions that constrain *and* enable their living of meaningful lives. Mayne's public and hidden transcripts demonstrate the agentic navigation of trans people through the interpenetrating circuitries of medical, legal, and mass-mediated discourses. The resulting analysis challenges those who characterize (and chastise) trans people as passive subjects determined by forces beyond their control, and instead illustrates how their inventiveness allows them to manage their relationships as citizens with strangers. Hence, the law affords individuals agentic modalities that do not always start or end with recourse to the law as a final or determining arbiter.[18]

To these ends, the first section of this chapter outlines a Butlerian perspective on agency emphasizing the performativity of identity and performative repertoires as a way to mitigate concerns about the political and pedagogical effectivities of promoting quotidian practices of resistance. Upon laying this foundation, the second section returns to the scene of Mayne's arrest to contextualize Butler's rereading of connections among interpellation, recognition, identity, and agency. Implicating performativity and agency with public and hidden transcripts clarifies their symbiotic relationship. The third and fourth sections explore Mayne's public and hidden transcripts to flesh out the concept of "performative repertoires" as an agentic practice. Reading Mayne's letters provides clues about how Mayne negotiated the constraints of medical and legal discourses and leveraged them to her advantage. Finally, I summarize the importance of recognizing performative repertoires as valuable agentic resources to help citizens cope with and transform cultural conditions not of their own making. In the end, such a perspective allows us to better understand how legal discourses generate the conditions for unruly legal subjects, as well as reminding us that the most important site of legal change may not be in the courtroom, but in the practices of our everyday lives.

Contesting Agency

The study of everyday negotiation of citizen subjectivities with and against the law is often met with skepticism, if not outright hostility, especially when situated within discussions of agency and resistance.[19] Michael McCann and Tracey Marsh suggest that the idea that "citizens can think for themselves is hardly pathbreaking."[20] Their concern centers on "the claims of significance" made by resistance scholarship, as these claims tend to be "overdrawn, underdeveloped, and often unconvincing."[21] In their eyes, the valorization of individual and isolated actions risks "imped[ing] collective political action over time."[22] Jeffrey Rubin similarly claims that the celebration of everyday modes of resistance "risks uncritically equating forms of collective mobilization with linguistic, artistic, and ritual expression and placing considerable energy, on the part of both scholars and activists, in activities that do not foster far-reaching challenges to power."[23] The primary opposition to studies of resistance, therefore, relies on the resurrection of deterministic readings of ideology and hegemony as well as the perceived zero-sum trade-off between everyday forms of resistance and large-scale political mobilization.[24]

Over and against this anxiety, a Butlerian understanding of agency can reframe the political effectivities of the identity work performed by such negotiations. Butler's most important intervention is often reduced to gender performance and/or performativity; in the process, what is often lost is Butler's larger project of envisioning nonstate-centered forms of agency, agencies activated in and by the performativity of identity.[25] Butler never explicitly defines agency, yet we can glean an operational definition from the following passage:

> One might say that the purposes of power are not always the purposes of agency. To the extent that the latter diverges from the former, agency is the assumption of a purpose *unintended* by power, one that could not have been derived logically or historically, that operates in a relation of contingency and reversal to the power that makes it possible, to which it nevertheless belongs. This is, as it were, the ambivalent scene of agency, constrained by no teleological necessity.[26]

In a seemingly paradoxical vision of agency, Butler's Foucaultian parsing of agency from the aims of power nevertheless accepts the disciplinary formations of power relations as the constraining and enabling
conditions of agency. Mayne's actions allow for a fuller consideration
of the possibilities for agency presented by this paradox and provide a
potent rejoinder to those concerned about agency after the critique of
the sovereign subject.

As Butler has argued in numerous places, the reduction of her work
to ironic theatricality misses the point in that performativity is not a
radically new project since "a theory of the performative is already at
work" in the living of our everyday lives.[27] Butler's politics of the performative navigates Althusserian conceptions of interpellation and Aus-
tinian speech act theory, both of which are typically theorized through
public actions, to account for mundane enactments of subjectivity. In
an argument I develop more fully in this chapter, Butler's recuperation
of interpellation embraces the importance of intersubjective recognition, real or imagined, without conceding the complete capture of the
ideologically-infused hail. The hail, or the moment of recognition, then,
does not present subjects with a take-it-or-leave-it choice of recognition restricted in advance by the logics of dominant ideologies. Instead,
the hail unwittingly opens up subjective latitude to rearticulate prevailing logics as a tactical strategy for surviving otherwise uninhabitable
spaces. Thus, the politics of the performative is not oppositional in the
way that some would prefer but neither can it be characterized as res-
ignation to one's own domination. The reworking of interpellative discourses or "the unsettling of 'matter'" is more than simply a "politics of
textuality" when it is "understood as initiating new possibilities, new
ways for bodies to matter," which, in turn, is an especially salient point
for those whose understanding of their bodies and gender identities lies
outside of conventional legal and medical discourses.[28] The constant
motion of performativity calls attention to the malleability of discipline,
exposing it as a dynamic force rather than as a determinative foreclo-
sure of agency. In opposition to claims about the disabling collapse of
the material into discourse, performativity generates sufficient antagonisms to produce agency; discipline and domination are constantly
reworked, from innumerable points and often in the operation of hidden transcripts, and expose structures as unstable sets of discursive

formations in a perpetual state of undoing. This distinction is relevant to understanding the operation of law in everyday life especially if we want to avoid mistaking the public transcript for reality and obscuring the more complex, dialectical negotiation of dynamic discursive networks.

It may be the case that hidden transcripts embolden subjects to take public actions but we should not assign a necessary location or teleological destination to agency; put differently, the proper response to anxiety over the loss of a sovereign subject outside of discourse is not necessarily the requirement that agency take the form of publicity. To respond thus forecloses investigations into the resistant possibilities of our quotidian practices and effectively resituates rhetorical practice as being solely within the logics of influencing others, in a move that negates the complexities of our subjectivities beyond their public trafficking. Moreover, evaluating agency through public optics makes us blind to the ways in which agency is a constant, embodied process rather than an endpoint marked by the legibility of one's actions. Here we should attune ourselves to instances of subject-negotiation that easily evade public detection as a way to account for the performative repertoire of hidden transcripts. To elaborate a Butlerian sense of agency, I now turn to Mayne's arrest to demonstrate how she reworked her interpellation in an agentic manner.

Debbie Mayne's Legal Transcripts

In a very literal sense, Mayne's provocation of her own arrest allows us an opportunity to revisit Althusser's exemplary scene of interpellation and, following Butler, to revise the relationship between recognition and agency. In the Althusserian rendering of subjectivity, subjects are constituted by the hailing of one individual to another. His primary example involves a police officer yelling, "Hey, you!" with the hailed subject turning around to accept the ideologically infused hail. For Althusser, "ideology 'acts' or 'functions' in such a way that it 'recruits' subjects among the individuals (it recruits them all), or 'transforms' the individuals into subjects (it transforms them all)."[29] Willing to meet Althusser somewhere in the middle, Butler concedes that our subjectivities involve the recognition, real or imagined, of another individual.[30]

However, the hail is not an autonomous or singularly efficacious speech act, as Austin would have it, determined by the intention of the person offering the hail. Arguing against both Althusser and Austinian-inspired readings of speech-act theory, Butler rejects linguistic determinism on the grounds that "human speech rarely mimes that divine effect except in cases where the speech is backed by state power . . . and even then there does sometimes exist recourse to refute that power."[31] In other words, "the mark interpellation makes is not descriptive, but inaugurative," and therefore, *contra* Althusser, we are not predetermined by the ideological intentions of the hailer.[32]

Recasting the relationship between interpellation and subjectivity allows Butler to explain how a subject "constituted through the address of the Other becomes a subject capable of addressing others." Thus Butler postulates that we must accept the possibility that "the subject is neither a sovereign agent with a purely instrumental relation to language, nor a mere effect whose agency is pure complicity with prior operations of power."[33] Butler's redefinition of the process of interpellation, in her own words, "founds an alternative notion of agency and, ultimately, of responsibility, one that more fully acknowledges the way in which the subject is constituted in language, how what it creates is also what it derives from elsewhere."[34] Butler's critique of agency and sovereignty is derived from Foucault's understanding of power, operating not from one center but from any number of points and in the service of various ends. Power relations, then, are productive as opposed to purely constraining forces.[35] As Butler states, the productive nature of power inaugurates subjects that it never imagined, as well as "instabilities, the possibilities for rematerialization, opened up by this process that mark one domain in which the force of the regulatory law can be turned against itself to spawn rearticulations that call into question the hegemonic force of that very regulatory law."[36] In this way, Butler addresses her critics who "mistake the critique of sovereignty for the demolition of agency." For her, "agency begins where sovereignty wanes. The one who acts (who is not the same as the sovereign subject) acts precisely to the extent that he or she is constituted as an actor, and, hence, operating within a linguistic field of enabling constraints from the outset."[37] Rather than fear this reformulation of agency as the loss of agency, we should instead embrace it as a strategic critical resource in resisting the expansion and sedimentation of legal hegemonies.

Mayne did not wait for the law to find her. Rather, by seeking out a confrontation with the law, she pre-empted her inevitable interpellation as a sexual deviant and criminal. Of course, Mayne's interpellation of the law could not compel its own effectivity because she could not escape the spatio-temporal regimes of truth governing the regulation of sex and gender. Thus she risked her own desubjugation within these regimes of truth as well as invited the violence of legal technologies. In spite of these risks, we might ask, along with Butler, how actions like Mayne's instigate critical interventions and expose "the fragility and transformability of the epistemics of power"[38] In this way, we come to understand the working of the weaknesses of hegemonies not as a concession to our own domination but rather as valuable acts of cultural critique that "maximize the possibility for a livable life," and "minimize the possibility of unbearable life, or, indeed, social or literal death."[39]

I want to clarify that in assigning a motive to Mayne's actions, I do not mean to imply a sense of self-mastery or radical sovereignty: the Nietzschean and Foucaultian influences at work in this discursive theory of agency and performativity caution against such attributions. As Butler has pointed out, we must not conflate "the subject" with "the person" or "the individual"; instead, "the subject" should be seen as a "critical category" marking a "linguistic category, a placeholder, a structure in formation."[40] Subjectivity operates within a representational logic—it is not a claim to unmediated access to one's soul or essence. Thus, subjectivity is better thought of as a discursive practice of relationality and recognition, meaning that there is an "opacity of the subject" to one's self and others; we do not control our subjectivities when they traffic in symbols and signs that we only partially command.[41] That is, we can give an account of ourselves to others, but this articulation of our selves or moment of subjectivity is a negotiated space of contextualized meaning saturated with the diachronic and synchronic baggage particular to the articulation in question. Open to various interpretations and misunderstandings, even seemingly successful intersubjective recognitions involve excesses and remainders that prevent unmediated access to the self. In other words, our selves are implicated by the historicity of our experiences. Performative repertoires remain a constitutive part of us even though they are not always consciously available to us as a source of reflective judgment. Mayne's historicity informed without determining her unruly legal subjectivity. The psychic spaces of resistance found between Mayne the individual and Mayne's subjectivities generated alternative articulatory pathways in the circuitries of recognition and power. But the critical task here is not to play the role of the psychoanalyst to excavate an originary moment of agency. Instead, we must be willing to expand the concept of agency to account for subjective negotiations of ideologies and hegemonies while also recognizing that these articulatory moments often operate in two registers: public and hidden transcripts. By recasting interpellation as a generative antagonism, our public and hidden transcripts represent valuable agentic practices implicated in the historicity of our performative repertoires. Further investigation into Mayne's archive uncovers a productive operation of hidden and public transcripts as part of her performative repertoire.

Debbie Mayne's Medical Transcripts

In 1953, Mayne began her correspondence with Harry Benjamin, who was at that time one of the world's only medical experts on transsexuality. Benjamin's ardent advocacy for the liberalization of laws concerning sexuality led to his interest in transvestites and transsexuals, populations he saw as particularly vulnerable to the violence of medicine and law.[42] Benjamin's research involved the collection of hundreds of narratives from trans people with whom he developed and maintained extensive contact. This included Mayne and her acquaintances. In her letters to Benjamin, Mayne oftentimes presented a public transcript of deference while pursuing a hidden transcript of defiance and resistance. When Mayne or her acquaintances exposed the operation of a hidden transcript, she would try to reframe the situation to fit within the logics of the public transcript to maintain her relationship with Benjamin. Their exchanges provide insight into Mayne's performative repertoire and how she developed a legal consciousness against the law's aims and hence created agential pathways for herself.

In a letter to Benjamin dated December 10, 1955, Mayne initially denied that she provoked her own arrest while also neglecting to mention that she had been arrested not once but twice. She wrote:

> I have recently been arrested by the police on suspicion of masquerading as a female. I am out on bail. The press was so disgusted with the masquerade charge that they left it out of the papers entirely. The police want to make a test case out of this charge so that they will have something to go on in the future. So my trial will be a test case, that will effect others to come. . . . I was not reported by anyone for masquerading. It is the police. They want a trial test. I am registered with the employment office both in Sacramento and Los Angeles as a female.[43]

Mayne's selective recounting of the situation highlights the ways in which she utilized public and hidden transcripts to manage her relationship with Benjamin. Benjamin saw himself as "a maverick or an outsider" of the medical establishment in his rejection of psychoanalytic cures for transsexuals, opting instead to advocate for hormonal and surgical therapies.[44] At the same time, Benjamin approached the reform of the medico-legal treatment of transsexuals as an incremental project to be pursued within the porous boundaries of medicine and law. Therefore, Mayne quickly learned how to frame her actions in such a way that they conformed to Benjamin's politics, such as portraying herself as a victim of police harassment. This experience would assist Mayne later on in dealing with the law and the press coverage of her case.

In one of their earliest exchanges, two years before her first arrest, Mayne disclosed to Benjamin her collaboration with a local afternoon tabloid, the *Los Angeles Mirror*, wherein they would pay for her procedures and travel expenses to Holland in exchange for exclusive rights to her story.[45] Performing an act of deference to Benjamin's expertise, in a later letter Mayne asked for his advice on the matter:

> I am most interested in knowing what you think about my plans in connection with the magazine (not money) as to if you would be for or against this magazine handling my release after operations. What are your

opinions on this matter, this to me is important. I have not yet signed the contract. I consider you one of my docters whether you go along with this or not and I will not go against my docters if they should advise against the magazine, so far they have not, but what is the word from you Dr. Benjamin? On my part I feel that they are better qualified to handle such a case than any other magazine (but I do not always know best as you well know and I feel that I do need your advice in this matter). I find less prejudice in this group than any other group that I know of. And on the other hand I will not go against the advice of my doctorers, but what is that advice? . . . Perhaps this is another decision I must make for myself (I hope not) with help. If such be the case, may the good lord guide me in this decision and that I will not make another blunder. There would be so much at stake. You are my most precious contact you know.[46]

Benjamin urged Mayne to be cautious in her associations with the press. "Be patient [Debbie], save your money, wait till you hear from Dr. [F] whether he and his associates would consider to perform the surgery at a lower fee and if not, you will just have to try and save up enough money to be able to afford it later on."[47] Without responding to Benjamin's request, Mayne continued her association with the tabloid.

When it came to dealing with Mayne's doctors in Los Angeles, Benjamin similarly encouraged discrete acts of cooperation instead of confrontation. After being informed by one of Mayne's acquaintances that she "blew her cork all over the place"[48] at a doctor's appointment, Benjamin advised Mayne to comply with her doctor's wishes:

I think it isn't very wise and very diplomatic of you to antagonize Dr. [W]. You must try to keep your temper under control because that will facilitate the fulfillment of your wishes in the future. Do try hard to give the impression of a well-balanced sensible person who does not expect miracles and would be satisfied and happy with whatever science can offer under the present laws.

He continued:

Don't get discouraged even if the struggle seems hard and the handicaps great. If you behave sensibly and well-controlled I have the best hopes for the future. . . . All my good wishes to you [Debbie] and do be a sensible girl.[49]

As he often did, Benjamin politely but sternly advised Mayne to be pragmatic about the situation, imploring Mayne to create a compliant public transcript to accomplish her goals.

Mayne's response to Benjamin was persistent and unrelenting. Mayne justified her actions in the following way:

> Dr. [W] is only interested in making (what in his eyes) is a good homosexual out of me. . . . Dr. Benjamin, Dr. [W] is a homosexual and he was dead set against my operations right from the start, although I didn't know it at first. . . . I will never go back to Dr. [W]. This girl is going to keep on raising hell until I get my operations and I will always remember that you stuck by me Dr. Benjamin. I will be a lady if it kills me.[50]

Again, Mayne was undeterred by the lack of medical cooperation while also refusing Benjamin's advice to take the more pragmatic and passive approach of submitting to her doctor's wishes.[51] By shifting the focus to the personal motives of her doctor, Mayne reassured Benjamin that she would continue to pursue the proper medical channels for her surgeries. Mayne eventually found a doctor in Mexico who agreed to perform her sex-reassignment surgeries, which were done in March 1955.[52] Mayne made arrangements to pay for the surgery on an installment plan. As a result, Mayne skirted the legal restrictions of the United States while remaining within the disciplinary technologies of the medical community.

After recovering from her surgeries, Mayne pursued a legal name-change by filing papers at the Los Angeles City Courthouse. Although it is unclear whether or not Mayne contacted the media to publicize her case, newspapers and tabloids published multiple stories about her request for a name-change. Sending Benjamin a copy of the story from the *Los Angeles Examiner*, Mayne recounted the situation to him:

> Three newspapers have already interviewed me, including pictures in male clothing. The interviews were about 2 hours long each. I seem to have made a hit with them, but that remains to be seen. The pictures

are bust pictures. I have been interviewed by the Mirror, Examiner, and Times. They all acted like gentlemen. The interviews were all at different times, not all together. Of course I have kept in touch with the Mirror for the last three years, but the other two newspapers, the Examiner and Times were new to me. I do not know when the newspapers will release their stories on me. I won the battle for my surgery and now I am in a battle for my change of status that would permit me to dress and live as a woman legally, if won. I am beginning to feel as though I am an old battle ship. (Well, I just don't know. Nov 5th will tell).[53]

Using her experience with the *Mirror* as a guide, Mayne felt competent and confident in dealing with the press, which in turn boosted her spirits about the outcome of her court case. However, Mayne also understood that she could not control the press coverage and had to hope for the best. In response, Benjamin informed Mayne that he had already received two copies of the stories from separate contacts. He also wished her the best of luck: "Now since the publicity occurred, I hope it will work out to your advantage, but especially hope that the decision on November 5 will be favorable."[54] In the same letter, Benjamin enclosed copies of articles about transsexuality that he thought might be useful for her attorney in the upcoming hearing.

As the preceding representative examples demonstrate, Mayne faced a variety of constraints when interacting with Benjamin. Aware that she needed to appear legally and medically compliant to obtain Benjamin's assistance, Mayne was willing to be more defiant when she was less dependent on Benjamin's advice or connections. At the time of her arrest, Mayne desperately wanted Benjamin to submit an affidavit or testify on her behalf. She stated: "I have tasted the sweetness of freedom, I was sick and I have been treated by surgery and am cured. If I am forced to turn back I will die. Please write me a letter that I am not masquerading."[55] Mayne, in constructing a more palatable public transcript responsive to Benjamin's biases, went out of her way to clarify the fact that she had been a legally compliant subject to increase the chances that Benjamin would assist her defense with some form of medical testimony.

Two days later, before receiving a reply from Benjamin, Mayne wrote yet another letter to Benjamin to further clarify the details of the arrest.

The police mentioned a month ago, that they would like to make a trial case; but they would not come to me so I went to them and we have forced the court to make a decision, the date of the trial for this decision is 12-22-1955. The opposition contends that I have had an illegal operation and therefore should not be recognized as a woman because the operation was illegal and therefore I am illegal. The opposition maintains I am masquerading, and we claim that I am not. . . . I wish you were here. Your help is most urgently needed.[56]

Understanding the possibility that her involvement could be read as unnecessarily provoking the police, Mayne repositioned the arrest narrative to argue that she was simply fulfilling the wishes of the police.

Benjamin's response to the initial letter indicated that he had already received copies of the articles from someone in San Francisco—a fact that suggests that Mayne's case had at least regional circulation. This development no doubt concerned the pragmatic Benjamin, especially given that he had been warned in advance by a few of Mayne's acquaintances of her plans to make her case publicly known.[57] After classifying Mayne as a "psycho-neurotic, not fully responsible for her action," in one terse response to one of Mayne's acquaintances, Benjamin said: "Should [Debbie] ever send me the clipping or write to me, I shall not hesitate to tell her what I think about it. The natural feeling of inferiority of people like her tempts them very much to see themselves in print which not only flatters their vanity and raises their ego, but also gives them hope (rarely realized) of making some money."[58] After her initial arrest, the same informant wrote to Benjamin: "She has told the police that she is looking forward to being arrested again! Being an overt homo and prodding the law at arresting her may eventually discredit all of us who were helped and consequently the public may look upon us as the same kind of pervert she is. I hope they lock her up and throw away the key or better yet, a padded cell!"[59] Benjamin wrote in response: "I am grateful that you are keeping me posted and I am as disgusted as you are that [Debbie] should be unable to keep out of trouble. You know, however, that I always considered her as much psychotic as neurotic, and we can only hope that the authorities will see the situation in the proper light."[60] The harsh words aside, Benjamin's exchange demonstrate that he had his own public and hidden transcripts regarding his relationship with Mayne.

Failing to follow through in the manner he had promised to Mayne's acquaintances, Benjamin instead politely warned Mayne about the possible negative repercussions of the press coverage: "I am sorry [Debbie] that you have been unable to prevent publicity. I have found out that all such publicity in the end does more harm than good. The people who are in authority and on whom we have to depend, are being antagonized by all such newspaper articles." Subtlety injecting some doubt concerning the innocence of her actions, Benjamin continued: "Your arrest is particularly unfortunate. I can imagine you looking very well dressed as a girl and I cannot see that you should be conspicuous unless you make yourself so by your actions or by the place you choose to frequent. Again I can only express my regret that you were unable to prevent such a happening." In conclusion Benjamin advised patience and cooperation with the law to prevent any harm to herself and other trans people:

> Our present laws, however, may look at the situation differently (purely technical) and the police are there to enforce these laws. You must try to understand that. You want understanding from others. In fairness you must do the same and try to understand them. They think they are doing their duty. They do not know of transvestism etc. as much as you and I do. Prejudices are slow to change and it takes still more time for unrealistic and illogical laws to be changed. In the meantime, it is the best policy to avoid any friction with the law and be more diplomatic than rebellious.[61]

These exchanges illuminate an important point about the public and hidden transcripts Mayne and Benjamin performed for one another. Public transcripts are not enacted solely by the dominated. Rather, as Steve Pile suggests, "each is a lie to the other, and each gives the lie to the other."[62] Those in authority are often aware of the artifice of the public transcript, yet, for pragmatic or egotistical reasons, they participate in it even as they understand the complex dynamics at work in the interaction. Benjamin's comments undoubtedly prove he was suspicious of Mayne's actions and motives—at this point he had been given far too many indications of Mayne's hidden transcripts to act otherwise—yet he still worked within the parameters of their public transcript to avoid a complete rupture in their relationship. Through these interactions, they both learned how to navigate the discursive networks governing their relationship.

In response to Benjamin's letter, Mayne restated the personal and possibly widespread importance of her case: "My trial is taking on more importance with each passing day." She also disclosed to Benjamin that she had "referred 25 patients to Mexico City so far. They got my address through the newspapers." Thus, rather than shaming her, the publication of Mayne's arrest provided her with an opportunity to connect with other trans people. Seemingly aware of Benjamin's concerns that her actions could be interpreted as contrived publicity stunts threatening the efforts of those pursuing more discrete actions, Mayne ensured Benjamin that "the press remains silent." Mayne further informed Benjamin that she had distributed copies of his articles to the press: "Much good has been done as a result. The press is educated here and they have been good boys ever since." However, in the same letter, Mayne allowed Benjamin a peek into the motivations of the hidden transcript underwriting her public transcripts:

> The reason I went to the police was because I had been threatened by them the day before I made my dress transformation, that they would pick me up if I was seen dressed. I met the officer who had threatened me and I stopped him on the street to pay my respects and was taken in. I will not live in fear of being molested by the police and so therefore a trial test will decide. I will not run or hide. I will stay here at home and fight this to the very bitter end, if God is willing. This decision will effect every case in the Country. (May be a blessing in disguise) My attorney has contacted an outstanding criminal lawyer to assist us. Needless to say there is a lot at stake. We are asking for recognition.[63]

As this letter demonstrates, Mayne resisted the state's interpellative gestures, seeing herself instead as an innocent victim who was simply trying to live her life as a woman. In asking to be recognized, Mayne wanted more than the state's blessing (she already had that from her legal name modification)—she wanted the ability to define her own identity free from government intrusion and regulation and, as a result, weaken the state's control over her body.

Benjamin initially refused to write an affidavit in support of Mayne's case because he was not her doctor.[64] However, upon some reflection, the pragmatic side of Benjamin got the best of him, and he submitted a general statement about transsexuality. In it, Benjamin did not speak to Mayne's case in particular; instead, he stated that transsexuality was a legitimate medical condition and should be treated as such.[65] For Mayne, the letter became a decisive factor in her acquittal. Mayne wrote to Benjamin to tell him about the results of the trial: "I will be eternally gratefull to you for the statement you sent us a couple of days ago. Your statement and articles played a very important part in my being aqqiuted. Without your help; a clear cut aqqiutal would not have been possible, and a precedent would not have been set." In the final lines, Mayne exclaimed, "You saved the day, and your statement arrived in the nick of time to save the day and set a precedent. That God I am free. You rascal, I love you for this. Gratefully yours, Always, [Debbie]."[66] From the archival evidence, Benjamin and Mayne exchanged only a few more letters discussing minor matters such as Mayne's moving and a new job before their correspondence ended.[67]

Doing and Undoing Citizenship

This chapter makes three related contributions to our discussions about agency and how citizens negotiate stranger relationalities in a liberal-democratic polity. First, agency is a product of performative repertoires, embodied practices of movement, action, emotionality, and culturally negotiated productions of identity. Returning to the body as a locus of identity and knowledge production does much to allay the fears of those who mistakenly read theorists like Butler as advancing a playful politics detached from the material conditions of our lives. At the same time, this perspective untangles agency from the logocentrism of instrumental rationality and the sovereign subject. Accordingly, agency is not created anew in each moment but rather is the mediation of the accumulation of one's life experiences that should not be narrowed solely to publicly legible acts. In other words, the public transcript is an incomplete explanation of how power is experienced because it fails to explain how resistance to interpellations continually challenge and modify the undergirding logics of recognition. My narrative reconstruction avoids assigning any necessary causal connections between Mayne's various enactments of performative repertoires. The issue here is not the demonstration of a linear narrative of cause and effect, but, rather, an exposition of the multifarious ways that Mayne traversed the discursive circuitries available to her. A fuller consideration of our performative repertoires is not meant to get at the true source of agency—a fundamentally impossible task if we faithfully embrace the concept. Instead, performative repertoires ask us to consider how agency is developed and practiced in ways that are not immediately apparent if we restrict ourselves to the immediate moment of the public transcript. The following chapters privilege public transcripts more than hidden transcripts, but Mayne's actions exemplify the need to acknowledge that citizens operate in myriad ways, sometimes in accordance with the state's wishes and more often not.

In addition, Mayne's case emphasizes the need to theorize quotidian practices as important sites of identity creation, agency, and politics. The examination of Mayne's hidden and public transcripts favors the demonstration of resistance and performativity to supplement our knowledge of invention and agency. The resulting analysis explains how Mayne navigated her way through the varied interpellations offered to her by legal and medical authorities, risking desubjugation at all times yet never settling for subjectivities that failed to reflect key parts of her sense of self. In comparison to emancipatory or revolutionary politics, a Butlerian politics of the performative, employing a rhetorical perspective of contingency and probability to work the weaknesses of dominant hegemonies, can never satisfy those who equate resignification with defeatism, especially when they position practices of resistance as zero-sum trade-offs with collective action. However, scholarship and advocacy that reminds trans and cis people alike that, absent overthrowing existing cultural logics, we live in a world of inflexible domination does little to foster progressive politics or coalitions. As Butler reminds us, "possibility is not a luxury" in a world of heterosexual hegemonies; "it is as crucial as bread." Thus, "we should not underestimate what the thought of the possible does for those whom the very issue of survival is most urgent."[68]

By extension, we should ask what is lost and, more importantly, gained when we privilege tactical operations of dialectical forms of resistance over the deterministic narrative of oppositional politics. Incrementalism and inclusion are the bad objects of much of queer studies today. Yet, the majoritarian logics of persuasion associated with a truly oppositional politics may not be a viable option, at least in the short term, for many gender and sexual minorities. Conflicting hegemonic and ideological regimes, with their attendant circuitries of power, create conditions in which we don't all share the same subject positions and so the results of rejecting dominant institutions and their logics are not equally beneficial. Some of our bodies, regardless of our wishes, are always already read as political acts of transgression or resistance, as vile bodies that must be punished for those transgressions. We aren't all fighting for the same thing, and it is far from clear that collective action over and against tactical individual action is necessarily more successful at creating social change. For some of us, large-scale political mobilization and the persuasion of the majority to accept us as equal citizens is not always possible. If we mistakenly "dismiss these momentary feints and ruses" as politically invaluable, we ignore the array of legal consciousnesses available to us.[69] In an era of identity politics, consciousness is still the issue. However, it is no longer clear that a preoccupation with demystification of false consciousness is relevant. Instead, the task is to raise awareness of domination and cultivate the actions necessary to counter it. Like Mayne, we need to envision, cultivate, and practice agencies that take the absence of full legal recognition not as a hindrance to living a meaningful life but instead as a moment pregnant with possibilities for tactically making life more livable. Legally speaking, then, Butler suggests, "we had better be able to use that language to secure legal protections and entitlements, but perhaps we make a mistake if we take the definitions of who we are, legally, to be adequate descriptions of what we are about."[70] In other words, we need to learn how operate within the limits and possibilities of recognition and intelligibility as this is "the juncture from which critique emerges, where critique is understood as an interrogation of the terms by which life is constrained in order to open up the possibility for different modes of living."[71] The performativity of identity and performative repertoires inform the following chapters in significant ways as we tease out the meanings of transgender practices of citizenship.

Finally, Mayne's case also beckons us to further interrogate our commitment to locating ourselves and our senses of agency in legal recognition, not only as a matter of practical outcomes but also as a question about how such a position enables and constrains the possibility for non-normative subjectivities capable of resisting different modalities of dominance. The move here is not to ignore or disengage the law, for none of us has the privilege of existing outside the law's disciplinary technologies. Rather, we must recognize first that the practice of law is not restricted to the courtroom and second that the state has limited ability to ensure the cultural recognition of official legal protections. As Austin Sarat and his colleagues suggest, the law "seeks to colonize everyday life and give it substance, to capture it and hold it in its grasp, to attach itself to the solidity of the everyday and, in so doing, to further solidify it." However, the law's imperial aims are frustrated by the fact that "everyday life is a force in motion, a clash of forces which never fully reveal themselves, law can never totally capture or organize the everyday." In this way, "law does not just happen *to* the everyday; it is produced and reproduced *in* everyday encounters."[72] In order to understand the disciplinary effectivities of legal ideologies and hegemonies, we must engage the law not only in its reified forms but also as a practice of everyday life as citizens move through time and space.

Mayne directly engaged the state for official legal recognition as a woman but she did not stop there for she understood the limits of the state's power to ensure her legibility and safety. To further widen the avenues of agency available to her, Mayne participated in an education effort with the press and circulated her stories of resistance to friends and admirers. The important point here is that official recognition by the state is in many ways a prerequisite for participation in a rhetorical culture; thus, at the very least, the lack of recognition can seriously hinder one's ability to be seen and heard as a citizen. However, legal recognition alone provides only limited benefits as the law is an actually practiced relationality among friends, kin, and strangers. As a result, to understand the rhetorical effectivities of the law and how to engage or resist them, we must conceptualize agency in non-state-centered terms to allow a greater multiplicity of identities to flourish.

A politics of performativity necessarily operates within one's spatiotemporal constraints, yet we must not forget that cultural constraints, including medical and legal ones, are dynamic and recursive, not static. Operating within and between these conflicting, competing, and contradictory logics of legibility, Butler argues, "we must be undone in order to do ourselves: we must be part of a larger social fabric of existence in order to create who we are." And, as a result, "until social conditions are radically changed, freedom will require unfreedom, and autonomy is implicated in subjection."[73] Butler's own subtle rhetorical move from troubling gender to a process of continual undoing represents an evolution of agential praxis, one that recognizes the important but limited value of isolated disruptions of sexual and gender hegemonies. This is not to suggest that the undoing of gender involves a radical break or that it supersedes the troubling of gender. Rather, the perspective of undoing, along with Butler's repeated usage of phrases such as "livable life," directs her and our attention to the stakes of tactically challenging the normativities governing our existence. In other words, the complete and constant rejection of normativities fails us as a sustainable ethics of subjectivity. Instead, we must learn to

> distinguish among the norms and conventions that permit people to breathe, to desire, to love, and to live, and those norms and conventions that restrict or eviscerate the conditions of life itself. Sometimes norms function both ways at once, and sometimes they function one way for a given group, and another way for another group. What is most important is to cease legislating for all lives what is livable only for some, and similarly, to refrain from proscribing for all lives what is unlivable for some. The differences in position and desire set the limits to universalizability as an ethical reflex.[74]

Mayne, like all of us, could not ignore or wish away the legal, medical, and other inaugurations of her subjectivity. Rather, Mayne had to navigate this discursive milieu with public and hidden transcripts. Even though this is a radically incremental approach to social change, "collective and diffuse, belonging to no single subject," nevertheless "one effect of these alterations is to make acting like a subject possible."[75] So the challenge issued by this Butlerian conceptualization of agency is can we allow ourselves, in the name of a limited but purposive autonomy, to become undone?

Of course, subjective negotiations such as Mayne's do not have to stay individuated. They can lead to political collectivities. We return to our opening scene in the following chapter to explore how public bathrooms are sites of identity-formation and coalitional politics. In the intervening decades between Mayne's arrest and today, even with all of the cultural and legal progress made toward LGBT equality, the policing of public bathrooms continues unabated. Transgender citizens know all too well the risks of relieving one's self in public, and public bathrooms continue to be the subject of important struggles.

2

PISSAR's Critically Queer and Disabled Politics

For most able-bodied cisgenders, public bathrooms are functional, unremarkable places for eliminating waste.[1] They may be judged to be spacious or cramped, clean or dirty, plush or industrial, but they are generally unreflectively entered, used, and exited as part of one's everyday routine. These places are not sites of interrogative and self-reflexive thought, at least not about the cultural logics of public bathrooms themselves. One may take the time afforded by this biological necessity to collect one's thoughts, but public bathrooms typically are a short pit stop as one moves from one task to another. Put simply, for many, public bathrooms just are what they are: toilets, urinals, sinks, trashcans, and maybe a changing table. Accordingly, these naturalized places are seemingly immune from and irrelevant to the practice of politics and citizenship, although even a cursory review of the history of public bathrooms illuminates their fundamental importance to cultural figurations of the body politic.

While it may be difficult for us to imagine a world filled with gender-neutral public bathrooms, we only need to look to the not-so-distant past to discover that sex-segregated public toilets are a thoroughly modern invention. In nineteenth-century Anglo-American culture, as Barbara Penner explains, Victorian morality and its "increasingly strict prohibition on bodily display and the emergence of a rigid ideology of gender," as well as the capitalist production of women as consumers and workers outside the home, dictated the design of separate bathrooms for men and women.[2] Of course, in the wake of the Americans with Disabilities Act (ADA) and the need to accommodate consumers with children, we now have some gender-neutral bathrooms. Bathrooms designed for people with disabilities are marked by a sign depicting a genderless stick figure in a wheelchair, and the designation of family bathrooms are typically represented by a male, female, and a genderless stick figured child. Yet despite their gender-neutral design, even these places are implicated in heteronormative, bigendered logics of public propriety. Signs for the family bathroom imagine a hetero-nuclear family, and facilities for people with disabilities are typically designed as a single-stall toilet in a sex-segregated bathroom. There-fore, returning to Penner's argument, the architectural design and planning of public bathrooms are influenced at least as much by "complex and often competing discourses on the body, sexuality, morality, [and] hygiene" as they are by concerns with structural integrity or construction costs.[3]

In the American context, these complex and competing discourses have produced rhetorical resources for advocates in debates about racial segregation, gender equality, and the aforementioned accommodation of people with disabilities. As for the opponents of racial integration, they fervently resisted relinquishing "Whites Only" bathrooms.[4] To isolate just one example of this ubiquitous struggle, city officials in Memphis, Tennessee, trading in the mythology of the sex-crazed African American, justified racially segregated bathrooms in an otherwise desegregated public library on the grounds that African Americans would spread sexually transmitted diseases to white patrons. When this policy was legally challenged, a federal court struck it down. In a con-voluted decision, the justices side-stepped the issue of race by inject-ing class into the judicial calculus and concluded that library patrons, on the whole and regardless of race, were less likely to have sexually transmitted diseases and, therefore, city officials could not continue the racially motivated practice under the guise of public health policy.[5] Even though the law worked against the interests of segregationists in this instance, it is worth noting that this was the exception rather than the rule for much of our nation's history.

As for debates about gender equality, the specter of unisex public bathrooms figured prominently, at least for a short period in the 1970s, in debates about the Equal Rights Amendment (ERA). Opponents of the ERA, led by Phyllis Schlafly, asserted that its ratification would legally prohibit sex-segregated bathrooms. The public circulation of this argument, Patricia Cooper and Ruth Oldenziel suggest, "tapped into deep fears about sexual mixing, transgressing social boundaries, and ending recognition of gender differences."[6] Jane Sherron De Hart further explains that "sexual fears, compounded by and intertwined with racism," created trepidation and confusion about the ERA's goals and effects, although its ultimate impact on American opinions of the ERA appears to have been limited.[7] Jane Mansbridge's study of the defeat of the ERA, one well-supported by extensive polling data on the "potty issue," concludes that "while this issue strengthened the morale of the [anti-ERA] activists, it had mixed results among the public and backfired in the legislatures." As Mansbridge explains, in one survey polling ERA opponents, "less than 3 percent gave unisex toilets as either a first, second, or third reason for their opposition," and another survey of the general public revealed 76 percent did not think the ERA would "increase the likelihood of integrated toilets." With regard to the circulation of this argument in debates in state legislatures, "the issue served to solidify the conviction of middle-of-the-road legislators that the opposition was irrational."[8] In the end, the "potty issue" may not have been decisive in the defeat of the ERA, although it is often remembered as a pivotal issue. Indeed, the fact that it circulated at all speaks to gendered and racialized anxieties associated with public bathrooms.

Taken together, these anecdotes demonstrate the inherently political nature of public bathrooms, even as their seeming banality encourages their users to eschew reflection on the underlying cultural logics of these public places. Far too often when we do discuss public bathrooms, the squeamishness initiated by the second term inhibits any serious reflection on the first, thus effectively securing current arrangements as they are to the great disadvantage of those who fail to see themselves or those who are not seen by others as welcome to use the facilities. In lieu of understanding public toilets as something instrumentally linked to the public sphere, a richer perspective views them as reciprocal forces in the figuration of publics and politics. Ruth Barcan does not overstate the case, then, when she directs our attention to the fact that public bathrooms are places where "we meet members of the public and where we interact with, and continually reproduce, an *idea* of the public."[9] Consequently, these public places reflect certain normativities, which are tenuously secured by a spatial ordering of citizens—an ordering just as capable of being remade as it is made.

The undoing of the privatizing logics of public bathrooms may be one of the most exciting and productive sites for queer coalitional politics as it opens up the potential for linking the everyday concerns of LGBTs and people with disabilities.[10] This suggested site of solidarity is not without risk. Many members of these communities, save those who live at the intersections of these identities, have labored to untangle the negative articulations of one with the other.[11] Thus, LGBT advocates have invested considerable time and energy in countering the medicalization and pathologization of their identities and desires, and the struggle continues today with campaigns against religiously based reparative therapies and the continued classification of transgender identifications as "gender identity disorder" (and now "gender dysphoria"). People with disabilities, on the other hand, have been figured as asexual beings, or as hypersexual deviants, like LGBTs. Therefore, to link the interests of people with disabilities and LGBTs may seem counterintuitive, regressive, and politically untenable. Yet, in a liberal-democratic polity that only sometimes tolerates LGBTs and people with disabilities, the continued vitality and vibrancy of LGBT, queer, and disability politics is dependent largely upon the ability of these advocates to develop forms of coalitional politics that articulate their modalities of discrimination to the interests of other similarly situated groups. Public bathrooms provide a scene for naming and exposing the otherwise neglected nexus of "hetero/homo-corporo-normativities" operating in public culture.[12]

Coalitions between LGBTs and people with disabilities are not unprecedented, as two short histories reveal, providing a backdrop for contextualizing the possibilities of these acts of solidarity in the process. In 1977, disability activists coordinated a nationwide protest to secure the enforcement of Section 504 of the 1973 Rehabilitation Act. In language mirroring the protections of Title VI of the Civil Rights Act of 1964, Section 504 prevented discrimination against people with disabilities by government agencies and federally funded entities. The legislative history of the provision is unclear, but the best evidence suggests that legislative aides working in concert with disability activists quietly inserted the simple yet expansive language into the legislation during a Senate markup of the appropriation. Except for some minor points of clarification, members of Congress did not debate Section 504 on the floor or in conference committees. The provision even survived two vetoes by President Nixon, who objected to the overall cost of the programs authorized by the act. After Congress reduced the funding for the act, Nixon signed the legislation on September 23, 1973. However, Nixon's Secretary of Health, Education, and Welfare (HEW) immediately realized the tremendous costs of following the provision and refused for the next three years to develop the regulations needed to enforce the law.[13]

With the election of Jimmy Carter, disability advocates lobbied the president to make good on his campaign promise to enact the necessary legal regulations. Faced with the wide-ranging and costly mandates of Section 504, Carter's administration avoided implementing the provision. In response, disability activists planned nationwide protests at regional HEW offices for April 5, 1977. In San Francisco, as in other locations, protestors occupied the buildings, refusing to leave until Joseph Califano, Carter's HEW Secretary, approved regulations to enforce the section. As the end of the first day neared and the protestors refused to leave, HEW officials across the country refused them access to phones, bathrooms, and food in the hopes that they could avoid sending in the police to arrest them. This strategy worked in almost all of the locations except for San Francisco. There, in response to reports of the protests, the Butterfly Brigade, a group that patrolled the Castro district to prevent violence against inhabitants and patrons, smuggled in toiletries and walkie-talkies so that the protestors could communicate with the press as well as with their families and the caregivers who could provide them with medications and treatments.[14] Whether the Butterfly Brigade was motivated by altruism, a sense of shared injustice, and/or suspicion of the treatment of minorities by law enforcement, their assistance, along with that of other groups such as the Black Panthers, allowed the protestors to outlast the initial measures designed to break their spirit. As a result, the San Francisco protest was the only one that lasted more than two days. After twenty-four days of protests, Califano signed off on the new regulations.

Seizing the momentum gained by the enactment of Section 504, disability advocates turned their attention toward more comprehensive legislation. Over a decade later, in what would culminate in the Americans with Disabilities Act (ADA), disability advocates and legislators included HIV-positive individuals as one of the act's protected classes. Opponents of the ADA justified their opposition in a number of ways, but the inclusion of HIV-positive individuals provided political cover for those hostile to LGBTs and the unfunded mandates contained in the act. Thus, while the Senate passed a version of the ADA without any exceptions for HIV-positive individuals, on the last day of debate in the House, Jim Chapman, a Republican from Texas, introduced an amendment to exclude restaurants from coverage out of the fear that HIV-positive workers would spread the disease through food preparation and service. Despite strenuous opposition on the part of disability advocates, the House narrowly approved the Chapman amendment on a 199–187 vote. Before and during the House and Senate conference committee, disability advocates continued to oppose the measure out of the conviction that HIV-positive individuals should be included in the act as well as the fear that one exclusion would justify future attempts to narrow the scope of the ADA. Over time, disability advocates threatened to withdraw their support of the ADA if the conference committee capitulated on the Chapman amendment. As a result of this pressure, the conference committee eliminated the amendment.[15]

In one way, then, the ADA demonstrates the political utility and necessity of coalitional politics. In another way, however, the passage of the ADA is a cautionary tale about the politics of exclusion in the service of political expediency. Senator Jesse Helms, for example, added language that excluded transvestites from the 1988 Fair Housing amendment (it's not altogether clear what Helms meant when he used this term), and then went on to insert explicit language in the ADA precluding transvestites, transsexuals, homosexuals, those with gender identity disorders not resulting from physical impairments, and other sexual behavior disorders, as well the practices of bestiality, pedophilia, exhibitionism, and voyeurism from protection.[16] In an effort to disentangle the issue of HIV status from sexuality, ADA advocates were more than willing to accept such a measure.[17] "The best that the gay rights community was able to achieve," according to legal scholar Ruth Colker "was to take 'homosexuality' and 'bisexuality' out of the sentence that listed 'sexual behavior disorders.'"[18] In the end, this clarification secured 99 votes for the ADA in the Senate—Helms was the lone dissenter. Even with the inclusion of his desired exceptions, Helms refused to support the ADA because of its protections for HIV-positive individuals who, he reasoned, were likely to be drug users and/or sexual deviants and therefore not worthy of legal protection. Thus, the inclusion of HIV-positive individuals in the ADA came at the expense and the further stigmatization of sexual and gender minorities.

These two examples of coalitional politics illustrate how issues of importance to LGBTs and people with disabilities have generated the inventional resources needed to forge coalitional politics. At the same time, the political struggle to secure the passage of the ADA demonstrates the ways in which the interests of trans people are often ignored in the coalitional work undertaken by gay and lesbian advocates, as well as how quickly disability advocates can distance themselves from the concerns of trans people. It is thus even more notable that trans people and people with disabilities have found common cause through their shared experiences. Despite differences between trans people and people with disabilities, they do tend to negotiate a number of similar issues in their daily lives, which can, in turn, prove useful in forging political alliances. These include: difficulties, if not outright discrimination, in securing an education, job, and/or housing; demonization and/or condemnation by religious officials; violence from perpetrators of hate crimes; familial and social rejection and shame; and finding a safe and accessible bathroom.[19]

Public bathrooms are far from trivial spaces, given how they both enable and constrain face-to-face public interactions. From the outset, the location and condition of public bathrooms provide explicit physical markers about expectations concerning gender and physical capabilities of the people in that area. The differences between the lines for the men's and women's bathrooms, as well as the use of bathrooms designated for people with disabilities by people without disabilities, speak volumes about the infusion of cultural norms into architecture. Moreover, as Rob Kitchin and Robin Law note, an individual's inability to find a safe and accessible public bathroom subjects him or her to "'the bladder's leash,'" which not only limits the amount of time that the individual can spend in a public location, but can also prevent him or her from even attempting to participate in a variety of public arenas.[20] As a result, people with disabilities and trans people must be uniquely mindful of the accommodations available in places such as restaurants, stores, airports, schools, and their places of employment.[21]

Instead of parsing out the differences between people with disabilities and trans people and furthering the able-bodied and bigendered normativities underwriting the regulation of public places, I see members of both of these identity groups wanting to be free from their bladder's leashes, which are tethered to the pole of an idealized, mythic, and normative body. Thus, in the spirit of promoting and developing radical democratic coalitional politics interested in challenging intersecting modalities of domination, this chapter will explore how these seemingly disparate groups have articulated, negotiated, and managed their differences, all while practicing a coalitional politics that questioned the safety and accessibility of public bathrooms.

In the process, this argument makes a case for taking more seriously the rhetorical undoing and doing of place, space, and identity. Academics often treat place and space as sites of rhetorical practice, noting them as material constraint without exploring the interpenetrating rhetorical relationship of individuals in place and space. To avoid this two-dimensional flattening of place and space, I treat these concepts as dynamic elements integrally linked to the rhetorical production of citizen identity and agency. More specifically, the examination of public bathrooms offers insight into the gendered and able-bodied logics actively undergirding these seemingly banal places. It also suggests how we can intervene in these cultural practices by attending to the identity work negotiated in and through the materiality and performativity of these spaces.

The second half of this chapter analyzes the actions of People in Search of Safe and Accessible Restrooms (PISSAR), a genderqueer and disability coalition composed of college students and staff dedicated to providing safe and accessible bathrooms. With the goal of demonstrating the productive potential of coalitional politics informed by critical queerness and disability, we will explore the inventional resources created by the interaction of genderqueer and disabled bodies in campus bathrooms. The members of PISSAR addressed multiple forms of shame directed at them, including the internalized shame of their own bodies, the shame associated with bathroom activities and politics, and the potential sources of shame created by the articulation of their stigmatized identities together. By surveying and actually meeting in campus bathrooms, PISSAR negotiated a spatially based consubstantiality of shame to challenge the homo/hetero-corporo-normativity of public places and spaces. Recognizing public bathrooms as sites of performative identity formation, PISSAR exemplifies a provocative model for theorizing and practicing critically queer politics outside of the hegemonic and increasingly ineffective logics of gay white male shame which guide much of contemporary LGBT and queer politics. To arrive at these positions, we first turn to a discussion of relationships among rhetoric, place, space, and identity.

The Rhetoricity of Place, Space, and Identity

In the context of this chapter, the concepts "space" and "place" are informed by Michel de Certeau's simple yet provocative maxim: "*space is a practiced place.*"[22] Place and space, in Certeau's formulations of the terms, are given meaning by the practices employed in them, with relationships between place and strategy and between space and tactics developing accordingly. For Certeau, the association of place with strategy signifies how locations are "circumscribed as *proper* and thus serve as the basis for generating relations with an exterior distinct from it."[23] Thus, in an attempt to dictate the proper set of actions and relationships of members of a polity, the "strong" use strategies to create places to manage the maneuvering of the "weak" by taking recourse to naturalized hierarchies outside of the context of the immediate physical locales.[24] Public bathrooms, then, are "places" in that they are designed and provided for a limited number of functions (urinating, defecating, changing a diaper, vomiting, washing hands, fixing hair and/or makeup, gaining composure, and brushing teeth), they are divided by the sexes through an appeal to a naturalized system of biological separation, and they are regulated and surveyed by the law to enforce these taken-as-given differences.

Of course, public bathrooms are used for a number of purposes unintended by their owners—some people fuck and suck in them, others use them to buy and use drugs, and individuals who are homeless may use them as a respite from the elements and the violence directed toward them. In these ways, by being associated with tactics or "calculated actions" that "play on and with a terrain imposed on it and organized by the law of a foreign power," the place of the public bathroom becomes a space.[25] Emphasizing the rhetorical conditions of contingency and probability, Certeau observes that those who are interested in turning places into spaces

> must accept the chance offerings of the moment . . . and make use of the cracks that particular conjunctions open in the surveillance of the proprietary powers. It [a tactic] poaches in them. It creates surprises in them. It can be where it is least expected. It is a guileful ruse. In short, a tactic is an art of the weak.[26]

The spatiality of resistance, inherently wedded to timing, relies on fugitive power relations, and these relations create the conditions to remake the material worlds we inhabit. Precisely because "spaces of resistance are multiple, dynamic, and weak (in their effectiveness, but also because resistance is also dangerous)," Steven Pile concludes, they are "only ever in part controlled by the practices of domination."[27] Therefore, challenges to cultural hegemonies are located primarily in the alterations of quotidian routines, and in spatializing the understanding of resistance, we can, as Pile and Michael Keith urge us to do, draw "attention not only to the myriad spaces of political struggles, but also to the politics of the everyday space, through which political identities constantly flow and fix."[28] This conceptualization of space and place, along with strategies and tactics, assists us in understanding the complex interactions of space, identity, and agency.

As should be clear, the concomitant construction of identity and space is inherently performative, and it deserves further theorization. Reminding critics interested in intervening in cultural formations that we must forego the notion that space is "a mere setting or an innocent background in, over, or across which cultural activities and practices are seen to be occurring," Raka Shome suggests that we opt instead for a perspective that acknowledges "the role that space plays in the (re)production of social power."[29] The implication of this move, according to Shome, is that we must account for the symbolicity of space as it "functions as a technology—a means and a medium—of power that is socially constituted through material relations that enable the communication of specific politics," while making others more difficult.[30] In the case of public bathrooms, Barcan's description of them as "technologies of division and separation" calls attention to the ways in which they privatize this public action and rely on and reinforce gender binaries through their appeals to a naturalized logic of sex segregation, individualized stalls, and the complex codes of permissible interactions in these places.[31]

Certeau's perspective assists us in understanding Shome's attention to the contextualized agentic effectivities of space and identity. In drawing attention to the spatial dimensions of power relations, Shome simultaneously problematizes acontextual understandings of identity to prevent the importation of stable subjectivities into the dynamic operations of space and identity.[32] As a result, agency is found in the localized interaction of subjects and the spaces in which they operate—which is to say in the performative co-production of identities and spaces. Nothing is guaranteed in advance as subjects necessarily work in between the constraining and enabling conditions found in the contingent and the probable, whether they recognize it or not.

Nonetheless, the regulation of place presents formidable obstacles to practices of resistance, and consideration must be paid to the contextualized nature of this dialectic. As Michel Foucault provocatively suggested, "a whole history remains to be written of *spaces*—which would at the same time be the history of *powers* (both these terms in the plural)—from the great strategies of geo-politics to the little tactics of the habitat."[33] In a lecture first presented in 1967, Foucault was particularly interested in the secularization of Western societies and the attendant spatial effectivities of these cultural transformations. Ever-concerned with the dispersion and dissimulation of power relations, he postulated that place was in a period of partial desanctification— meaning that a unilateral exercise of power and hence determination of subjectivity had transferred from the centralized location of the church to innumerable points exercising differing forms of power, and thus enabling resistant subjects to increasingly challenge the naturalness and centrally controlled meanings of places. The complete desanctification of places remains incomplete, however, because our cultural logics are arranged around "oppositions that remain inviolable, that our institutions and practices have not yet dared to break down," including those spaces and places defined by the split between public and private matters.[34]

Cultural geographer David Sibley locates the limits of desanctification in micropolitical and biopolitical exercises of power. Sibley argues that in spite of the continual undoing of places into spaces, "there seems to me to be a continuing need for ritual practices to maintain the sanctity of space in a secular society." He concludes, however, that today's "guardians of sacred spaces are more likely to be security guards, parents or judges rather than priests."[35] In the case of public bathrooms, these are treated by many as places of gender regulation as they are policed in the both the figurative and literal senses of the word.[36] Trans people often face the possibility of being treated as gender transgressors for using the "wrong" bathroom. In response to a survey taken by the San Francisco Human Rights Commission, trans people documented negative reactions to their use of public restrooms, with stories ranging from security guards harassing them to losing jobs to "[getting] the shit kicked out of me for using the 'wrong bathroom.'" One respondent wrote that they "almost got killed."[37] "The bathroom problem," according to Jack Halberstam, "illustrates in remarkably clear ways the flourishing existence of gender binarism despite rumors of its demise."[38] That is, in spite of increasingly fluid notions of gender, the binary logic of sex remains the dominant ideology of corporeal legibility, which is defined primarily by visual cues. Ironically enough, then, as Halberstam notes, "gender's very flexibility and seeming fluidity is precisely what allows dimorphic gender to hold sway"; as he further elaborates, the "definitional boundaries of male and female are so elastic, there are very few people in any given public space who are completely unreadable in terms of their gender."[39] In turn, these codes of cultural legibility authorize the biopolitical practice of gender policing, thereby allowing anxious individuals to punish those who trouble the stability of sexual and gender categories. Thus, even with the malleability of gender codes, "the transphobic imagination," according to Richard Juang, allows the bathroom to "become an extension of a genital narcissism (which could be expressed, roughly, as 'my body is how sex should be defined for all other bodies' and 'the presence of other kinds of body violates the sex of my own body')."[40] In these ways and others, the fluidity of sex and gender are understood to have its limits.

Anxieties about public bathrooms are heightened by the fact that, in using the bathroom, we perform a private act in a public place with strangers. Moreover, using the bathroom leaves us vulnerable. We are in compromised positions that limit our lines of sight, be it because of a stall or a urinal. We expose parts of our bodies that are otherwise hidden from view—parts of our bodies that we typically don't want strangers to see. We pass fluids and objects that make a mess, can be noisy, and smell. In order to allay some of our anxieties, we invoke state-based protections to ensure that public bathrooms are places regulated by a variety of legal technologies. Transgender individuals are especially prone to this regulation, and sometimes concomitant violence, because of naturalized assumptions about bodies, genders, and sexuality. Kath Browne explains that transgender transgressions of public bathrooms are especially threatening "in part because the leakiness of bodies cannot be associated with the fluid possibilities of sexed bodies" for "where bodies are revealed as unstable and porous, flowing between the sexes may be more threatening; where one border (bodily) is contravened others (man/woman) may be more intensely protected" by those exhibiting genital narcissism.[41]

Of course, women's and men's restrooms are policed in similar yet different ways. According to Patricia Cooper and Ruth Oldenziel, for women, more than men, the bathroom is a space "where they take care of their bodies and where they might remove themselves from public scrutiny or surveillance, exercise some authority, or forge bonds of solidarity."[42] Public bathrooms for women are areas where non-excretory activities are more likely to take place—women may, among other things, go to the bathroom in groups to have private conversations, reapply make-up and fix their hair, or regroup after a confrontation. In contrast, men's public restrooms involve what Halberstam terms "an architecture of surveillance" where each man stands at his urinal and looks straight ahead at the wall for fear he might be spotted sizing up the competition; talking at the urinals or between stalls is reserved only for the closest of friends and only when other men are not around. However, Halberstam continues, the men's bathroom is also a space for "homosocial interaction and of homoerotic interaction." For Halberstam, the distinction between men's and women's bathrooms is that whereas men's bathrooms "tend to operate as a highly charged sexual space in which sexual interactions are both encouraged and punished, women's rest rooms tend to operate as an arena for enforcement of gender conformity."[43] For trans people, then, pissing and shitting always carries with it the chance for legal and physical violence for they can be read as violating the sanctity and semiotic stability of these public places.

Taken together, the works of the preceding theorists provide useful heuristic tools for understanding the spatio-temporal modalities of power as well as the need to focus on the actions of specific bodies in particular spaces. As Tim Cresswell astutely notes, "the geographical ordering of society is founded on a multitude of acts of boundary making—of territorialization—whose ambiguity is to simultaneously open up the possibilities for transgression."[44] Attention to the communicative acts associated with space-making practices helps to bridge the practico-theoretical aporias identified by geographers in scholarship on the politics of gender and queer resistance. For example, Doreen Massey reads Certeau as offering too strict an opposition and distinction between place and time, privileging the latter while negating the dynamism of the former and thereby having the inadvertent effect of stabilizing the meaning of space and obscuring its constitutive political potential.[45] Massey interrogates this dualism as one complicit with feminizing space and masculinizing time, and thus connected to larger logics underwriting the naturalization of gender ideologies.[46] Similarly, Lise Nelson identifies the lack of spatial consideration in many invocations of performativity as a limiting condition to effective political intervention.[47]

With these criticisms in mind, I want to suggest that we work with Certeau's and Foucault's arguments in order to decode contextualized communicative acts in a spatio-temporal context. In this way, we can revalue quotidian practices like those associated with public bathrooms and address the concerns of those who are rightly worried about acontextualized understandings of space and identity. If, like Robyn Longhurst, we take seriously the notions that "bodies are also always in a state of becoming with places,"[48] and that practices of resistance are inaugurated by the fluidity of both bodies and places/spaces, we can comprehend more fully, as Lynn Stewart suggests, how "space [is] a *product* of the human body," and how the "ability to *produce* space, rather than just to *conceive* space, is the means by which people can take back power in their everyday lives."[49] Accordingly, the histories of power, space, and place that remain to be written must be sensitive to the gender, racial, and able-bodied discourses (to name only a few

categories of analysis) that animate these spaces. Using these perspectives, we turn to PISSAR's actions to demonstrate how the performativity of identity is informed by spatial politics and how, at the same time,
spatial politics are informed by the performativity of identity.

PISSAR Patrols and Politics

The students and staff that formed PISSAR met at the 2003 University
of California Students of Color Conference hosted on the University
of California-Santa Barbara campus. In a case of serendipitous sched-
uling, the conveners slated the transgender and disability caucuses at
the same time in adjacent rooms. However, as each group noticed they
had attracted only a few attendees, the two caucuses merged together
to share their concerns about the campus. In the course of the meeting, the disability caucus disclosed their intention to survey the accessibility of campus bathrooms. Understanding the possible convergence
of their interests, the disability caucus asked the transgender caucus if
they would be interested in jointly undertaking the project. Painfully
aware of how transgender students are especially vulnerable to harassment and violence in and around public bathrooms, the members of the
transgender caucus eagerly accepted the invitation.[50] In one recollec-
tion of the event, "everyone in the room suddenly began talking about
the possibilities of a genderqueer/disability coalition, and PISSAR was
born."[51] The choice of the name PISSAR was not merely an extension
of the group's playful attitude; it also embraced and projected a queer
attitude to challenge euphemistic discussions of bathrooms that impede
the interrogation of what they termed "pee privilege."[52] Members of the
group described the name as a "tool" that drew attention to the fact that
all of us need to piss and shit and "warned" others that they were "about
to talk about something 'crude.'"[53]

PISSAR soon discovered that another campus group with a blunt
name meant to call attention to bodily functions was similarly interested in bathroom politics. Aunt Flo and the Plug Patrol had been vol-
untarily stocking tampon and pad machines on campus after the university failed to hire a new company to supply them. Stocking over two
hundred bathrooms on campus with tampons and pads bought from a
wholesaler, Aunt Flo and the Plug Patrol made about $100 a month in

profits that they funneled to student groups on campus.[54] Recognizing the intimate connections of the gendered politics of bathrooms, PISSAR allied themselves with Aunt Flo and the Plug Patrol to make the campus a safe place to piss, shit, and bleed.[55] Aunt Flo and the Plug Patrol provided PISSAR with start-up funds to purchase the materials needed for their "PISSAR patrols" including gloves, tape measures, clipboards, and their signature bright yellow t-shirts with spray-painted stenciling: "PISSAR" on the front and "FREE 2 PEE" on the back. In return, PISSAR included information about tampon and pad machines on their checklist. When they were constructing their checklist, a member of PISSAR raised the issue of changing tables, and this consideration was also added. As a result of this attitudinizing frame, one that in their own words "refuse[d] to accept a narrow definition of 'queer' that denie[d] the complexities of our bodies,"[56] PISSAR broadly defined themselves in their mission statement as a group dedicated to making the campus a space where "people with all sorts of bodies and all sorts of genders should be free to pee, free to shit, free to bleed, free to share a stall with an attendant or change a baby's diaper."[57]

PISSAR's actions invite further investigation given their practice of radical democratic politics concerned with bodies and identities in space. More specifically, PISSAR enacted critically queer and disabled politics designed to counter the shame and stigma attached to their bodies. By directly confronting stigma and shame in the place of its inscription, PISSAR transformed campus bathrooms into a space of coalitional politics. PISSAR provides valuable lessons for LGBT, queer, and disabled advocates about how to challenge their own and others' attitudes about the safety and accessibility of campus bathrooms.

Consubstantial Spaces of Shame

Shame is often understood as a private, individualized emotion. Yet, as Janice Irvine highlights, "shame acts politically when it reinforces social boundaries about which citizens are worthy and acceptable and which are not."[58] PISSAR's members negotiated three interdependent levels of shame. First, they had to overcome the shame associated with the assertion of public bathrooms as a politically important issue. In this context, both the disabled and the genderqueer members had to face the fact that

public bathrooms are easily branded as an unimportant or fringe concern when compared to "real" political issues such as access to medical care, equal employment and housing opportunities, and lobbying
for partnership rights. In addition, the disabled members had to contend with the mistaken perception that the ADA had already resolved
the issue of bathroom accessibility. Like other protected classes before
them, people with disabilities have felt the pain of formal equality's dou-
ble-edged sword, and of being assured that they are treated equally in
spite of their experiences to the contrary. The discourses of equality and
accommodation associated with the ADA, David Serlin cautions, cannot be counted upon as a "sophisticated mechanism designed to generate respectful difference between parties with shared access to social or
political power."[59] Unfortunately, these discourses are available equally
as a "blunt instrument used to flatten difference" as minimal accommodations negate any further questioning about systemic inequalities faced
by people with disabilities and simultaneously sidestep sustained interrogation into the "the tension between autonomy and equality at the core
of classical liberalism."[60] Unlike the disabled, genderqueers are generally
not afforded legal access to discourses of equality and must turn to their
supposedly natural allies: gays, lesbians, and bisexuals. However, gays,
lesbians, and bisexuals are often hesitant to lend their time and energy
to bathroom politics as they do not want to associate themselves with
the shameful subject of public sex in bathrooms.[61] Trans people are even
less likely to find support outside of LGBT communities, as Olga Gershenson notes, because "transgender toilet provision stirs public controversy, even among those sympathetic to the campaigns for civil rights
of those who have come before."[62] For both of these minority groups,
although for somewhat different reasons, safe and accessible bathrooms
are difficult to get on the political agenda of their allies.

On a more personal level, PISSAR members dealt with a second
source of shame when they confronted their feelings about their own
bodies. The genderqueer-identified members of the group harbored
varying degrees of "internalized shame" generated by their "visible
queerness" and "genderqueerness."[63] In a visual economy tolerant of
LGBTs as long as they seamlessly assimilate or operate within "acceptable stereotypes of gay appearance," the trans members felt the gravitational pull of the politics of respectability practiced by a number of

LGBTs.[64] When LGBTs align themselves with or adopt normative cultural markers of sex, gender, and sexuality, they can marginalize those who operate outside these dominant logics. As a result, the genderqueer-identified members reported a general sense of internalized shame compounded by the need to discuss their unique needs, as well as the private topic of bodily functions. According to PISSAR, open discussion was an exceptionally difficult task because "we're trained from an early age not to talk publicly about what happens in the bathroom; we don't even have *language* for what happens in there; many of us still rely on the euphemisms our parents used when we were three."[65] In this way, the genderqueer members had to embrace their doubly stigmatized difference by publicly articulating themselves as pissing and shitting trans bodies.

The disabled members similarly negotiated their identities over and against the corporeal normativities and the discursive propriety associated with public bathrooms. As for the pressure to minimize their differences from the nondisabled, the members stated, "In striving to assimilate to nondisabled norms, many of us gloss over the need for the assistance some of us have in using the bathroom."[66] In a culture defined by ableist norms that can project shame onto disabled bodies, people with disabilities have an incentive to minimize their differences to prevent further stigmatization. For PISSAR's disabled members, these normalizing regimes are compounded by the fact that "particularly in mixed company (that is, in the presence of nondisabled folks), we are reluctant to talk about the odd ways we piss and shit." In the absence of these frank discussions, they felt that "this reticence has hindered our bathroom politics, often making it difficult for us to demand bathrooms that meet all of our needs."[67] These needs, identified on PISSAR's checklist, included: signs denoting the accessibility of the bathroom, stall doors wide enough for wheelchairs, toilets mounted at an accessible height with a generous amount of space around them, the presence of grab bars, accessible toilet paper dispensers, and sinks, soap dispensers, and mirrors placed at an accessible height.[68] Hence, like the genderqueer members, the disabled members had to place their own bodies at risk by publicly marking their differences as pissing and shitting human beings.

Finally, the members had a third level of shame to deal with in relation to the mutual articulation of their struggles. In trumpeting

PISSAR's coalition-building efforts, I do not mean to suggest that it was an easy endeavor. In a published history of PISSAR, the members suggested that the shame and stigma associated with queerness and disability proved to be formidable obstacles in their alliance:

> Our shame isn't always directed outward, toward the society and institutions that helped create it. It often drives a wedge between communities that might otherwise work together. And it is *precisely* this kind of embodied shame—the shame that we feel in our bodies and the shame that arises out of the experience and appearance of our bodies—that drives the divisions between queer and disability communities. PISSAR initially had trouble bridging this gap, in that some of our straight disabled members worried about the political (read: queer) implications of our bathroom-mapping work.[69]

As this quotation suggests, instead of reading the hesitation of the straight-identified disabled members of PISSAR as a mark of their fear or hatred of gender-transgressors, it can be read within the context of the shame produced by the nefarious intersections of compulsory heterosexuality and disability. As suggested by Alison Kafer, a queer feminist with disabilities who was coincidentally a member of PISSAR, "compulsory heterosexuality accrues a particular urgency among some segments of the disability community" as "many have wanted to appear 'normal,' 'natural,' and 'healthy' in other aspects of their lives." Therefore, it should come as no surprise when "the larger culture's heterosexism and homophobia are thus reproduced within the disability community."[70] At the same time, the non-disabled genderqueer members of the group had to interrogate their abelist assumptions to overcome the divisions engendered by their desires to "distance themselves from disabled people in an effort to assert their own normalcy and health."[71] Thus, the members of PISSAR encountered what Kenneth Burke would call the "characteristic invitation to rhetoric" in that they needed to bridge the symbolic divisions generated by these interpenetrating discursive constellations of shame.[72]

These internalized and projected discourses of shame produced division, yet they also contained the seeds of identification through the rhetorical construction of consubstantiality. For Burke, consubstantiality is achieved when the interests of two distinct individuals are articulated together through "common sensations, concepts, images, ideas, [and] attitudes," or what Burke would term the substance of rhetoric.[73] Importantly, especially for those interested in the politics of identity, consubstantiality requires constant renewal, for even as consubstantiality is an "*acting-together*," it is also a temporary identification between those who are "joined and separate, at once a distinct substance and consubstantial with another."[74] Consubstantiality, then, is a fragile union, one in need of continual rhetorical renewal, as the competing motives of the concerned parties are negotiated. As an important addendum to Burke's thought, we must consider how the spatial locations of consubstantiality constrain and enable the potential for identification. Contextualizing this discussion in PISSAR's spatial politics engages this problematic while also demonstrating the possibilities of reanimating shame as a productive discursive element of critically queer and disabled politics.

Critical Queerness and Disability

According to the members of PISSAR, the act of coming together in the campus bathrooms and "repeatedly talking openly about people's need for a safe space to pee helps us break through some of the embodied shame and recognize our common needs."[75] When the disabled members patrolled with the genderqueer members, many of them reported a greater understanding of the fear and anxiety generated by sex-specific bathrooms. In one memorable case of consubstantiality, the members of PISSAR recounted the evolution of a straight-identified disabled man's attitudes toward gender-neutral bathrooms. Once skeptical and dismissive of the need to accommodate genderqueer students and staff, after going out on a few patrols he was able to link his own struggles with his trans counterparts through the language of accessibility. This is not to say that he understood these accessibility issues as equal to one another. Instead, as they state, he was able to "make the connection between disability oppression and genderqueer oppression" which then created favorable conditions for his continued participation in coalitional politics.[76]

Likewise, after the trans members of the group worked together with their disabled colleagues, they understood the spatial dynamics of campus bathrooms in a way that fostered connections between them. Using their checklist, the nondisabled together with the disabled members measured the width, height, and overall accessibility of numerous parts of the bathroom. As they describe it, the checklist operated as a "consciousness-raising tool" among their own members. Several trans/genderqueer members did not understand the inaccessibility of campus bathrooms for many of the disabled students on campus. For one nondisabled member, "going through the PISSAR checklist caused her to view the entire built world through different eyes."[77] "Rather than focusing on the alleged failures and hardships of disabled bodies," the PISSAR members directed their attention to "the failures and omissions of the built environment—a too-narrow door, a too-high dispenser."[78] By reframing the issue as one of the architectural privileging of "the 'normal' body and its needs," the nondisabled members of PISSAR could start to understand how they and the disabled were both working against corporeal normativities. As they described it, "this switch in focus from the inability of the body to the inaccessibility of the space makes room for activism" between groups that may not initially notice their shared sources of struggle.[79] The nondisabled members realized that ability, like sex and gender, is a naturalized, as opposed to a natural, condition, and that the accommodation of ability is a choice that could be made differently to better account for bodies of different sizes, shapes, and mobility.

In this way, PISSAR, unlike many LGBT and queer advocates before them, effectively addressed *both* the shame and stigma directed at their bodies to bolster their coalition. Michael Warner demands that queer coalitions attend to the interrelated and divisive pressures of stigma and shame; otherwise, these coalitions will inevitably incorporate themselves into and thus strengthen, rather than weaken, the social hierarchies that authorize the violence directed at LGBTs. Drawing upon Erving Goffman's work, Warner explains the relationship between stigma and shame as one of identity (stigma) and acts (shame).[80] Unfortunately, too many LGBTs, in Warner's words, have dealt with the "ambivalence of belonging to a stigmatized group" by "embrac[ing] the identity but disavow[ing] the act," meaning that LGBTs, with their rainbow flags and Human Rights Campaign bumper stickers, latch onto pride in their identity as *the* countervailing affect to the shame directed at their sexual and corporeal practices.[81] However, LGBT investment in pride in their identity often involves a distancing of themselves from the shameful acts informing their identities, which then manifests itself in divisions between "normal" and "deviant" LGBTs. As a result, Warner suggests, the "incoherence and weakness" of LGBT politics are rooted in the decision to "challenge the stigma on identity, but only by reinforcing the shame of sex" and thereby choosing to "articulate the politics of identity rather than become a broader movement targeting the politics of sexual shame."[82] In response to these normalizing pressures, Warner offers an ethics of queer life that repurposes shame and abjection as that which binds together and hence should guide queer politics.[83] PISSAR's simultaneous challenging of the stigma and shame of disabled and trans pissing and shitting bodies reflects this ethic and provides an instructive example for how we can initiate coalitional politics to trouble the sexual and corporeal normativities of public spaces.

By articulating their coalitional work in the particular space of campus bathrooms, PISSAR avoided the potential pitfalls associated with single-issue identity politics—namely, allowing the differences between similarly situated individuals to overwhelm their synergistic merger. When crafting their mission statement, the members of PISSAR, composed primarily of graduate students with an interest in queer and/or disability studies, stated their commitment to "multi-identity organizing" as well as "working in tandem with other interest groups on campus and elsewhere."[84] Explicitly identifying themselves elsewhere as a queer organization, they further clarified their investment in a "*queer* queerness" that "encompasses both sexually and medically queer bodies, that embraces a diversity of appearances and disabilities and needs." PISSAR translated this critical attitude into their checklist, which they described as "a manifesto of sorts" that "models *queer* coalition-building by incorporating disability, genderqueer, childcare, and menstruation issues into one document, refusing single-issue analysis."[85]

PISSAR, a self-described "coalition group of disability and genderqueer activists," may be best understood then as the fusion of critically queer and disabled politics. First advanced by Butler, the concept of critical queerness is meant to highlight the fact that queer, as a category of identity and site of cultural agency, must "remain that which is, in the present, never fully owned, but always and only redeployed, twisted,

queered from a prior usage and in the direction of urgent and expanding political purposes."[86] Seeing it as a necessary precondition for the
radical democratization of queer politics, Butler asks us to resist the
temptation to circumscribe queerness by embracing and "affirm[ing]
the contingency of the term: to let it be vanquished by those who are
excluded by the term but who justifiably expect representation by it"
and "to let it take on meanings that cannot now be anticipated by a
younger generation whose political vocabulary may well carry a very
different set of investments."[87] Embracing a critically queer attitude,
PISSAR's mobilization of queerness refused to define it narrowly along
identical lines of sexuality, choosing instead to inaugurate an interrogation of the bigendered and abled normativities associated with public
bathrooms.

Of course, assigning temporal and spatial fluidity and contingency
to queerness is not meant to render it a completely empty signifier.
Rather, the emphasis here is on resisting the stable noun form of *queer*
in favor of its usage as a contextual adjective and an active verb.[88] Crip
theorist Robert McRuer further differentiates between virtual and critical queerness, a distinction based on action and intention. As McRuer
argues, "a virtually queer identity" can be "experienced by anyone who
fail[s] to perform heterosexuality without contradiction and incoherence (i.e., everyone)" while a "critically queer perspective [would] pre-
sumably mobilize the inevitable failure to approximate the norm, col-
lectively 'working the weakness in the norm.'"[89] McRuer's interest in
these terms rests primarily in their translation to disability contexts to
differentiate between living a disabled life (virtual disability) and acts
where disabled individuals and groups "have resisted the demands of
compulsory able-bodiedness and have demanded access to a newly
imagined and newly configured public sphere where full participation
is not contingent on an able body" (critical disability).[90] These distinctions prevent the all-too-easy equivocations made in the declarations
that everyone is queer and, if they live long enough, disabled—a move
meant to universalize these identities while simultaneously neutralizing
their potential to unsettle unquestioned institutional, corporeal, and
spatial normativities.

In this particular case, PISSAR's attention to the material effectivities of the spatial normativities that failed to account for disabled and

gender-transgressive bodies provided the inventional resources necessary to animate a critically queer and disabled politics. Composed primarily of educators, the members of PISSAR identified their activism
as "a teaching model in and of itself" by "combin[ing] education with
social change," and we would be well served by further investigating
how they embodied a critical corrective that challenges the devalua-
tion or ignorance of material space in radical democratic theory.[91] As
outlined above, I understand critical queerness and critical disability
to be radical democratic projects. With that said, as critical geographer Michael Brown rightly notes, the theorization of radical democracy generally "lacks any sort of geographical imagination" as it often
fails "to consider that citizens are always engaging in politics in actual
locations."[92] Like Shome, Brown finds the use of spatial metaphors (e.g.,
"creating space" for a practice or group) especially irksome as it risks
"import[ing] fixed, essentialized notions of space into the geographical
imagination of political theory (to the extent that it actually has one)."[93]
Figurative or discursive space alone could not solve the issue of safe and
accessible campus bathrooms. Therefore, out of logistical and political
necessity, PISSAR's enactment of radical democracy had to take place
in the actual space of the campus bathrooms.

The PISSAR patrols provide a potent rejoinder to those who dismiss
queer and disability studies' potential for praxis. Situated on a university campus and composed largely of graduate students with an interest in queer and/or disability studies, PISSAR actively articulated their
theoretical training to their political activities. In their description of
the PISSAR patrols, one group of members framed the connections
in the following way: "Because the bathroom is our site, and the body
in search of a bathroom is our motivation, we recognized early on the
need to be concerned with the body and theory together. PISSAR's
work is an attempt at embodying theory, at theorizing from the body."[94]
PISSAR patrol members armed with rubber gloves and tape measures
utilized a checklist that covered disability accessibility and gender safety
issues as well as the accessibility and supply of tampons and pads and
the presence of a changing table. Fully aware of the risks associated with
their actions, yet still wanting to gather the necessary information in an
"unapologetically public way," PISSAR established guidelines to reduce
the risk of harassment and violence, including working during the day

in groups of three; ensuring that at least one person wore PISSAR's bright yellow t-shirt to raise awareness of the group while also establishing a justification for their spatial transgression; and, finally, making an effort to include persons of varying gender identities.[95] By coming together and working together in bathrooms, the different members of PISSAR placed their own bodies at risk while also experiencing the discomfort and anxieties experienced by others. As a result, PISSAR members enacted a radical democratic politics that utilized space as a generative locus for critically queer and disabled politics built upon the appropriation of shame.

Pissing Off Institutions

At the conclusion of their patrols, PISSAR confirmed their suspicion that their campus bathrooms presented serious obstacles for disabled and trans students and staff. With regard to disabled accessibility, PISSAR reported that of the "approximately 50 single-stall restrooms identified by UCSB as both accessible *and* gender-neutral . . . a majority of restrooms (including those at Health Services) [were] not fully wheelchair accessible and up to ADA codes."[96] PISSAR also found the gender-neutral bathrooms to be riddled with problems as "many 'gender-neutral' bathrooms were incorrectly marked with poor signage, and most [were] functioning as de facto men's rooms because of their placement directly next to specifically marked women's rooms." Moreover, these bathrooms were far from safe in that they created "embarrassing and dangerous" situations for genderqueers.[97] Armed with these results, PISSAR met with university administrators, including the chancellor of the UC system, to demand a solution to these problems, and according to a report put together by the Transgender Law and Policy Institute, the Santa Barbara campus recently "converted 17 single-occupancy restrooms from gendered to gender-neutral and are investigating the feasibility of converting an additional 17."[98] In addition, all future major construction on the UCSB campus will include gender-neutral bathrooms.[99]

In the end, PISSAR seems to have been a temporary coalition, one that withered away once their rhetorical exigencies were addressed by the university administration. Their website is defunct, and many of the members have moved on to other campuses or taken jobs elsewhere. Such are the strategic conditions of coalitional politics.

Reconsidering Time, Space, and Resistance

PISSAR's particular enactment of coalitional politics, one motivated by the overcoming of stigma and shame and emphasizing the rhetoricity of place, space, and identity, brings to light three important issues about the practice of critically queer and disabled politics. First, public bathrooms reflect cultural biases in their erection of potential barriers for individuals who want to participate in public life. For genderqueers and people with disabilities, the seemingly natural system of sexual segregation creates limiting and dangerous places hostile to extended public engagement. Rather than accept these conditions as unfortunate realities, PISSAR used their bodies and voices to remind us that these architectural choices are precisely that—choices to conform to hetero-corporo-normativities and therein accommodate the mythic norms of sex, gender, and able-bodiedness.[100] More importantly, PISSAR called attention to other ways of arranging, marking, constructing, and equipping public bathrooms to lessen the already incredible stigma and shame associated with pissing and shitting in public. Although people with disabilities have some avenues of legal recourse to address issues of accessibility—assuming of course that they can afford the legal representation needed to initiate such challenges—trans people generally do not enjoy comparable legal status as a protected class. If Lisa Mottet is correct in her assertion that the courts will generally treat bathroom access for trans people "as just a minor inconvenience that they do not want to micromanage," this work will have to take place in venues outside of the courts.[101] It is my hope that this chapter makes a compelling case for why all of us should be willing to examine our own pee privilege, or lack of it, and thus support efforts like PISSAR's in the name of securing safe and accessible spaces for everyone to piss and shit in peace.

PISSAR's embodied politics raise a second set of issues concerning the rhetorical undoing of place, space, and identity. We often treat the space/place of rhetoric's enactment as an inert material reality that serves as an innocent backdrop to the reception of the spoken word. Or, on the other end of the spectrum, the occasion is seen as a determining factor in how individuals respond to rhetorical situations. What I want to suggest is that neither of these perspectives fully captures the ways place/space relate to the rhetorical production of identity and agency. PISSAR's activism, including the choice to meet in their campus bathrooms to confront their shared and different forms of shame, demonstrates Certeau's principle that space is a practiced place where individuals can challenge the power relations meant to exclude them from creating publics more hospitable to their needs. Also, in line with Foucault's theorization of space, PISSAR's embodied resistance to the hetero-corporo-normativities governing public places reminds us that spaces are given meaning through the contestation of identity in those spaces.

Finally, PISSAR's negotiation of stigma and shame provides an instructive example of the kinds of correctives needed to energize critically queer politics and resist the normalizing pressures of liberalism. LGBT investment in pride as the antidote to sexual shame can result in the normalization of LGBT politics. However, instead of trying to rid ourselves of shame, might we mobilize it instead as the nodal point for a broader-based critique that refracts social processes and projections of shame? As Eve Sedgwick eloquently argues, shame cannot be quarantined as stigmatized individuals and groups cannot escape the "permanent, structuring fact of identity" performed by shame. They can, however, explore the "powerfully productive and powerfully social metamorphic possibilities" of its affect, as Sedgwick suggests.[102] PISSAR's refusal to be shamed perfectly captured the spirit of Sally Munt's observation about the political possibilities of shame: "When you no longer care that you are being shamed, particularly when horizontal bonds formed through communities of shame can be transmuted into collective desires to claim a political presence and a legitimate self, that new sense of identity can forge ahead and gain rights and protection."[103] PISSAR's explicit articulation of the needs of genderqueer and disabled bodies negotiated, through the idioms of shame, spatially based identifications as a necessary component of political coalition and action.

PISSAR's explicit declaration of their intentions to animate a "queer queerness" that addressed the various ways in which bodies are disciplined and regulated in public bathrooms provides a useful model for countering the logics of shame that dominate LGBT and queer politics. Queer studies and activism, on Halberstam's reading, must divest itself from "white gay male identity politics," motivated by white gay male shame, "that focuses its libidinal and other energies on simply rebuilding the self that shame dismantled rather than taking apart the social processes that project shame onto queer subjects in the first place."[104] He continues: "If queer studies is to survive gay shame, and it will, we all need to move far beyond the limited scope of white gay male concerns and interests." Echoing Butler's commentary on critical queerness, Halberstam suggests that queer theorists and activists must be willing to learn from and adopt the intersectional critiques forwarded by those steeped in feminist and ethnic studies, and I would add crip theory/disability studies to the list.[105] Critically queer groups like PISSAR that define themselves broadly as coalitions countering related forms of domination provide a provocative model for thinking outside of the logics of gay white male shame. We now turn to our attention to a statewide trans activist coalition to further explore the difficulties and benefits of coalitional politics.

3

INTRAAventions in the Heartland

On January 22, 2004, Bree Hartlage, president of the Indiana Transgender Rights Advocacy Alliance (INTRAA), and John Clower, chair
of Indiana Equality (IE), met with the mayor of Bloomington, Indiana,
Mark Kruzan, to discuss the amendment of the city's Human Rights
Ordinance (HRO) to include gender identity as a protected class.
Despite Hartlage's and Clower's efforts to convince Kruzan that gender identity should be explicitly added as a discrete identity category
to Bloomington's HRO, the mayor remained unwilling to endorse an
effort to revise the municipal codes.[1] Kruzan's refusal surprised many,
given his previous support for local gay and lesbian causes and events.
Motivated not by any detectable animus toward trans people, Kruzan's
opposition to the proposed amendment relied instead on his reading of
the codes, as well as the counsel of city attorneys who had advised him
of ways to handle gender identity discrimination claims within existing
legal frameworks. Prior to meeting with Hartlage and Clower, Kruzan
conferred with the city attorney and executive director of Bloomington's Human Rights Commission (BHRC), Barbara McKinney, who
explained to the mayor the possibility of treating gender identity discrimination as sex discrimination, an already protected category under
federal law. For McKinney and Kruzan, the best strategy for dealing
with gender identity discrimination claims would be an administrative interpretation of sex to include gender identity because it would
trigger all of the investigatory mechanisms provided by state and federal anti-discrimination laws. The proposed amendment, according to
McKinney, could not extend a comparable set of resources.[2] Without
the stable footing of a protected category, the BHRC's hands would be
tied, and they would only be able to recommend voluntary mediation

for incidents involving individuals in identity categories not protected at the state or federal level. Although sympathetic to arguments about the symbolic importance of an explicit prohibition against gender identity discrimination, McKinney explained that "an ethical obligation to argue for the strongest possible interpretation of the law, consistent with sound legal reasoning," guided her opposition to the amendment.[3] For the trans advocates, McKinney's offer of an administrative interpretation was an unacceptable compromise in that it failed to codify permanently the prohibitions against gender identity discrimination— depending on the charity of future mayors to interpret the HRO in a trans-affirmative manner could not substitute for an explicit inclusion into the ordinance. Undeterred by Kruzan's and McKinney's objections to their efforts, Hartlage and Clower, along with other members of INTRAA and IE, took their amendment to the members of the BHRC for a public hearing.

After a year and a half of working with the BHRC, the trans advocates persuaded the commissioners to consider the adoption of the amendment at a meeting held on September 26, 2005. When I first heard of this meeting, I decided to attend it as a concerned citizen, not as an interested academic, although my budding academic interests in queer studies made me more than a little skeptical about LGBT appeals to government institutions for protection. In spite of these reservations about the normalizing pressures of the law, I wanted to bracket this critique to show my solidarity with trans people and support their claims of equality. What I did not yet know was how this meeting and the subsequent campaign would inform my work, first by obliging me to confront the sharp discrepancy between situated articulations of equality and queer studies' normative critique of these claims, and second, by forcing me to reconsider the minoritizing logic of my initial interest ("gender identity protections are for other people, not me") and thus to seek a more expansive, universalized understanding of the disparate yet shared forms of gender discrimination LGBTs face on a daily basis.

As I waited outside of the small conference room where the BHRC met, I overheard a small group of what I assumed to be advocates for the measure divide up who would answer what questions. They noticed me, too, and it seemed as though they were not sure if I was friend or foe. Not wanting to distract them from their work but wanting to clarify that I was an ally, I whispered, "Good luck!" and they smiled in return. When the BHRC commissioners arrived and unlocked the door, we all filed into a small room with a conference table in the center and chairs lining the perimeter. I grabbed a seat on the outer ring as the trans advocates exchanged pleasantries with the commissioners, and then the meeting began. As it did, I sensed a level of familiarity between the trans advocates and the commissioners, and processed it as a sign that the stakes of this meeting were low as much of the groundwork had already been laid for this particular discussion.

Jeff Harlig, the chair of the commission, along with fellow commissioner Emily Bowman, sponsored the amendment before the BHRC. Bowman, a graduate student in sociology, explained her support of the amendment as an important step toward LGBT parity before the law: "I know there are several examples of cases where gay, lesbian, and bisexual people have derived benefits from legal or social triumphs and that transgendered and intersexed people have been left on the outside looking in." Referring to the city's prohibition of sexual orientation discrimination since 1993, Bowman concluded, "I personally don't want our Bloomington city ordinance to be another one of those cases."[4] According to the minutes of the BHRC meeting, recorded and reported by McKinney herself, McKinney responded to this line of argument by appropriating arguments about the symbolic importance of the law when she stated that "if the BHRC decided on the voluntary option when legally enforceable options are available, it was sending the message that gender identity discrimination was not a serious issue."[5] Chair Harlig, unmoved by McKinney's attempts to usurp the moral high ground, reiterated the importance of a public declaration against gender identity discrimination, branding McKinney's approach a "stealth option." Another commissioner also voiced a preference for an explicit ordinance that would allow "employers [to] be able to look at the ordinance and know who was protected."[6] Throughout the meeting, McKinney strenuously and repeatedly objected to the amendment, arguing that "symbolic inclusion made no legal sense." At one point, Hartlage, who was in the audience, interjected: "not having the words 'gender identity' in the ordinance was 'not acceptable.' She [McKinney] said it would be better not to be voluntary," referring here to the voluntary mediation of gender identity discrimination claims, "but if it has to be legally, 'so be it.'" Following a short discussion, and against McKinney's recommendation, the commission unanimously approved the amendment to the HRO and forwarded it on to the city commission for their approval.[7]

When the interested parties turned their attention toward the city council, what had started out as an honest disagreement between the trans advocates and the mayor's staff quickly developed into an openly antagonistic relationship. As Clower described it, "a rift opened up between BHRC and transgender community members on one side and McKinney and the mayor's office on the other."[8] The gulf between the two sides widened as McKinney adamantly defended her proposed administrative interpretation as the only legitimate and legally defensible solution, thereby dismissing all other options as imprudent from her position of legal expertise. McKinney's insistence on her interpretive monopoly exacerbated the disagreement as she argued from a doctrinaire perspective emphasizing legal limits and how to work within the law as it already was understood, while the trans advocates operated from a future-oriented frame interested in what the law could become. Whatever her intentions, McKinney's defense of the administrative interpretation strategy exposed the law as an indeterminate system of meaning open to any number of policy translations, thereby undermining her ability to invoke her reading of the law as a reliable guide as to how future city attorneys might construe the relationship between federally protected categories and local ordinances. When McKinney appealed to firm legal grounding, the trans advocates envisioned patches of quicksand lubricated by political expediency, now and possibly in the future. Nothing short of an explicit inclusion of gender identity into the HRO would do.

Aggravating matters even more, McKinney repeatedly claimed that the mayor had assured her that he would not support the proposed amendment; nor would he meet with trans advocates to clarify his position. On the other hand, according to Clower, Kruzan had privately pledged his support, but was "obliged to take a 'better safe than sorry' approach until he [saw] the Council's actual proposal."[9] Whether it was a case of a politician speaking out of both sides of his mouth or a miscommunication between a tone-deaf attorney who valued legal process and protection over trans people's desire for legal recognition, the impasse and mutual distrust between the trans advocates and McKinney and Kruzan stalled the amendment. In the absence of McKinney's blessing, the trans advocates and BHRC members had to expend a great deal of time and energy convincing city council members of the merits of the amendment. McKinney's legal credentials and her certitude about the proper course of action imposed additional hurdles for the amendment's advocates. After months of hard work, two members of the council finally agreed to sponsor the gender identity amendment, and, in contrast to the intense controversy generated by the city council's addition of sexual orientation to the HRO in 1993, the council unanimously adopted the measure on April 19, 2006, with very little public opposition. At the time of the amendment's adoption, Bloomington could count itself as one of the first one hundred jurisdictions to adopt gender identity protections in the United States. While not pathbreaking in its actions, Bloomington was still ahead of the national curve with its decision to provide a remedy for gender identity discrimination, even if it relied upon voluntary compliance and mediation.

INTRAA's statewide advocacy efforts and the campaign to include gender identity into Bloomington's HRO offer us an opportunity to reassess the "T" portion of LGBT politics in two ways.[10] First, INTRAA's advocacy actions provide insight into transgender activism outside of the urban context. Much of what we know about transgender activism comes from major metropolitan areas in North America such as New York, San Francisco, Los Angeles, Quebec, and Toronto.[11] Given their size, both in terms of population and area, these urban locations possess certain resources that are more likely to produce particular forms of visibility politics: community centers dedicated specifically to LGBTs, which carve out safe spaces for communal gatherings; local offices of national organizations such as the Human Rights Campaign and Lambda Legal, which are capable of financing and coordinating targeted protests and campaigns; neighborhoods with higher concentrations of LGBTs and LGBT-friendly and LGBT-owned businesses tolerant of LGBT publicity; and local organizations designed to provide social support. Moreover, an assumed anonymity in a city of strangers, wherein one is less likely to be noticed by acquaintances, family, and friends, allows for particularized forms of being one's self in public. Without inscribing a binaristic, essentialist, or deterministic relationship between the practice of politics in urban and non-urban areas, I want to draw our attention to a state where a city nicknamed "The Crossroads of America" (Indianapolis) sits at its center, yet is not necessarily the center of transgender activism in the area. For transgender advocacy groups and advocates outside of metropolitan areas, politics can take different forms that may not necessarily rely on a visible or sizable population as the implicit warrant undergirding their claims for equality. Accordingly, we need to account for how transgender advocates agitate for cultural intelligibility outside of the big city. In this way, this chapter contributes to a nascent, yet significant, set of literatures challenging the "metronormativity" associated with most LGBT/queer scholarship.[12]

Second, as LGBT and queer theorists and activists wrestle with what it means to be a citizen in a nation that only sometimes tolerates them, INTRAA's activities also provide an opportunity to reconsider the assumed normativity associated with advocates' claims of equality. Many legal and queer theorists remain suspicious of the efforts by LGBTs to gain equal protection before the law due to the expected articulation of these claims to discourses of normalcy. However, my archive, which consists of interviews with INTRAA members, debates on a LGBT radio show, and public deliberations about legal reforms, challenges the proposition that claims to legal recognition and equality require assimilation or acquiescence to hetero-corporo-normativities. This is not to say that discourses of normalcy don't exist or that all transgender advocates want the same thing. Yet, when trans advocates articulate themselves as citizens who want the ability to be recognized as equally valued members of a polity, it may be the case that this is a public transcript, and one that allows for entrance into the cultural imaginary without being beholden to all of its trappings of liberal individualism. The charge of assimilation holds only if discourse and legal subjectivity are figured as fixed processes divorced from particular contexts and located within cultural logics with inalterable scripts whereby culture is reproduced without a difference. It might also be the case that these advocates do not want to be absorbed into dominant culture as much as they want to be able to participate in it, which inevitably transforms the terms of who counts as a legitimate citizen. To read this mode of address as an additive process without any other consequences is both totalizing as a hermeneutic and not sensitive to the diversity of motivations at work in these claims. The advocacy actions discussed in this chapter provide a potent rejoinder to those who suggest that we must reject citizenship or queer it *before* we enter its discursive-material domain. A great number of people do not have the privilege of such a position, and I want to use this archive to demonstrate how advocates work within, outside, and against the law, sometimes vacillating between positions at a moment's notice. This might seem like a contradictory strategy for engaging the law, but it is a strategy that allows trans people a number of articulatory pathways to engage strangers and those who would see them as strangers to the law.

To address these issues, the first section of this chapter surveys the conflicting interpretations of the stakes of asserting a claim to citizenship, especially for LGBTs and queer communities. If we refuse the tendency to condemn these practices as trafficking in and thus legitimating further unaltered normativities, we are not forced to conclude that citizenship must be refused as a remedy to the injustices directed at LGBTs and queers. Instead, we might value these acts as a two-track approach to legal reform wherein advocates both employ legal discourses and critique legal authority at the same time. In so doing, we will appropriate the work of critical legal scholars to outline this conflicted mode of legal subjectivity in our archive. In the third and fourth sections, I analyze the actions of INTRAA on a broad level and then their efforts in Bloomington to contextualize these specific rights-assertion claims as something other than inherently normative claims to citizenship, or what we might call an enactment of the transgender rights imaginary.

Queer Citizenships

In polities where LGBTs, and especially trans people, are treated as second-class citizens, the desire to be recognized as equal citizens is more than understandable. There are, of course, several strategies available for articulating this desire. In an era when LGBT identities and other forms of queerness are caricatured and commodified so as to be easily digested by intrigued publics, whether in the form of television shows, movies, art displays, music, and even academic research, the question of whether or not LGBTs can maintain a distinctive and dissident identity is frequent and pronounced. In response to the question "What's queer about queer studies now?" David Eng, Jack Halberstam, and José Esteban Muñoz skeptically, yet optimistically, suggest that queerness can still generate challenges to sexual, racial, class, and nationalistic hegemonies if it successfully avoids the traps of "queer liberalism." For them, queer liberalism "marks an unsettling though perhaps not entirely unexpected attempt to reconcile the radical political aspirations of queer studies' subjectless critique with the contemporary liberal demands of a nationalist gay and lesbian U.S. citizen-subject petitioning for rights and recognition before the law."[13] More recently, Eng's book-length treatment of queer liberalism develops a sophisticated critique of what he reads as a privatized form of citizenship invested in rhetorics of colorblindness and normative familial and kinship structures, thereby inhibiting any critical traction for those who want challenge these naturalized cultural formations. Eng implores us to "reflect on the political and economic costs that underwrite the current inscription of queer U.S. citizen-subjects into a national order," including "the instability of a rights-based discourse that enables political legitimacy while exacerbating evolving relations of capitalist exploitation, racial domination, and gender insubordination in a domestic as well as global context."[14] These critiques of queer liberalism, motivated primarily by the privileged position of same-sex marriage as the centerpiece of LGBT politics, remind us of the importance of a vigilant defense against the purchase of legal recognition if the cost is uncritically articulating one's self within the logics of normalcy and affirming their status. For me, however, what remains unpersuasive about this essentializing positioning of legal subjectivities as always and only normative is that it is not informed by contextualized articulations of these demands.

For example, Lisa Duggan's much-cited writing on this topic cautions us against the enticements of "homonormativity." Understanding this as "a politics that does not contest dominant heteronormative assumptions and institutions, but upholds and sustains them, while promising the possibility of a demobilized gay constituency and a privatized, depoliticized gay culture anchored in domesticity and consumption," Duggan further calls our attention to the ways in which homonormativity comes equipped with a rhetorical recoding of key terms in the history of gay politics: 'equality' becomes narrow, formal access to a few conservatizing institutions, 'freedom' becomes impunity for bigotry and vast inequalities, in commercial life and civil society, the 'right to privacy' becomes domestic confinement, and democratic politics is something to be escaped. All of this adds up to a corporate culture managed by a minimal state, achieved by the neoliberal privatization of affective as well as economic and public life.[15]

Homonormativity is an incremental, privatized approach to politics that relies primarily on lobbying and/or the work of LGBT and allied lawyers and sympathetic judges. This approach, according to Duggan, leaves little for LGBTs and their allies to do beyond donating money, attending rallies and protests, signing petitions, and acting "normal" in public. In other words, it leaves us with an impoverished sense of agency that disempowers LGBTs and their allies to effect real or direct change in their own lives. Agency thus becomes synonymous with the visibility and then the invisibility enabled by legal recognition. Cultural change is delegated to someone else, someone with access to institutions that will do the serious work of politics for us. On this reading, appropriately enough, citizenship in a neoliberal service economy is contracted out for someone else to do or it is something that can be bought. My issue with Duggan's work is not so much her reading of some disturbing forms of gay and lesbian respectability politics, but more its uptake as an inescapable condition of any and all claims to citizenship. We would be served better by reading the conditions of homonormativity and neoliberalism as a mapping of a conjuncture, to use the language of cultural studies, against which specific articulations of citizenship would be judged.

This critique of queer liberalisms has led some, like Amy Brandzel, to advocate a queer politics premised necessarily on rejecting citizenship and attempts to queer it. Both legal incrementalism and the hope that citizenship can be queered, for Brandzel, require negotiations with heteronormativity that irreparably taint queer world-making projects. This sweeping indictment deserves further scrutiny. For Brandzel, "citizenship is necessarily exclusive, privileged, and normative," and "those who are privileged and well off enough to do so, should refuse citizenship and actively subvert the normalization, legitimization, and regulation it requires."[16] Brandzel defines citizenship to include not only state-based forms of recognition but also civic engagement and "citizenship as identity and the collective experience of belonging to a community."[17] On this expansive definition of citizenship she and I can agree. However, we part ways on the possibility for queering citizenship because the complete rejection of citizenship does not seem like a viable or pragmatic option for coalitional LGBT/queer politics, especially given that many queers, including many trans people, do not enjoy the privilege necessary to *reject* citizenship. Brandzel's commentary, along with Duggan's and Eng's work, on the dangers of norms and assimilation are important reminders about the regulatory force of norms, but their strong structuralist reading of power relations runs counter to a dialectical understanding of the interpenetrative and performative articulation of power and identity. Thus, I cannot agree with my interlocutors that agency is found in the form of some radical autonomy from norms if for no other reason than that complete autonomy, free from the logics of citizenship, is impossible. Therefore, I propose a different conception of agency and politics, influenced by the performativity of identity, which engages these critiques of liberalism but nevertheless understands that for many of us rejecting the state will not make law's violence go away.

To begin to recuperate citizenship from its queer dismissal, we can align ourselves with more generous interpretations of the intersections of queer identities and citizenship, most importantly the work of Lauren Berlant and Shane Phelan. Working from the assumption that "practices of citizenship involve both public-sphere narratives and concrete experiences of quotidian life that do not cohere or harmonize," Berlant offers a more expansive vision of citizenship that moves beyond formal rights and recognition to understand our affiliations with these ideals.[18] Phelan similarly asks us to consider the prospects of queering citizenship: "The question, then, is not 'queer or not' or 'how to make citizenship queer,' but how to queer citizenship—how to continue the subversion of a category that is nonetheless both crucial and beneficial for millions of people around the world."[19] For both Phelan and Berlant, the critical task is not predetermined judgment about legally proscribed subjectivities. Rather, we have to reframe citizenship from a rarified understanding of the political to the ground level of everyday life so as to call attention not only to the ways that the personal is political but also to how the political is negotiated in our daily lives. Finally, such a perspective recognizes that the public transcript of rights claims may not accurately reflect the way that individuals actually live their everyday lives. More than simple strategic essentialism, which relies on instrumentalist views of language and action, I am suggesting that the law is transformed by its performance and that the possibility of transforming hegemonic cultural arrangements is still possible while laying claim to the law.

With this background in place, the current state of LGBT/queer politics is a provocative if not a paradoxical one, as LGBTs/queers and their allies face difficult decisions about how best to advance their interests within a liberal-democratic polity. These difficult decisions include whether or not we want state-based recognition of our identities (such as civil marriage rights, adoption rights, legal protection from workplace and housing discrimination, etc.), how those identities should be defined, and who can lay claim to the categories (e.g., trans, gay, lesbian, bisexual, queer). Rather than decry the conflicting answers that arise to these questions, I see the myriad perspectives and strategies of LGBT and queer politics as a critical resource and a vibrant means for intervention. The question is not citizenship or its refusal. Here I want us to forego the forced choice of one and only one path to equality. Evolving contingencies require the adaptability of political subjectivities, and we need more agile political tactics to respond to them.

Thus far I have established the stakes involved in LGBT and queer claims of citizenship as a frame for understanding the problematics of the relationship between citizenship and the pressures of normalization. The queering of citizenship, the twisting of it away from its normative tendencies, has to be something more than just legal recognition or radical separatism. Neither of these options holds much promise because each of them misconstrues the cultural flows of law: legal recognition alone places too much emphasis on formal equality as a strategy for cultural acceptance, and radical separatism ignores the material consequences associated with legal unintelligibility. Legal recognition, if understood only as a site of normalcy, underinvests itself in the productive threat posed by unexpected articulations of equality, and radical separatists' claims to autonomy and sovereignty from the exercise of state power misunderstand the sources and possibilities of agency. As a corrective to this unproductive binary, I suggest that we address contextualized articulations of the law to understand the effectivities of claims to equality and the law. Similar debates in Critical Legal Studies (CLS) about legal subjectivity may prove to be a useful guide to bridge this theoretical impasse between uncritical acceptance of the law and complete rejection of it. What these debates show is the need to critique state power, if not reject its legitimacy, as one works within its logics, and thus they can serve as a rich context for our reading of INTRAA's actions. Queer critics of rights claims may not be explicitly indebted to CLS, but similar controversies in CLS work analogously to demonstrate the short-sightedness and liabilities of the outright rejection of citizenship as a productive category of cultural intelligibility.

CLS and Rights-Assertion

In the late 1970s and early 1980s, CLS, influenced by Marxist thought and poststructuralist theories of language, hegemony, and ideology, rapidly developed a devoted following of legal scholars willing to challenge the dogmas of legal education and institutions. Born out of dissatisfaction with the limits of reformist legal scholarship, the first wave of CLS scholars, or "crits," interrogated legal liberalism and advocated a strategy of "trashing" the current legal system.[20] In short, trashing required a thorough deconstruction of legal ideals and institutions to expose the various modes of ideological and hegemonic domination enshrined in liberal-democratic governance. The assertion of rights particularly worried CLS scholars because of the false sense of security and equality created by these rights. According to Jason Whitehead, CLS, at least in its formative period and to varying degrees, based its perspective on two principles: the ideology thesis and the indeterminacy thesis.[21] Both of these theses, like the traditional scholarship that they were critiquing, treated rhetorical claims to rights with a great deal of suspicion, since legal language enabled the mystifications and contradictions exploited by elites to maintain their hegemonic positions. The ideology thesis assumed the legal system served the interests of the elites and their property rights while providing only the most minimal of protections and resources for the less privileged. Equality, by almost any measure, is therefore paradoxically prevented by the ways in which individual rights trump collective concerns. The privileging of individual rights over the collective good hinders the ability of disadvantaged groups from bonding together and demanding legal changes. Accordingly, a false dichotomy between the rhetorical and material is reproduced as any rhetoric that works within or reforms the current legal frameworks is seen as the adoption of a false consciousness of legal agency.[22] As one travels further down this deterministic road, it becomes clearer that liberation from this false consciousness is possible only through collective action that does away with, or trashes, the current system. In its place, a new legal order, one that eschews liberal-capitalist ideologies, would need to be constructed. In many ways, the critiques of queer liberalism track nicely along with the ideology thesis in their dismissal of the ability of individuals to transgress and transform the normativities of citizenship.

The second principle of CLS, the indeterminacy thesis, creates tension with its first principle, which made it difficult for the crits to produce a viable political alternative. The indeterminacy thesis assumes that the law's rhetoricity renders it "internally and externally inconsistent" as abstract concepts such as equality, privacy, and freedom of expression can be interpreted in any number of ways.[23] The internal indeterminacy of the law stems from the inherent tensions in a liberal democracy wherein the balancing of individual rights with the collective good gives birth to contradictory case law and necessarily incomplete and fragmented answers to complex social issues as individuals try to make sense of their obligations to one another. Internal consistency breeds external inconsistency because the constellation of case law is not uniform or reliable as a guide in every case. In this skeptical view of rhetoric, legal texts, be they cases or statutes, are seen as liabilities rather than potential assets in that the instability of language allows for a wide range of outcomes. Queer theorists make a similar move when they agree that legal inclusion will help only the most normal-appearing and normal-acting LGBTs. If these two principles are adopted as an accurate rendering of law's grasp on its subjects—meaning that first, the law is a source of ideological domination and that second, the rhetoricity of legal language hinders social progress—the task of imagining a legal system free from these conditions is difficult, if not impossible.

Long on critique but short on practical alternatives, legal scholars across the ideological spectrum leveled charges of legal nihilism against CLS advocates, paying particular attention in the process to the unintended outcomes that would become possible if we trashed the law. For our purposes, we can learn from feminist and critical race scholars who engaged the sexual, gendered, and racial blindspots of CLS's conception of hegemony and ideology to produce more viable legal subjectivities. These revisions to CLS are useful for our purposes in that they engage the complex subjectivities inaugurated and negotiated through legal discourses.

For many feminist jurisprudence scholars, CLS did not adequately interrogate the dynamics of patriarchy either within the exercise of law or in its own critical practice. The diversity of perspectives associated with feminist jurisprudence makes it difficult to generalize about their objections to CLS. For example, Catherine MacKinnon's work forcefully argued for more sustained interrogations into the ways in which male dominance is maintained by a legal system that explicitly and implicitly assumes and promotes male norms.[24] Others, such as Mary Joe Frug, took issue with MacKinnon's "totalizing theory" of domination and wanted to wrestle with the implications of postmodernist theories of identity—theories that understand legal categories as discursive constructions with multiple meanings, thereby denying the thrust of dominance feminism.[25] Met with varying degrees of acceptance, feminist critiques of CLS exposed the heteropatriarchal assumptions of the law and injected gender into conversations previously dominated by class-based concerns.

Critical race scholars provided some of the most productive criticisms of CLS in that they questioned the privileged assumptions underwriting the critical practice of trashing. Like the feminist crits, critical race theorists approached the topic from a number of perspectives. In general, though, the main thrust of their criticisms focused on how Marxist influences directed CLS scholarship to questions of economic equality to the exclusion of questions about the legal and cultural importance of race, gender, and their intersection. Some of the most notable authors in this tradition include Derrick Bell, Kimberlé Williams Crenshaw, Richard Delgado, and Patricia Williams.[26] Of particular importance for our purposes—namely, investigating relationships of identity, hegemony, ideology, and the law—the work of Crenshaw and Williams provides instructive insights for how to address issues of legal recognition and reform.

The central concern of both Williams and Crenshaw is the relationship of rights-assertion, hegemony, and ideology. For Williams, the characterization of rights-assertion as an act of false consciousness or complicity with forces of domination is unacceptable because it ignores the cultural work done by and through rights-assertion. As Williams reminds us, "the country's worst historical moments have not been attributable to rights-*assertion*, but to a failure of rights-*commitment*."[27] Although this statement does not directly refute the possible entrenchment of hegemonic norms, it does remind us that we cannot blindly assume that ridding ourselves of rights talk will necessarily result in a more just society. On Williams's reading, CLS's deconstructive tendencies cannot serve the interests of disadvantaged groups if CLS scholars begin with the assumption that all citizens experience law's hegemony and ideology in the same manner. Formal legal recognition is but one aspect of our cultural lives and other axes of identity must be accounted for to understand how individuals operationalize these terms in their everyday interactions. As we have established earlier, laws and cultures are not two distinct spheres of life such that one exerts control over the other. Rather, laws and cultures mutually undo one another as they are performatively reproduced through each other. To ignore the multiplicity of cultural forces which authorize law's violence risks making a bad situation worse. There is not one dominant legal ideology but rather multiple cultural ideologies of oppression that try to erase entire groups of citizens. Therefore, the assertion of rights can be a valuable tool for countering these oppressive ideologies as one moves from the category of stranger and gains cultural legibility as a citizen. As Williams states, "rights imply a respect which places one within the referential range of self and others, which elevates one's status from human body to social being," who is deserving of "the collective responsibility properly owed by a society to one of its own."[28] Even if one concedes that deploying rights claims associated with a dominant ideology entails some risk of becoming complicit with it, according to Williams, it is certainly better than the alternative of trashing rights or avoiding rights talk. In the here and now, there are not any other plausible discursive arrangements for effecting a sense of communal obligations apart from rights talk. Not all rights claims are equally effective or advisable, but they can announce and establish a set of relationalities conducive to further negotiations of what strangers owe each other.

Crenshaw more directly addresses the deficiencies in CLS's theorizing of hegemony. In particular, she excoriates the critics for their relative ignorance of racism and how race is a hegemonic formation sustained by coercion. CLS's theorizing of domination and hegemony, as in many other critical approaches, is heavily indebted to one reading of Antonio Gramsci.[29] Crenshaw repurposes the vocabulary of hegemony to put an emphasis on the importance of coercion in securing a hegemonic formation:

> In examining domination as a combination of both physical coercion and ideological control, Gramsci developed the concept of hegemony, the means by which a system of attitudes and beliefs, permeating both popular consciousness and the ideology of elites, reinforces existing social arrangements and convinces the dominated classes that the existing order is inevitable.[30]

For CLS, hegemony is a useful concept for explaining how elites garnered consent through legal ideologies. Unfortunately, consent is only part of the condition of hegemony, and Crenshaw argues that the crits often forget to address the forms of coercion used in tandem with consent to produce hegemonic effects.[31] Thus, Crenshaw calls for critical attention to both consent and coercion to more fully account for influence of racism in the practices of domination.

Coercion, as defined by Crenshaw, includes "all non-consensual forms of domination—that is, all forces external to the individual or group that maintain that individual or group's position in society's hierarchy." Thus, coercion can include anything from "baton-wielding police officers to court injunctions to 'White Only' signs. More importantly, it also refers to more subtle forms of exterior domination, such as the institutionalized oppositional dynamic—the vision of 'normative whiteness' that pervades current forms of race consciousness."[32] For our interests, in addition to race, class, and other forms of privilege, trans people face coercion in the form of heterosexual hegemonies that rely on stable bodies with essentialized opposite-sex desires. In making this claim I am not equivocating racism and transphobia, but, they are each forms of social hierarchy reliant on coercion to try to secure the stability of the hegemonic order. As a result, coercion sets into motion certain parameters for cultural arrangements, but they also contain the seeds of their own undoing. Legal rhetorics cannot be reduced to fixed ideological positions. Marginalized groups can use the law to "confront beliefs held *about* them" to "become participants in the dominant discourse rather than outsiders defined, objectified, and reified by that discourse," even if this is not the speaking position that might be chosen in a perfect world.[33] As such, rights-assertion must not be confused with consent to all of the underlying ideological assumptions and hegemonic enticements associated with a legal identity category—the law, as the case of Debbie Mayne demonstrates in the first chapter, is performatively produced, oftentimes at cross-purposes with the intentions of the elites. Marginalized individuals, such as trans people, can use legal identity categories as a way of gaining recognition without falling prey to the law's ideological and hegemonic traps.

So far, our interest in the legal articulations of trans people has been to decipher how their legally inflected discourses enable certain political formations and subjectivities. Having reviewed the criticisms of CLS, we will now focus our attention on outward strategies for engaging legal institutions. If, like some advocates, we adopt a two-track approach to the law that is a politics of *both* legal inclusion *and* perpetual critique of the legal system, we can appreciate the complexities of transgender negotiations of the law. Since trans individuals are acutely aware of the power of identity categories, both for good and ill, transgender activism must be understood, according to Bente Meyer, as "embodying the key concerns of politics and theory today—the complex commitment to and suspicion of identity."[34] Confronting the fact that the law cannot be escaped and the need to embrace it sometimes, this two-track approach to legal engagement maintains a critical distance from law's hegemonic/normative desires. As Harold Dalton explains, we need to view critique of and engagement with the state as a "symbiotic" strategy wherein "the former launches the latter and keeps it on course, whereas the latter saves the former from petulance and self-parody."[35] From this vantage point, arguments for legal recognition should not be read as conceding to the state's authority to define and determine one's sex. Trans advocates often occupy this position by engaging politics at a local level while also challenging the state's ability to determine one's sex.

Paisley Currah outlines how transgender rights imaginaries can move beyond our current situation to envision a world of gender pluralism. Building upon Crenshaw's work, Currah describes the transgender rights imaginary as a way to conceptualize the aggregation of trans legal strategies from inclusion to dis-establishing the state's ability to exclusively define sex and distribute resources, rights, and privileges through this category. As Currah explains:

> Even as activists work to unmoor legal gender from the confines of the sex gender system and its attendant assumptions—that sex is binary and biologically transparent, that gender maps easily and predictably onto sex—they (we) have framed their arguments in terms intelligible to those outside the "gender community" by strategically deploying the language of identity. As a movement, however, the ultimate goal of transgender rights does not seem to be to contain gender nonconforming identities and practices within slightly expanded yet still-normative gender constructions and arrangements. Indeed, in other legal and policy contexts, many of the same activists are working to "dis-establish" gender from the state by ending the state's authority to police the relation between one's legal sex assigned at birth, one's gender identity, and one's gender expression; by attempting to stop the state's use of "sex" as a marker of identity on identification documents; and by ending the state's reliance on sex as a legal category to distribute resources—through bans on same-sex marriage, for example.[36]

Currah's explanation of the transgender rights imaginary makes clear that engaging and using legal categories and institutions does not guarantee the uncritical complicity with their underlying assumptions; much the opposite appears to be the case as legal engagements open up the opportunity for oppositional subjectivities. As trans people argue for legal inclusion and protection, they are also working to make sex a category of self-identification, rather than a medically determined category, that dis-establishes sex as a locus of state benefits and protections. The self-determination and dis-establishment of sex is a lofty goal—maybe it's an impossible goal. But it is an example of this two-track strategy that creates neither a contradiction nor a distraction, and instead involves mutually reinforcing actions. To contextualize this strategy, I now turn to the actions of INTRAA and the passage of the gender identity amendment to Bloomington's HRO.

INTRAA's Educational and Advocacy Efforts

When I first started this project, INTRAA was a relatively small organization with thirty dues-paying members, twelve board members who regularly attended meetings, and around three hundred members on an email distribution list. Cianán, the chair of INTRAA at that time, spent almost 160 hours a month checking up on fundraising projects, sending emails, reading, and contacting people to help with the organization. When I first met Cianán, he was a transman transplanted from Iowa where he had been very active on the University of Iowa campus, succeeding at establishing a gender-neutral floor in a dormitory as well as securing a few gender-neutral bathrooms on that campus. At the time of my initial research, he was living in West Lafayette and pursuing a graduate degree at Purdue. Cianán found Indiana to be far more dangerous than Iowa. As he described to me, he was afraid for his safety when he walked down the streets of this college town. This hostile climate extended to the Purdue campus, where, he claimed, it would be a "fifteen-year battle to get a gender-neutral floor in a dormitory."[37] Citing a number of reasons for this protracted battle, Cianán stressed the political apathy of Purdue students in general, along with the apolitical goals of the Queer Student Union, an undergraduate group concerned primarily with social functions. Describing his interactions with the Purdue undergraduates, Cianán characterized them as "frustrating" because "it's not give and take, it is all give." Unable to find a satisfactory political outlet on campus, Cianán turned his attention to West Lafayette, Indianapolis, and INTRAA.

The association's primary activities include gaining trans protections through the amendment of local ordinances and educational efforts aimed at countering the stigmas associated with trans identities. As Cianán explained, local organizing and successes are part of a bottom-up approach to create pressure to pass statewide protections and a gender identity-inclusive hate crimes bill. INTRAA's educational efforts include a speaker's bureau, which sends out members to address interested parties, and Reel Gender, a film series that provides trans people and their allies a chance to watch and discuss mediated representations of trans and gender issues. This latter forum provides a politics of visibility that moves beyond the simple consumption of mediated texts to a collective critical interrogation of what these mediations provide in terms of cultural resources for understanding genders, sexualities, and bodies. Together, these different activities give INTRAA members a variety of outlets for involvement.

Claire, for example, a self-identified female-to-female transwoman, described herself as "not really a political person who can't speak to legislators," but she enjoyed "supporting those efforts" in other ways, especially through educational activities.[38] Thus, Claire was so moved by one Transgender Day of Remembrance that she asked to lead the following year's activities. When asked why she involved herself with these educational efforts, Claire explained:

> To me, education is the most important function of INTRAA's work and because I see education as coming first and then people will understand what legislation needs to be done. Because if you convince legislators, that's great, but just because you have a law doesn't mean people will understand it and respect it and say, "Oh, yeah, that is a good idea," because, you know, first of all because you know people have bias against laws and legislators and people don't like to be regulated. But if you can bring people to understand through personal experience, by meeting people such as myself who you know, "I have friends who are trans people" to use the old cliché, it can remove the fear of the unknown and that is what INTRAA's mission is.

Similarly, Nick, a transman living in Indianapolis, preferred educational activities to legislative lobbying because he did not want to be placed in a position where he had to distance himself from others through discursive markers of normalcy. As he put the matter,

> It seems like you have to like disavow association with so many people, the fringes, you can only talk about the center to get to, in order to get to,

to get things done legislatively, the most palatable people have to go forward to talk to the legislators and not talk much about anything potentially subversive or upsetting about the things they're saying. And I'm
skeptical about the possibility of the gains trickling down to those who
weren't mentioned in that process.[39]

Demonstrating a nuanced understanding of the public transcripts,
legal norms, and a lack of false consciousness about rights-assertion,
Nick further stated, "I mean I am very much opposed to a politics
of pity us, we can't help it, we're just like you, and that sort of thing,
so I am not really interested in that political form of things." Both
participants in the speaker's bureau, Claire and Nick are interested
in expanding the speaking engagements to populations outside of
schools and campuses, especially to medical personnel and first
responders, given the ways that these people actually hold their lives
in their hands.

Beyond INTRAA's educational work, the organization campaigns
across the state to gain legal protections for trans people. One of
their most successful strategies of engagement involves face-to-face
meetings with city, county, and state officials. At these meetings,
they often use stories of discrimination to provide concrete evidence of the effects of the lack of legal protection.[40] Cianán was
the manager of the Discrimination Stories Project (trans people
can submit stories online, anonymously if they wish), and he often
used these anecdotes to get the attention of lawmakers. As Cianán
recounted,

Personal stories are probably more useful than statistics. They just need
to be honest and coming from a real person. Our stories collection really
exists for the purpose of being able to share things that have happened
in Indiana with the people whose constituencies they happened in. And
most of the time, the person who is telling the story is too afraid to tell
and that in and of itself has a huge impact on the person we're telling it
to. And that the person doesn't have the confidence to come and tell it to
them for themselves because they're in fear for their life or their job and
that has a huge impact and so us being able to tell these honest stories
from the perspectives of Hoosiers that also shows the vulnerability of the

people in this community, I think that it has an impact that people don't really expect necessarily.[41]

Cianán said that most of the officials they encounter are "shocked that this happens in Indiana" as they assume that "it is as safe for everyone as it is for them." He found particularly effective the story of a trans-woman with cerebral palsy who could neither get social services nor file a discrimination suit because she lacked legal standing. As Cianán recounted the story to me, "she cannot shave any better than she does, her appearance is the best that she can do, it as much a disability claim as a gender identity claim but no one sees it that way." While she is discriminated against because of her gender presentation *and* her disability, her discrimination suit is treated only as a gender identity claim, and thus one that is outside of the purview of the law. However, even though the law structurally prohibits an intersectional claim of disability and gender identity discrimination, advocates such as Cianán are able to leverage legal concepts in such a way as to make a persuasive case to sympathetic officials. Instead of being constrained by strict interpretations of the law, Cianán is able to articulate this narrative as a reason for changes in the law.

When dealing with legislators, INTRAA members understand the importance of sticking closely to issues of discrimination and legal language. They do not try to counter claims made by the religious right about the immorality of their identities. To illustrate his point, Cianán discussed with me the problems created by LGBT advocates in South Bend who tried to push through a LGBT-inclusive amendment to the city's HRO by countering the influential religious organizations in the area:

> It was a freight train, way too fast, faster than we could get involved in it. They tried to counter the religious right's arguments and you can't do that. You need to ignore them and continue to make your points, especially in places like South Bend where they outnumber us, so it's important to ignore ridiculous arguments about leading to bestiality protections or whatever, just ignore it and move on. Instead, they tried to counter everything they were saying, and it failed because they didn't get enough of their points out because they spent so much time trying to counter what everyone else was saying.

Cianán later added:

> I've had to defend myself to enough people, to strangers who don't
> deserve my time. So it's not worth it to me for that reason, and I don't
> really feel that it's productive in terms of trying to sway some third party
> to bicker amongst the opponents, between you and your opponent. I
> guess that's an accurate representation of how I deal with the religious
> right. I just kind of ignore it. I don't see it as a very professional mecha-
> nism for dealing with a debate or whatever.

Cianán went on to explain that the rest of organization tends to
think the same way about this strategy of ignoring the religious right.
INTRAA has quickly learned that they do not need to convince everyone, only the officials who will actually vote on the protections. In the
end, city and state officials are not refereeing a debate between the two
sides, and INTRAA members try to focus on personally convincing the
city official or legislator, as opposed to someone from the religious right,
through adherence to existing legal rhetorics of fairness and equality.

Like any successful organization, INTRAA continues to adapt its
strategies and learn from its failures. As Cianán recounted, "the first few
battles taught us how to start, the more of these battles we fight, the
more prepared we are for the next one." Unlike a partisan political unit
that measures its success purely by wins and losses, INTRAA takes a
different attitude: "It doesn't even matter, the win-loss ratio, or any of
that stuff because we expect more often than not that we'll only take
baby steps and when you go in not expecting to sway everyone but to
make an impact, first off, you aren't crushed and ruined when you don't
win so you're able to start back up again." Cianán continued:

> Second, you can learn a lot more from what happened because you can
> see more clearly where your mistakes were and you focus less on infight-
> ing or picking apart what everyone else did. We started to take a stance
> of, I mean I don't want to call it pacifism, but I mean that's really what it
> is. You know we don't really expect to win very often and I think that's
> really good for us because it allows us to relish in our successes. It also
> gives us a really good perspective on our losses that it just lets us see
> that from a much more level-headed place than had we expected to win

every fight that we take on. I think that we also have learned about how the dialogue works, you know what a person needs to know, or how a person needs to speak, just sort of what's expected in that political dialogue to be able to be recognized as a viable figure and that's, you know, extremely useful for us as we grow and we try to take on more projects.

Using South Bend as an example of this attitude, Cianán said:

> We never would have approached South Bend that way, to fight the religious right, to try to win that battle. It isn't the right way to do that and when we sat down and started talking about South Bend it was too late for us to get involved. We started to strategize what we would do the next time around in South Bend and how to get people and work South Bend. I think that we have honed a more sophisticated political understanding of the ways to reach Indiana people in the process of doing this.

The South Bend activists' unsuccessful deviation from legal concepts left an impression on Cianán as other grounds of argument failed to yield favorable results.

In addition to their independent efforts, INTRAA participates in Indiana Equality (IE). IE describes itself as a "coalition of organizations from around the state that focus on ensuring basic human rights for Indiana's LGBT citizens." At the time of my interviews, INTRAA members were often frustrated when working with other parts of the IE coalition because the organization was not especially sensitive to their needs and goals. For Nick, the problem lay in IE's inability to live up to its coalition status: "I feel so much like sitting at that table is about defending my right to be there or defending the worthiness of trans stuff and all of that. I really resent having to do that." Nick also felt "the focus on gay marriage makes it difficult to talk about trans people," as the marriage issues seems to dominate the group's agenda. Cianán echoed these frustrations, explaining that INTRAA members are also "fighting the marriage amendment, it's not our number one priority but it's our coalition's number one priority so we get sucked into it a lot." Although INTRAA has expressed concerns about this direction of the coalition, the objections have largely been ignored. Cianán observed that the insensitivity of the rest of the coalition members was stemmed

partly from its being "very easy to believe that you are more accepting and more capable of understanding, welcoming, et cetera than the
people you are trying to understand actually experience you being."
Cianán continued: "Makes sense. To see yourself in the light that those
people see you is more difficult but is necessary in a coalition." When
asked about the future of the coalition, Cianán carefully said, "We are
hopeful."

As these interviews with members of INTRAA demonstrate, the use
of the law and engaging the state do not necessarily entail the assumption of all of their ideological and hegemonic baggage. INTRAA participates in legal reforms but also has educational components that
address the broader cultural forces authorizing trans discrimination
and violence. That the organization continues to evolve and transform
its mission should allay the fears of those who worry that legal reform
will always only normalize its subjects. As in Debbie Mayne's case, we
should not mistake the public transcript for the whole story as the law
is a source of subjectivities unintended by the law. To further contextualize the discussion of how trans advocates engage and challenge legal
subjectivities, I now turn to the campaign to amend Bloomington's
HRO.

Bloomington City Council

As stated earlier, the executive director of the BHRC posed one of the
biggest obstacles for advocates of the amendment. McKinney did not
appear to be transphobic nor did she object to protecting trans people under the law. McKinney, as a lawyer arguing on behalf of the city,
asserted that she was acting in everyone's best interest. A discussion on
BloomingOUT, a Bloomington-based radio program concerned with
LGBT issues, succinctly captured the tension between the trans advocates and McKinney and Kruzan. McKinney reiterated the mayor's preference for including trans issues under the rubric of sex as opposed to
creating a new category, emphasizing the argument that only sex-based
claims would allow the city to issue subpoenas and obtain documents.
Deana Lahre, an advocate of the gender identity option, questioned
McKinney's understanding of the law and trans identity, observing that
trans discrimination is often rooted in issues of gender and sexuality

more than it is purely an issue of sex. Dismissing Lahre's point as an academic division between sex and gender that is not recognized by the law (meaning that gender discrimination claims are filed under the legal category of sex), McKinney again warned that the addition of a protected class not recognized by state or federal law would open up the law to legal challenges and harm the credibility of the BHRC. McKinney stated, "if it's a serious problem, and I think it is, then it needs a serious solution, not just a symbolic solution." One of the show's hosts, Helen Harrel, immediately suggested the sex-only option was a "cop-out" on the part of the city, to which McKinney replied, "the cop-out is to trivialize it" by enacting a law with voluntary mediation. As the segment ended, Harrell asked Lahre if she had any final comments. Undeterred by McKinney's opposition and willing to accept what McKinney characterized as "symbolic" legal status, Lahre sharply replied: "we live in two worlds, the legal world and what we have to live in, the real world," thereby drawing attention to the fact that symbolic inclusion may be more important than legal doctrines in providing resources for negotiating one's way in the world and in relationships with others.[42] This seemingly simple statement marks a critical self-awareness about the limits of legal subjectivities as well as the possibilities for mobilizing legal categories in ways contrary to normative expectations.

While McKinney's position as the executive director of the BHRC obliged her to argue for the most legally sound method of addressing trans discrimination claims, her condescending tone and failure to recognize the importance of the distinct category of gender identity unnecessarily complicated the debate. To the ears of the trans advocates, McKinney's position and comments, while undoubtedly well-intentioned, erased the specificity of everyday struggles that are not adequately captured solely by the legal category of sex. Moreover, the collapsing of gender identity claims into sex avoided a public declaration that explicitly recognized the unique forms of discrimination aimed at trans people. Speaking in another forum, Bree Hartlage declared that even if the move was only symbolic, "Adding the words would be an open expression of support and an indication of buy-in from the city, that it's interested in preventing discrimination and mediating complaints." Hartlage further stated: "The words need to be written down. Transgender people have lived in the closet long enough.

We don't want the language to remain in the closet."[43] Here it must be noted that Hartlage's investment in the explicit category of gender identity was more than symbolic as it was equally rooted in pragmatic political calculation. One of the trans advocates' strongest arguments against the administrative interpretative strategy was that future city administrations could choose to ignore this generous interpretation of the municipal code and that trans people would be left without any recourse.[44] Therefore, McKinney's repeated disparagement of adding a new category to the HRO as simply symbolic was not a fair or complete depiction of the situation.

As the amendment languished, waiting for a sponsor on the city council, the trans advocates lobbied all of the council members willing to listen to their case. Frustrated by IE's giving priority to defeating a proposed prohibition on same-sex civil marriages, Hartlage and Lahre teamed up to do the majority of the lobbying on behalf of INTRAA. Lahre, a self-described "solid Reagan, business Republican" trans-woman, and Hartlage, described by Lahre as a "hard core Democrat," approached the issue from different perspectives which allowed them the ability, on Lahre's account, to "bring down any wall."[45] In Lahre's meetings with city council members, Hartlage presented arguments about human rights and equality while Lahre addressed issues associated with businesses. Operating from what Lahre termed "a business view of life," she would inform the council members that she worked for the Kelley School of Business at the University of Indiana, "the most Republican place in the state of Indiana," and that since her colleagues did not have a problem with her trans identity, neither should anyone else. As Lahre explained to me, the main obstacle to finding a sponsor was that none of the Democrats on the council was willing to be the first to propose the measure. In her view, they were "cowards or hypocrites" who supported the amendment only behind closed doors because they wanted a Republican to provide them with political cover. After Lahre and Hartlage found a Republican sponsor, a number of the Democratic members pledged their support.

Lahre credited the success of their face-to-face interactions with the council members to the ways in which they challenged the "freak show" stereotypes perpetuated by exploitative talk shows. In addition to the logical arguments she and Hartlage made, their physical presence was

also persuasive: "I don't want to say that I am responsible for something, but the dialogue changes when I walk in the room, I am not into
combativeness. . . . The thing is that when they see me and what I can
do, are you prepared to throw me in the trash heap?" Lahre continued:
"I put them on the defensive because I said that this was not a freak
show, I came in with a business suit and every time Bree came in with
a suit," and they engaged the council members' concerns. Armed with
statistics about businesses and the experiences of other municipalities
that had adopted similar measures, Lahre and Hartlage convinced a
majority of the council to support the measure, setting the stage for a
public battle over the amendment. Once this occurred, Lahre and Hartlage knew that they had enough votes to pass the amendment. The only
issue left was whether or not they could get all of the council members
to support it. Lahre's statements might be read as normalizing claims of
respectability, but they must be placed within a larger context of how
trans people can use these cultural expectations to demand intelligibility as citizens worthy of being heard and of being protected from the
discrimination of others.

In preparation for the first public hearing about the amendment,
the city council, with help from INTRAA and IE, prepared and distributed a legislative packet. After a perfunctory explanation of terminology, the report cited a 2003 study from the Transgender Law Center and the National Center for Lesbian Rights: "Transgender people
experience the following rates of discrimination: employment—49%;
public accommodation—38%; housing—32%; and health care—31%."[46]
All of these areas were covered by the amendment in some fashion and
immediately established the need for the amendment. The introduction also clearly stated the council's support for adding gender identity
as opposed to simply using the category of sex. The report stated: "the
Commission and other advocates for gender identity inclusion argued
that amending the Code sends an important public message. First,
inclusion points out that gender identity warrants protection. Second,
it educates the public about this form of discrimination. Third, codi-
fication assures that protection of gender identity is consistent from
one City Administration to the next."[47] Finally, the packet offered up
resources for those who needed more information about how to comply with the amended code.

Bathrooms were the main topic in this section. Suggesting that they be dealt with this on a case-by-case basis, the city council assured this could be done easily. Indeed, they went even further to say that

> According to one expert we consulted, instead of creating new problems regarding bathroom use, this ordinance will actually help solve some existing ones. Notably, people are *already* using the restroom of the gender with which they identify. The ordinance will help prevent the obvious disruptions and problems that arise when a person is required to use a bathroom inappropriate to her/his gender identity (e.g., when transgender women are forced to share bathrooms with men, or transgender men are forced to share bathrooms with women). Furthermore, the ordinance will help members of the community better understand gender identity and encourage employers to work with employees on arriving at a solution.[48]

The city council also clarified that the ordinance would not lead to more "cross-dressing" at work, a red herring often lodged against similar measures by those who feared that individuals would identify as transgender for lurid reasons:

> 87 jurisdictions (consisting of millions of people) have already extended their local non-discrimination ordinances or statutes to cover gender identity or expression. We spoke to Christopher Daley, Director of the Transgender Law Center, about this issue. According to Chris, the argument is really a red herring—there is no evidence that such protection leads to any increase in the number of employees who cross-dress on the job. Employers in jurisdictions that have passed similar ordinances have not reported or complained of any such increase in cross-dressing, and human rights departments in those jurisdictions have not been inundated with complaints from cross-dressing employees. The City of Minneapolis has had a gender identity inclusive non-discrimination law since 1975, and there has been no influx of cross-dressers into the workplaces in that jurisdiction.[49]

The tone of the packet suggested that the amendment would easily pass and pre-empted some of the most obvious arguments against it. Thus,

INTRAA's work was, in many ways, already done in that they had convinced the council members to support them. What remained was to engage their fellow citizens in the public hearings about the amendment.

At the first reading of the amendment, Harlig, the chair of the BHRC, introduced the commission's recommendation and, in not so many words, declared a compromise with McKinney. Accordingly, the BHRC would allow someone who experienced gender identity discrimination to choose if he or she wanted the claim to be pursued under the category of "sex" or "gender identity." Hartlage was the first person to speak from the audience, identifying herself as a "resident of the city of Bloomington," "a property owner and a landlord." Some might read Hartlage's opening lines as comporting with neoliberal formations of citizenship, but we must keep in mind that citizens must establish themselves as interested parties before a city council, and residence and land ownership in the jurisdiction are particularly effective ways to mark oneself as a citizen. Also, Bloomington is a university town, and so Hartlage's identifications signaled an investment in the community that transient students may not have. Wasting no time, Hartlage immediately called attention to the personal stakes she had in the amendment: "At the moment, I am not part of that thirty-one percent. When the amendment before the council is passed, the percentage will not increase significantly but it will still be very significant to me. I will join that thirty-one percent group of people who do live in a jurisdiction where transgender people are provided equal rights and protected from discrimination." Without recourse to discourses of normalcy, Hartlage still made a claim to being treated equally. Recounting her own good fortune to work at a company that did not fire her before, during, or after her transition, Hartlage spoke about those less fortunate than she: "Those who are brave enough to try to transition on the job are generally fired or harassed to the point that they end up leaving out of fear for their safety, health, and well-being. Most transgendered people quit their jobs before transitioning and start a new career after they have transitioned." After defining the terminology of transitioning, Hartlage redirected the shame from trans people to those who enforce cultural normativities on them: "After transitioning, most transgendered people hope beyond hope that no one finds out about their past. Thus, they have jumped out of one closet and into another. What a sad testimony this is to our society." Near the conclusion of her statement, Hartlage mentioned religious objections, but only once: "I recognize that there are people who are opposed to what we are doing this evening and for those who would like to throw out Biblical references, I would certainly ask that they keep them in perspective of where they are written." And that was one of the two comments from the trans advocates about religion for the entire night. Rebecaa Jimenez, an ordained American Baptist minister, provided the only other comments about religion a short while later. Consistent with INTRAA strategy, Hartlage and the other speakers in favor of the amendment were not about to be dragged into a debate about religion when the debate should remain focused on the law.

When it came time for public comments, a number of religious officials from local churches offered their interpretations of biblical passages that spoke to the sins of promoting trans identities. Again, the trans advocates did not take the bait. When Caleb Colbard, a transman, got up to speak, he did debate those opposed to the amendment—he was speaking truth to power in the form of the city council. After some introductory comments, Colbard explained his experiences in the following manner:

> Because my gender expression frequently defies traditional stereotypes, I have been the object of stares, whispers, or jokes, been delayed from receiving or denied services, have received harassing emails, have been specifically intimidated, have been dismissed or ignored, have been called dyke or fag depending on whether someone thinks that I am a woman or a man.

Calling attention to the fuzzy boundaries of sex, gender, and sexuality, Colbard asked:

> How does one classify this treatment? Have I been harassed on the basis of my sex, my gender, or my sexual orientation? The truth is that the public perception often blurs these categories together; transgress one and you have transgressed them all. But the current HRO only makes provisions for protection on the basis of sex and sexual orientation, so what does someone do when the discrimination they experience is not so easily defined?

After stating that the issue was one of valuing all citizens ("It makes a clear and public statement about who and what the city of Bloomington values. It makes a statement to those with less traditional gender identities and expressions are considered equal citizens under the law and that they are worth protecting"), Colbard identified the three benefits of the amendment: (1) it would be a way to educate the public about transgender discrimination, (2) it would improve the image of the town for people who look for LGBT-inclusive places to live and visit, and finally, (3) it would protect cisgenders who are discriminated against because of their gender transgressions. Using an estimate that 2 to 3 percent of the population is transgender, Colbard contextualized the number for a town the size of Bloomington:

> In Bloomington, if three percent of the population is transgender, over 2,000 residents are not explicitly protected by the current anti-discrimination ordinance. If only two are transgender, around 1,500 are not protected, and if only one percent, as little as one percent, are transgender, hundreds of Bloomington residents are not explicitly protected by the current antidiscrimination ordinance, and that is hundreds too many. These figures do not include the non-transgender portion of the gay, lesbian, bisexual, or heterosexual communities whose identities or gender expression may vary from traditional norms, or the countless numbers of family members or friends and allies who would also benefit from this amendment.

In emphasizing the wide-ranging effectivities of the proposed amendment, Colbard refused the stability of identities and identified the interpenetration of different forms of gender non-normativities. Rather than resort to claims based on similarities between transgender and cisgender people, Colbard focused the audience's attention on the discrimination aimed at those who do not conform neatly to expectations about body, gender, and sexuality.

Finally, Colbard addressed the issue of sex versus gender identity, framing it as one of visibility:

> It's about visibility. I would and do choose this option because trans people have been told to hide and stay quiet for too long, that we are not

welcome because we are freaks, that our concerns are not valid, that 'we brought this onto ourselves' and that violence and discrimination are the consequences of our choices. I am here tonight to say, "No!" I will not run and hide to receive under the table concessions as long as I do not have to be publicly acknowledged. The addition of gender identity to the human rights ordinance is right, it is just, and it is long overdue.

Again, Colbard's comments do not rely on strategies of normalization— in fact, Colbard does not apologize for what others may understand as the violation of gender norms. Instead, Colbard moves the discussion away from the issues of personal choice to focus on how the culture discriminates against trans people. Shifting the burden of proof onto those who impose and enforce gender norms on others, he justified legal inclusion on the grounds of others' behavior. At the same time, Colbard is unapologetic about non-normative gender modalities.

The religious opponents, as well as a man who claimed that trans people were pedophiles, shifted the discussion to the topic of how the amendment trampled their rights. Near the end of this discussion, Lisa Williams, someone who had been watching the hearing on television, came into the council chambers to speak in defense of the amendment. So outraged by the discussion that she did not have time to change out of her pajamas and slippers, Williams was one of the only people to make explicit rights claims in what we might typically consider rights talk. Although not transgender herself, Williams self-identified as disabled and related her experiences of discrimination and protection to the issue at hand:

I speak as a specially protected class of person as you can easily see I am a disabled woman, a rather severely disabled woman. Some years ago I was not in a special protected class of person, first because I wasn't disabled and earlier because there wasn't any protection for somebody like me. And there needs to be such a thing.

Williams continued to explain why discrimination laws are needed:

Let's be practical about things. The people who are discriminated against are not the people who are really healthy, or really attractive, or really heterosexual, or really gender-specific to what their biology is. That's not who is discriminated against, it's those of us in the minority.

Near the end of her comment, Williams articulated this issue to common legal themes:

> There is no fulfillment of the right of life, liberty and the pursuit of happiness if things like the ability to get a job based on your qualifications and your merit doesn't exist; there is no life, liberty, and the pursuit of happiness if you have nowhere to live because you are being discriminated against. . . . However, I do see the law as a step to changing the hearts of people, when the state deems it fit to recognize the worth and the dignity and the inalienable rights of all human beings, change starts happening in people's lives.

Williams conceded the importance of legal standing and recognition, but not as ends in and of themselves. To the contrary, as she extrapolated from her own experiences, legal recognition can alter the cultural coding of identities for the better. Making arguments that the trans people did not necessarily make, Williams shows that rights claims are one way, but not the only way, to make legal claims about one's identity.

After the religious opponents again stated their opposition, the council spoke. While many of the members had planned to save their comments for the following week, Commissioner Sturbaum spoke about the impact the face-to-face engagement had had on his support of the amendment. He then chastised the religious opponents for claiming a monopoly on morality and the word of God. Again, INTRAA members did not have to engage religion, although others were happy to do it for them, including Sturbaum, who grew increasingly frustrated by the tactics of the religious opponents:

> I was a little bit offended at the presumption that you know what God says to people in their hearts. I think you can know what God says to you, but it's very presumptuous to know that is what God says to everyone. And that's the interesting thing about how we're all different. And I think when God speaks, it's on a very personal basis, on a very personal level. And I have a lot of problems with why the expression of your

Christian faith would involve discriminating against a party of people that are part of the diversity of our world. I don't see that it affects the practice of your religion, unless part of your practice is to actively discriminate against others, and that's a little confusing to me.

Another council member, Tim Mayer, then chose to speak. After outlining the ways that religion has been used both to persecute Native American peoples and to justify slavery, he condemned the religious speakers:

We are a tolerant nation and for me as long as person lives a decent life, and does not affect other people, who am I to judge them? I think that we should be a tolerant society. I personally don't see that religion has anything to do with this, this has to do with people living their lives as they choose to live them and as long as they are not affecting other citizens of this community, I say that is fine with me.

Of course, tolerance may not have been the operative attitude hoped for by the transgender advocates, but then they could not control all of the interpretations of their messages. After one more council member spoke briefly, and the council voted 7-0-1 to advance the measure to a final reading.

The following week, with the writing on the wall, only one opponent of the measure showed up. Again, the council allowed the supporters and opponent to speak about the relative merits of the amendment. Then it came time for the council members to speak and cast their votes. David Sabbagh, a Republican co-sponsor of the bill, went first. In a serious tone with a paced delivery, he said:

I am a Republican, I don't apologize for it. I am a Republican first, I am a human first but I am a Republican, and I bring this forth in the best tradition of being a Republican because what we are saying is people, individuals, should be able to rise to the fullest of their ability and not be hindered by government.

Referring to the debate from the previous week, he then read a letter from a transwoman who was too afraid to speak in public on this issue and concluded: "I think they are the brave people because they look honestly at their lives and they say 'I can't live a lie, I've got to be honest with myself,' and they take that step. They are the ones, I tell you, who are the brave people. I have nothing but admiration for them." Dave Rollo, another council member, explained his support as a matter of civil rights:

> Although we have come a long way in our society in extending equal rights and equal protection under the law I think we still have a long way to go. In supporting this tonight we take another step in that process of affirming tolerance, equality, and basic civil rights. . . . I find that this ordinance harms no one but I hope that it helps to advance fundamental civil rights and I hope that this debate has worked in the interests of tolerance for our community.

For Chris Gaal, who refuted the argument that the amendment interferes with the exercise of religion, affirmed his support for the amendment in the following manner:

> is a statement of city policy saying that the city condemns discrimination on the basis of our ordinance on the basis of gender identity when it comes to employment, when it comes to public accommodations, and when it comes to housing. Someone should not be denied a job or housing or denied entrance to public accommodations based on their gender identity. I am happy to support this ordinance amendment.

Similarly, Andy Ruff said that the religious opposition crystallized his own thoughts on this issue and convinced him to support the amendment:

> It doesn't protect behavior, it protects people from behaviors. It protects people from intolerance, incivility, uninclusiveness, discrimination, it protects people and not adopting this would protect those behaviors, would protect the behavior of intolerance and incivility and discrimination of people they personally disagree with or disapprove of and those are behaviors the rest of us are protected from under the law. And those are behaviors and attitudes that the rest of the member of our

community, Bloomington, Indiana, reject. Bloomington is a place of inclusiveness, diversity, tolerance, and civility and I'm proud to pass this legislation tonight.

Council member Jason Banach, who had missed the previous meeting, was the one person whose support was uncertain to the trans advocates. Even though his vote would not make a difference to passage of the amendment, it could prevent unanimous passage. Banach's first comments about the fact that the ordinance could be opposed on grounds that had nothing to do with religion were not encouraging. Then, he described his friends' reaction to the issue at a dinner party he'd just thrown:

> I have never seen my friends get more into it and have stronger feelings one way or another, and it wasn't based in religion. The concerns they raised were what do we do about the restrooms, what do we do about the locker rooms, what do we do about the dressing rooms, it wasn't religious-based concerns at all. So I mean I thought that was interesting that it got me thinking about all sides of the issue and I have never, not even the smoking ordinance, caused that big of a debate, but it surprised me that there was that much contention over the issue.

Banach stated that this exchange among his friends led him to ask the city's legal experts about what effect the amendment would have on public accommodations and they assuaged his fears. Banach then said that the question

> boils down to a civil rights issue and I agree with that and I know that I am going to take a lot of smack at my next dinner party for this position, from at least half of my friends, but that's politics. So I think that also the fact that not only the past governor, Governor Kernan, issued transgender as a protected class, but also the current governor, Mitch Daniels, same proclamation. I think this is the right thing for us to do, so I plan to support it.

A few more commissioners had brief comments and then they voted— 9-0 in support of the amendment.

Lessons Learned

INTRAA's actions and the efforts to amend Bloomington's HRO provide two related yet distinct insights into legal subjectivity, citizenship, and trans/queer identities. First, there is a rich history of critical legal scholarship that is concerned with the implications of rights talk and the articulation of one's identity to rights.[50] As LGBT/queer critiques enter this discussion, one concern is that LGBTs/queers will be pressured to assert their normalcy and perform their citizenship in that way. However, we should not assume that all rights claims orbit around the normal or that we are dictated by its gravitational pull. To translate the lessons learned from the feminist and critical race engagements with CLS, rights-assertion is one useful method for gaining recognition as a citizen and being treated not as a stranger but as an equal worthy of respect. To assert one's rights is not to be complicit with all of the underlying assumptions and baggage of those rights. As stated earlier, citizenship is a performatively produced category that can be done and undone in a number of ways, some of which will counter the hegemonic desires of the law. When individuals position themselves in relation to mundane activities, such as working, shopping, or eating at restaurants, they may not be working with discourses of normalcy or aligning themselves with neoliberal consumer citizenship. Making claims to one's legal equality translated through these activities should be read more as a means than as an end since it is one utterance in a chain of contextualized articulations, not a claim to an essentialized identity.

Second, it is possible for advocates to work within and against the law at the same time. This may seem contradictory, but it is a crucial strategy for navigating one's way through the world. INTRAA and other trans advocates operate within a transgender rights imaginary that understands that the law will continue to rely on sexual classifications for the foreseeable future and therefore the ways in which these privileges are distributed must be confronted. However, this does not mean that they completely agree with all of the current order of things. They are also working through cultural engagements to alter the meaning and power of sex. Through outreach programs and educational efforts, they are able to reach people in ways that typical lobbying efforts don't. Their campaigns thus work both within and outside of the law. As a result, we should not assume that trans advocates are hegemonically trapped by the law for they are quite clearly reworking it as they engage it. Claire reminds us that the legal protection of gender identity is a starting point, not an end point. From this perspective, the goal of protecting gender-variance and educating people about it is to allow everyone, not just trans people, to be who they want to be:

> You know the motto for the group now is fighting for your right to be who you are. That's it, not what gender you are, but just who you are. And to me that is a really important shift in the discussion because to me, that is the core of the whole discussion that you have a right to be and also express who you are, within certain, I don't necessarily want serial killers to be expressing themselves, right, but for people to understand that there is nothing to be afraid of if people do not conform to what they expect gender expression to be. So, for example, if you see someone who you think is male wearing a dress, there is no reason to freak about it. There is no reason not to rent them an apartment, it doesn't mean they'll be a bad tenant, it doesn't mean they will be a bad parent, it doesn't mean they will have wild parties. It's to recognize that it's just the person's business, unless you want to date them, it's not significant in the legal way, in the social interaction way, in a "Oh my god, is that person going to use the same bathroom?" kind of way.

The articulation of trans identity as a protected class in and of itself worthy of legal protection is one productive strategy for addressing inequality. Recourse to legal concepts also allows one to be addressed as a citizen. We now turn our sights toward a national struggle for securing employment protections at the federal level and the question of whether or not these protections should be trans-inclusive, to understand better how the law can be a location of solidarity.

4

GENDA Trouble

For better or worse, the struggle for same-sex civil marriage rights continues to dominate the agendas of many LGBT advocacy organizations. A quick glance at the websites, promotional materials, and mailers from the Human Rights Campaign (HRC), Lambda Legal (LL), and other national organizations reveals the importance of civil marriage campaigns to their mission and fundraising efforts. As we saw in the last chapter, advocates are drawn to this issue for a variety of reasons, and the growing support of national leaders is emboldening same-sex civil marriage advocates to push more quickly and loudly for marriage equality in the United States. For example, after President Barack Obama announced his evolution on this issue, same-sex marriage activists redoubled their efforts to secure civil marriage equality, armed with a presidential imprimatur to buttress their claims for equal protection under the law. With subsequent newspaper headlines such as the *Los Angeles Times*'s "Gays May Have the Fastest of All Civil Rights Movements," a story detailing relatively rapid changes in public opinion on marriage equality, the subject has become increasingly framed as an inevitable outcome of liberalism's self-correcting impulse toward tolerance and inclusion.[1] In contrast to the frame of inertia, we should not forget the time and energy expended to force institutional logics in this direction.

In these campaigns, LGBT advocates often assert the centrality of equal marriage rights as the lynchpin to achieving cultural acceptance and full equality under the law. If we measure this claim against the vociferous opposition voiced by the so-called defenders of traditional marriage, including their conspiratorial accusations of a radical gay agenda, full and equal civil marriage rights may make one inroad into greater cultural tolerance of LGBTs. Of course, the fantastical projection of a monolithic LGBT rights movement capable of wielding such coercive and persuasive powers is crude propagandist hysteria meant to fill homophobic coffers. If anything, the cultural right and its venomous articulations of the threat posed by LGBTs have strengthened the political resolve of many LGBTs.[2] On Jodi O'Brien's reading of the situation, "to the extent that a 'gay agenda' does exist, it can be defined as the collective spirit of defense that has coalesced *in response to* an anti-gay political movement."[3] Rather than assign a positive political valence to this discursive formation of community, O'Brien warns of what she terms the "tyranny of solidarity" wherein LGBTs, regardless of their own political inclinations, are obliged to coalesce around issues such as same-sex civil marriage rights simply because of their perceived membership in a larger imagined community under attack. That is, if LGBT unity is imposed by a reactionary one-to-one relationship between identity and politics, this unity may come at the expense of shutting down the robust and generative antagonisms necessary to keep movements, activists, and identities vibrant and healthy. Consequently, the centrality of the struggle for same-sex civil marriage rights may be paradoxically fueling and suffocating LGBT politics. The material benefits of marriage are but one concern for LGBTs who face varied forms of inequitable institutional distributions of rights and privileges. Moreover, the suggestion that securing civil marriage rights is the last hurdle to full and equal citizenship rings hollow for many LGBTs. Civil marriage equality cannot address the discrimination directed at the other parts of their identities, including race or class, or their ability to secure and maintain employment.[4]

Without fully entering into the debate about the desirability and wisdom of the centrality of civil marriage equality for LGBT politics, I raise the issue here to draw our attention to how the time, energy, money, and mainstream media coverage afforded to marriage equality often come at the expense of another issue of equal or greater importance to many LGBT citizens: legal prohibitions against employment discrimination.[5] If we compare the polling data on public support for same-sex civil marriage rights and equal employment opportunities for LGBTs, the numbers fail to justify the disproportionate focus on marriage as the top priority of many LGBT organizations. Although civil marriage rights for same-sex couples now enjoys the support of the majority of Americans by a slim margin, an overwhelming majority of Americans favor employment protections for LGBTs.[6] In fact, the disparities of support for these issue is shocking. The Gallup Organization has tracked American attitudes on whether or not "homosexuals should or should not have equal rights in terms of job opportunities" since 1977. In its first poll, Gallup found 56 percent agreed that they should, and by 2008 the percentage had grown to 89 percent of respondents answering in the affirmative.[7] The Gallup poll did not include trans people in its questions, but another recent survey indicates almost three-quarters of Americans would support employment protections for trans people—a figure backed by hard data as far back as a 2002 survey commissioned by the HRC.[8] Given these statistics, the emphasis placed on civil marriage equality over a federal prohibition on employment discrimination is nothing short of dumbfounding. To be sure, an ardent advocate for civil marriage equality might rightfully point out that more Americans live in states with employment protections than in states with full civil marriage equality, thereby justifying their efforts in marriage activism. Moreover, these campaigns do not have to be positioned as an either-or propositions. The reality of resource availability, however, often forces a choice as to which issue is privileged. The hard-won advances made by activists at the local and state level to secure employment protections need not preclude the push for a federal remedy—not when it is still legal to fire gay, lesbian, and bisexual employees in twenty-nine states because of their sexual orientation, and when employers are free to discriminate against transgender employees in thirty-five states.[9]

Employment discrimination is pervasive in the lives of trans people. Using data collected from six different surveys of state government employees, the Williams Institute reports that between 20 to 57 percent of gender respondents experienced consistent and varied forms of employment discrimination, including denial of employment and promotion, verbal, physical, and mental harassment, and termination.[10] As shocking as these statistics may be, incidents of employment discrimination are likely to be underreported, partly because many trans people guard their identities, and partly because some participate in "job tracking," meaning they "avoid the prospect of employment discrimination by seeking out positions only in fields or with employers that have a record of supporting diversity in sexual orientation or by self-employ-ing."[11] The most comprehensive survey of transgender discrimination, recently released by the National Center for Transgender Equality (NCTE) and the National Gay and Lesbian Task Force (NGLTF), found that 90 percent of their respondents "directly experienced harassment or mistreatment at work or felt forced to take protective actions that negatively impacted their careers or their well-being"; trans members of racial minorities and those with lower incomes bear unequally the brunt of this mistreatment.[12] Unsurprisingly, then, the Transgender Law Center's (TLC) finding that trans people in California, when compared with their cisgender counterparts, are "almost twice as likely to hold a bachelor's degree" but are also "twice as likely to be living below the poverty line of $10,400," further confirms the hostile environment cre-ated by ignorant, if not transphobic, coworkers and employers. Of those trans people who lose their job(s) because of their gender identity, TLC reports over half of them find employment in another field after self-identifying as transgender or gender non-conforming, which, in turn, contributes to rates of episodic or extended homelessness approaching 20 percent.[13]

Although these rates of discrimination are alarming, they are in fact consistent with our surprisingly low opinions of our fellow citizens' behaviors. A Kaiser Family Foundation survey of the general public revealed that 67 percent of respondents answered affirmatively when asked if "LGBT people experienced discrimination 'often' or 'some-times' in applying for or keeping a job."[14] Although the situation is undeniably improving—and corporate America is ahead of the curve on this issue, given that 87 percent of the Fortune 500 companies have instituted policies prohibiting sexual orientation discrimination and 46 percent have similar policies related to gender identity discrimi-nation—the workplace cannot be considered a safe space for many LGBTs.[15] Moreover, it must be kept in mind that these internal company policies are not necessarily enforceable in a court of law; they are more aspirational than actionable, more public relations than practiced pol-icy if the self-reported experiences of discrimination are as numerous as the aforementioned studies suggest.

In response to these unfortunate realities, LGBT advocates have long fought for a federal legal remedy, known in its current form as the

Employment Non-Discrimination Act (ENDA). Like most controversial legislation, ENDA's long slow march through Congress began in 1974 when Bella Abzug introduced the first piece of legislation, the Equality Act of 1974, to address discrimination based on sexual orientation.[16] First proposed as ENDA in 1994, the bill gained steam and co-sponsors during the latter parts of the Clinton administration, but it reached the floor of the Senate only once before the Bush presidency and then languished in congressional committees for most of his term. When Democrats gained the majorities in both houses of Congress in 2007, though, and when Barney Frank and Tammy Baldwin, self-identified gay and lesbian members of Congress, took the lead, passage of ENDA seemed within reach, at least at the congressional level. No doubt President Bush would have vetoed the measure, and the House and Senate would probably not have been able to override the veto. Nonetheless, LGBT advocates felt that public pressure, the tacit support of the business community, and newly invigorated lobbying efforts might finally bring about congressional endorsement of ENDA. Then, however, over Baldwin's objections, Frank unilaterally excised gender identity protections from ENDA, justifying this decision on the grounds that their inclusion would doom the bill. Instead, Frank planned to introduce two bills to increase the likelihood of passage of an ENDA dealing only with sexual-orientation. The second bill, including gender identity, would come to be known as GENDA. And then this calculated move backfired in ways unimaginable to such a shrewd politician.

Almost every major LGBT organization, excluding the HRC, withdrew its support for the sexual-orientation-only ENDA. Not only had trans advocates labored for years to gain representation in the legislation, but all of the major LGBT advocacy organizations had previously declared their support for a gender-identity-inclusive ENDA. When Frank separated the act into two separate pieces of legislation, heated debates erupted on blogs, in LGBT publications, and the halls of Congress about how to proceed with them, as well as about whether solidarity could lead to the defeat of ENDA. Over four hundred LGBT organizations, from local to state to national groups, formed an alliance named United ENDA, and they pledged to actively work to delay, if not defeat, the bill if it excluded trans protections. Nonetheless, even in the face of this opposition, the House of Representatives voted 235-184 to pass ENDA, with thirty-five Republicans joining the Democratic majority, but then the measure failed to gain a vote in the Senate and died at the end of the session.

In what might be seen as a counterintuitive move, I want to suggest that the failure of ENDA and GENDA signals the success, and not the defeat, of queer identity politics. It would be easy to dismiss ENDA's demise as identity politics gone wrong, as so many disgruntled commentators did, or as the snatching of defeat from the jaws of victory, but these responses confuse a legislative result with a political one. Unlike other issues, ENDA brought the question of solidarity to the forefront of discussions among LGBT advocates, and the resounding show of support for a unified community unwilling to leave behind some of its members may have more profound and longer-lasting consequences than the passage of a bill doomed for veto. Unlike the tyranny of solidarity O'Brien sees in intracommunity discussions of same-sex civil marriage, wherein gays and lesbians must support these rights claims simply because of their membership in an identity category, the GENDA controversy opened up for debate the very ideas of community, affiliation, and solidarity. ENDA and GENDA concretized the amorphous and abstract acronym LGBT in such a way as to force those under its supposed umbrella to focus on the similarities and differences among these imagined and actual communities. The dispute over the goals and limits of LGBT unity and solidarity excavated the often sublimated, yet simmering, question about what these seemingly distinct groups share as common points of identification in the past, present, and future.

The choice of "queer identity politics" as the descriptor of the actions under consideration in this chapter may strike some as odd since LGBT and LGBT politics are often positioned as being distinct from and antithetical to queer and queer politics. And sometimes it is indeed useful to demarcate such differences, given that some advocates argue from a position secure in the assumption of stable, distinct identities (LGBT) and others operate from a more fluid, performative sense of identity (queer).[17] In this case, however, the rhetorical strategies employed by the supporters of a gender-identity-inclusive ENDA productively troubled these boundaries when they articulated the shared experiences and interests of LGBTs not by emphasizing their non-normative sexual identities (or lack thereof), but by attending to how LGBTs experience discrimination because of the performativity of their genders. In reviewing this situation we can map some of the contemporary sites for political alliances as well as the fault lines of this contested terrain.

With the public disputes over ENDA prompting my inquiry, my particular interest here is in the successful negotiation of a queer identity politics premised on the concept of wholeness versus that of oneness, which, as we have seen, helps to rescue identity politics from the problematics of purity and essentialism that often plague them. We should not abandon the centrality and necessity of the negotiation of identity as a generative element of political action. Identity and identity politics still matter, and we do the ideological work of dominant normativities when we dismiss debates about identity as roadblocks to political gains. In previous chapters we have not attended to intracommunity disputes about LGBT identity in the way that we will in this chapter. In the following pages we will engage the textual strategies employed by trans advocates and allies to unify LGBTs in common cause as a whole community working toward equality for all of its members. The campaign to resurrect a fully inclusive ENDA models how we might craft articulatory pathways for a queer identity politics premised on shared interests beyond sexuality. By articulating themselves as similarly situated targets of employment discrimination, the LGBT advocates for the gender-identity-inclusive ENDA reconstituted LGBT commonality around gender nonconformity, which includes and exceeds the confining logics of community based solely on the transgressions of normative heterosexuality. In this argument, the emphasis on gender should be seen as an attempt to supplement, rather than displace, sexuality as the basis of community since each can be understood only in a relational dialectic with one another.

From this perspective, I read the rhetoric of the supporters of a fully inclusive ENDA as a homonormative critique of LGBT political formations premised solely on sexuality as the common denominator for solidarity. My reference for homonormativity is not Lisa Duggan, the scholar most commonly cited when this term is employed, but Susan Stryker, who employs this concept in an imminent critique of LGBT politics. Whereas Duggan wants homonormativity to signify the processes involved in depoliticizing sexual minorities, Stryker twists it to hold sexual minorities accountable for their own gender-normative assumptions. In Stryker's words, homonormative critiques expose the "extent to which these gay and lesbian social formations have predicated their minority sexual-orientation identities on the gender-normative notions of *man* and *woman* that homosexual subcultures tend to share with the heteronormative societies of Eurocentric modernity."[18] The various defenses of a fully inclusive ENDA offer us fruitful examples of how LGBT communities can work against their own homonormative tendencies.

To properly contextualize the continued importance of identity as the source and site of collective political action resistant to homonormativity, I will begin by reconstructing a short history of identity politics and its repudiation over the last three decades. What follows is not so much a recuperation of an unreconstructed identity politics, as it is a rehearsal of these enduring arguments to contextualize the GENDA controversy as part of an ongoing struggle about the bases, forms, and goals of collective LGBT/queer political action. Internal debates about shared identities need not always derail coalitional forms of politics, and here we have a case where trans advocates and allies successfully redefined gender identity in universalizing, rather than minoritizing, terms. By moving the debate out of the minoritizing frame's emphasis on the importance of gender identity protections for trans people to a universalizing frame stressing the fact that everyone has a gender identity (or gender identities if we think in the logics of performativity) that can be read as violating normative expectations, United ENDA argued from a position of wholeness to demand that we recognize how we are all potentially vulnerable to unfavorable treatment because of our gender identities.[19] This did not require an equivocation of essential sameness in a homogenizing sense; instead, the approach emphasized the shared conditions and experiences of discrimination as a site of unification of seemingly disparate identity groups, and did so in a way that is distinct from the insular sense of self imagined by the critics of identity politics. In this process of organizing and advocating, the law does not fix and cement one's separatist sense of self in legal categories, but the process can result in an undoing of the self by unmooring certitude about the bases of identity and political action. By the end of this chapter, we will see that sometimes the legal remedy itself is not as important as the work done in its name.

Although a multitude of issues were involved in the ENDA controversy, I narrow the textual archive to three domains of argument to make sense of the discursive field. A review of Frank's arguments about the legislative reasons for separating ENDA into two bills will come first and serve as a backdrop for responses from LGBT leaders and organizations. For them, two key issues dominated the dispute over the best strategy for moving forward. Those who supported ENDA without gender identity provisions questioned the historical basis of the LGBT community. In effect, they asserted that LGBTs did not share a common past and that overall they were an inconvenient collection of disparate groups forged together by a shotgun wedding, with the leaders of national organizations holding the guns. In response, trans advocates and allies not only disputed these claims, but also emphasized the importance of closing the gender identity loophole. From their point of view, the removal of gender identity protections opened up the possibility for employers to discriminate against everyone, regardless of their sexual orientation, for failing to conduct themselves in accordance with expected gender norms. By reframing the issue as one of gender, the proponents of an inclusive ENDA reflected and produced a more responsive sense of a whole LGBT community comprised not by an acronym but by a shared interest in providing legal protections for everyone in this imagined community. Even though Frank proceeded with ENDA as planned, we can still value the efforts of United ENDA as a model for moving forward into the future. Now, though, let us review the discursive lives of identity politics.

Identity Politics

Identity politics is both old and new. In the broadest sense, debates about citizen identities have been a constant concern and source of tension from the earliest formations of American communities, but here I will restrict the arena to more contemporary contexts.[20] Thus, beginning with post–World War II United States, we can recall how minority groups increasingly gained cultural traction with regard to the omission of their concerns and demanded that their voices be heard, respected, and attended to by institutional actors, their peers, the media, and society writ large.[21] Those who identified as feminists, racial minorities, sexual and gender minorities, people with disabilities, or some combination of these categories, as well as others, focused some of their efforts on the public recognition of their similarities and differences. Their strategies varied widely from direct action protests, street theater, letter-writing campaigns, forming identity-based organizations, lobbying legislators, creating music and other modes of cultural production.[22] With uneven results and some inevitable backsliding after modest gains, members of these groups gained differential levels of recognition; most, if not all, the advocates for these causes would agree there is much work left to be done before they can declare, if ever, a full and unequivocal equality.[23]

In the 1980s and 1990s, those who were skeptical of or hostile to such claims tried to contain the challenges posed by minority groups by accusing them of practicing *identity politics*—a phrase that was almost always accusatory and was leveled at those who were seen as creating divisions in the body politic.[24] Whether or not the targets of this accusation actually intended to mark their difference in their words or deeds was largely irrelevant because the charge of identity politics lay in the eye of the beholder. The label of "identity politics" quickly accumulated a heavily saturated cluster of connotations fusing together distinct causes and groups into one specter of leftism and political correctness run amok. Speech codes, affirmative action, university policies attentive to any kinds of differences, multiculturalism, multilingual signs and documents, and indeed anything else that dared to propose, in ways great or small, the decentering of the self-sufficient, white, middle- to upper-class, able-bodied, straight man as the universalized exemplar of the good citizen could be lumped together under the label, which in turn allowed for dismissing grievances as illegitimate and redirecting attention to the supposed separatist and self-boosting tendencies of those practicing "identity politics." For many conservatives, the more trivial the action or policy in question, the better it served for a wholesale condemnation of the Left as a failed, dangerous experiment whose reincarnation in its various forms must be stopped at all costs. "Debates over *identity politics*," Lisa Duggan contends, "cover over and stand in for more significant disputes about democracy." Thus, it should not be surprising that similar indictments of identity politics came from the Left, too.[25]

For some on the Left, the critique of identity politics could serve to purify political space and defend its borders from invasion by what they saw as cultural matters divorced from or subordinate to the more pressing problems associated with material inequalities, militarism, and exploitative labor practices. Take, for example, Todd Gitlin and Arthur Schlesinger, Jr., authors whose ideas converged much more neatly in the 1990s than their politics would have suggested in the 1960s.[26] Gitlin, a former president of Students for a Democratic Society, and Schlesinger, a historian of the Kennedy family and the public intellectual most identified with defending their political legacy, both penned numerous works warning of the dangers posed by identity politics. Indeed, Schlesinger declared a state of emergency: "the historic idea of unifying American identity is now in peril in many arenas—in our politics, our voluntary organizations, our churches, our language."; for his part, Gitlin described identity politics as "a turning inward, a grim and hermetic bravado celebrating victimization and stylized marginality," and argued that this tendency was itself responsible for the rise of the Right: "they have been fighting over the English department while the right held the White House as its private fiefdom."[27] The lack of self-reflexivity on the part of these (old) guards of the Left is most definitely lost on them as their refusal to re-examine their own commitments is both the cause and the target of those practicing the identity politics Gitlin and Schlesinger so despise.

From the 1980s and now into the 2010s, many on the Left have reserved a special disdain for queer politics and the institutionalization of LGBT/queer studies, deeming them as further fragmenting the already precarious coalitions that march under the Left's banner. The in-your-face attitude of queer politics and queer studies' questioning of stable subjectivities dared to deny the Left its unexamined universalisms by placing on the order of business the very questions of who is speaking for whom and why in this fashion and to what end. With some on the Left successfully caricaturing queer studies' attention to sexualities and gender identities as a self-indulgent concern with representation and discourse rather than with "real" or "legitimate" politics, the aims of queer politics were cast as second- or third-order political issues.[28]

Take, for example, Walter Benn Michaels's much-discussed *The Trouble with Diversity*, in which some of the most pointed criticism of queer studies and politics appears in the concluding paragraphs:

> The more kinds of difference they can come up with to appreciate (not just many races but mixed races, not just gay and lesbian but gay, lesbian, bisexual, and transgendered), the more invisible becomes the difference that a truly left politics would want to eliminate: class difference.[29]

We would be remiss here if we did not pause to note Michaels's derisive sigh when he accentuates the inconvenience imposed by considerations of sexual and gender minorities beyond gays and lesbians, namely, the naïve excess and unnecessary distraction from real politics arising from the inclusion of bisexuals and trans people. Striking a similar chord, Sherry Wolf's *Sexuality and Socialism* accuses "identity politics activists and scholars" with privileging "separation from others as opposed to unity, as their key organizing principle," and criticizes the result as a "profoundly pessimistic, even paralyzing, worldview in which people are all just atomized beings for whom common group identity acts as a sort of social kryptonite or Achilles' heel that somehow weakens or lessens us each."[30] In each case, queer studies, theories, and identities are positioned as antithetical to collective politics and action in spite of substantial, empirical evidence to the contrary.

Similar debates generated both heat and light within intellectual and activist communities concerned with gender and sexuality. Judith Butler and Nancy Fraser exchanged the most well-developed arguments on the value of cultural critique as it relates to heterosexism. Objecting to the positioning of challenges to heteronormative cultural logics as "merely cultural" issues counterposed and detrimental to the more important struggle of anticaptialism, Butler observed: "Considered inessential to what is most pressing in material life, *queer politics is regularly figured by the orthodoxy as the cultural extreme of politicization*."[31] Butler's refusal to demand unity about the sources and remedies of oppression is read by Fraser as a misunderstanding of how capitalism distributes privileges and resources, once again subordinating concerns of one's sexuality and gender identity to "real" material concerns.[32] Even a generous reading of Fraser's position cannot counter Butler's claim that "the problem of unity or, more modestly, of solidarity cannot be resolved through the transcendence or obliteration of this field, and certainly not through the vain promise of retrieving a unity wrought through exclusions, one that reinstitutes subordination as the condition of its own possibility."[33] When understood from this perspective, reflexive critiques of identity authorize alternative discursive formations more responsive to the exigencies animating the need for a collective response. Further examination of these topoi of argument assist us in understanding how different versions of LGBT and queer communities see themselves and how others see them.

A full review of the sometimes-strained relationships between trans people and LGBs is beyond the scope of this chapter, but let me draw a brief historical sketch to establish the context for the ENDA controversy. As David Valentine explains in the brilliant *Imagining Transgender*, before the widespread use of *transgender* as a category of identity, many people who would now identify as trans or gender non-conforming identified as gay.[34] *Gay*, much like *queer* today, served as an umbrella term to lump together LGBTs, but the erasure of lesbian, bisexual, and trans experiences under this sign led to new categories to account for the differences between gay men and other sexual and gender minorities. More than a linguistic politics, the rise of these new categories sprang forth from divisions in LGBT populations about their common goals and whether or not they shared sufficient experiences across their differences to form a coherent whole. Some lesbian feminisms questioned the assumptions of gay male liberationist politics, and many of these same lesbian feminists questioned their alliances with transwomen and transmen, as well. Many academic feminists such as Mary Daly and Janice Raymond, as well as cultural icons like Robin Morgan, vociferously attacked transwomen for their patriarchal privilege and trafficking in feminine stereotypes. Transmen received similar scorn for taking advantage of and trafficking in male privilege. Some gay men, fearful of the loss of what little cultural respectability they had attained, kept (and too often today keep) trans people at an arm's length, especially if they understood same-sex sexuality as the distinguishing factor in generating communal interests. While gays and lesbians fought to remove the pathological classification of gay and lesbian sexuality from the American Psychological Association's Diagnostic Statistic Manual, some trans people welcomed their inclusion in it to medically validate their identities. As LGBT advocacy organizations gained greater access to institutional actors and developed national networks of influence, some organizations refused to officially recognize trans issues as relevant to their purposes, and some went so far as to exclude trans people from public marches and events.[35] In brief, then, the contestation of the role of identity in LGBT/queer politics has been and will continue to be a central concern. If we cannot wish it away, and we should not want to, we will have to learn how to negotiate debates about identities and political strategies in productive ways and with a finely tuned appreciation for the contingencies of the situation at hand.

One complicating factor in this task is the ability of *transgender* to function as an incapacitating marker of difference for both trans people and LGBs. As we just established, if the basis of community for some is rooted in same-sex sexual-object choice, those who identify as trans or gender non-conforming may not find immediate affinity with LGBs. At times, sexuality and gender are articulated as separate and unrelated axes of identity so that LGBs are defined by their sexualities and trans people by their genders. In many ways, the attractiveness and success of *queer* as a site of identification rested and continues to rest on its avoidance of these thorny issues. In no small part informed by HIV/AIDS as an intracommunity crisis indiscriminately impacting vulnerable populations, *queer* made available a sign of identification, and as the epidemic ravaged LGBT communities, it also named a political attitude. Yet, with the onset of AIDS fatigue, the distancing of some LGBTs from queer political aesthetics, and the increasing currency of *transgender* as an identity category, the linguistic shift from *queer* to the increasingly popular *LGBT* had wide-ranging implications. As Stryker observes, this shift ushered in "a retreat from the more radical concept of alliance, resistance, and rebellion" as well as the adoption of "a liberal model of minority tolerance and inclusion—sometimes amounting to little more than a 'politically correct' gesture of token inclusion for transgender people."[36] As with all identity categories, the evolutions of the meanings of these terms reminds us that we must remain vigilant about their constitutive exclusions.

Although well-intentioned in many respects, the sometimes token acknowledgement of transgender in LGBT can paradoxically initiate divisive distinctions even as it serves as a unitary impulse. For instance, Valentine concedes the vital necessity of transgender as a category of recognition, yet, at the same time, he notes that the juxtaposition of transgender against lesbian, gay, and bisexual sometimes secures sexual practices as private behaviors and gender nonconformity as a public concern, thus resurrecting a public/private dichotomy that serves the interests of LGBs who argue against the regulation of private sexual acts. In this way, Valentine concludes, *transgender* "has become useful to accommodationist gay and lesbian groups (apart from its usefulness to transgender-identified people) precisely because it has been able to absorb the gender transgression which has doggedly been associated with modern (and especially male) homosexual identities for more than a hundred years."[37] With these cautionary tales in mind, I will now chart out alternative possibilities for a more effective identity politics which are rooted in common concerns and can avoid the pitfalls described above.

In defending identity politics the invocation of Wendy Brown as an intellectual ally may initially strike some as curious, given her indictment of what she terms the "wounded attachments" associated with certain formations of politicized identities. For Brown, when identities are constituted by and through injury, individuals are encouraged to understand themselves as oppressed and disadvantaged by their mere membership in a population; the result, ironically, is the production of atomistic politics over and against collective politics because political subjects fixate on their own individual subjugation instead of addressing the conditions disadvantaging the group as a whole. For example, according to Brown, a gay man might fixate on his own oppression as a gay man, assuming himself to be disadvantaged and politically impotent simply because he is a gay man. Employing Nietzsche's treatment of *ressentiment*, Brown argues that if one's identity is dependent on injury and exclusion, one's sense of self is vexed by the pleasure derived from the narcissistic reincorporation of grievance as the foundational gesture of subjectivity; in other words, it is a source of frustration but also supplies a self-fulfilling narrative of one's exclusion. In turn, according to Brown, "the moralizing revenge of powerlessness" associated with identity politics seldom actualizes effective collective action. This can be due to a self-induced passivity that justifies the aggrieved subject position ("I can't do anything about it so why try?") or, alternately, to identity groups aligning themselves with the state to exact revenge or gain recognition through legal protections and therein fix their identities as victims ("I need the state's protection because of my disadvantaged identity"). Either way, as Brown explains, this political orientation steers toward the past, not the future, as it locates already realized or past wrongs as the authorizing force of the subject in the present. And this is where Brown's arguments generally trail off for critics of identity politics—with a disavowal of identity as an animating force of collective political action and thus, I fear, participate in a misreading of Brown's work.

What is often overlooked is Brown's call to reanimate identity in a collective idiom to ward off both the subjective pressures of *ressentiment* and the ossification of identity into a stable subject position dislodged from the plane of contestation and revision. Brown advises political advocates to transform their communicative habits from arguing from the position of purely self-interested identity ("who I am") to a more communal perspective ("what I want for us"). As Brown puts it, more productive figurations of identity emerge when we articulate our demands "from explicitly postulated norms and potential common values rather than from false essentialism or unreconstructed private interest."[38] This shift in attitude and perspective requires the advocate to set aside self-interested revenge or compensation as the goal of the demand in an effort to implicate identity claims in larger fields of social relations. Framed thus, these articulations are motivated not by wanting something for someone else or yourself alone, but by working together toward a shared goal. Translated into the context of coalitional identity politics, collective demands can be understood, as Susan Bickford does, as "political relations between partially constituted and partially constituting subjects in a context of variegated power."[39] If we combine these attitudes with Danielle Allen's call to imagine ourselves as whole instead of one, we can envision a politics guided by the accommodation and acceptance of differences as the very resources needed to maintain robust publics and renew our civic obligations to one another. In Allen's words, "the metaphor of wholeness can guide us into a conversation about how to develop habits of citizenship that can help a democracy bring trustful coherence out of division without erasing or suppressing difference."[40] The preceding prescriptions for communicating identity in more productive articulations than what often passes for political discourse today may seem too idealistic to serve as a model for actually existing political controversies, but before we dismiss it as academic fantasy, we should consider the rhetoric of advocates for a fully inclusive ENDA, which reveals the potential for this version of identity politics.

ENDA, GENDA, and Gender

Legislation designed to prohibit employment discrimination based on one's sexual orientation existed in one form or another for two decades before the 1994 introduction of ENDA in the House and Senate. Unlike previous incarnations of such measures, however, ENDA enjoyed greater support in Congress due in part to the increased visibility of gays and lesbians and in even greater part to the growing political strength of LGBT advocacy organizations. Originally championed by Senator Edward Kennedy and Representative Gerry Studds, ENDA initially failed to make it out of committee in both chambers. In the next congressional session, even as it was doomed to fail in the Republican-led House, Senator Kennedy forced a floor vote in the Senate, where ENDA fell one vote short of passage.[41] Although introduced in all but one of the subsequent congressional sessions, it was not until 2007, following vociferous debates about the bill's scope and the means for gaining a House vote, that ENDA's sponsors could shepherd it out of the necessary committees. After two decades of lobbying, gender advocates and allies had secured the inclusion of gender identity as one of ENDA's protected classes. The bill defined gender identity as "the gender-related identity, appearance, or mannerisms or other gender-related characteristics of an individual, with or without regard to the individual's designated sex at birth."[42]

In spite of his own support for this language, Frank abruptly scuttled the broader legislation for a new bill limited to prohibitions against discrimination based on sexual orientation. Frank claimed an official whip count revealed the reticence of legislators to endorse the gender identity provisions, leaving him with no option other than to move forward with the watered-down ENDA. Frank then suggested that a separate bill covering gender identity discrimination could be proposed, some-times referred to as GENDA, so as to not disturb the momentum of the sexual-orientation-only ENDA.

Frank's political maneuverings were entirely predictable, given his pragmatism and his resistance to expending political capital for the benefit of trans people. Unfortunately, this incident mirrored Frank's actions in the late 1990s when, again with the tacit blessing from the HRC, he betrayed trans people on this same issue. At that time, Frank excised trans protections from ENDA, claiming he didn't want to revisit the bathroom and showers issues that he felt had derailed the repeal of "Don't Ask, Don't Tell." Frank and the HRC explained their exclusionary move as necessary to prevent the loss of thirty votes right from the outset, leading trans advocates and allies to paint them both as traitors who were willing, in a variation on Judas's betrayal of Jesus, to trade "thirty pieces of silver" for ENDA.[43] A decade later, these old wounds reopened in the renewed push for ENDA. By then, trans advocates and allies were already wary of Frank and his political tactics. Their suspicions were confirmed when, as Currah notes, Frank "insisted on adding statutory language that would prevent a trans-gender woman who had been barred from a women's shared shower or dressing facilities from making an actionable claim (and vice versa for transgender men)" in the 2007 version of ENDA.[44] To understand Frank's motivations, we will read closely Frank's justification for jet-tisoning the gender identity provisions and then track the public pro-gression of these arguments to demonstrate the utility of arguing from the perspective of wholeness.

On the day after announcing ENDA's division into two separate pieces of legislation, in a widely circulated press statement doubling as a blog post on outlets such as the *Bilerico Project* and the *Huffington Post*, Frank defended his cleaving of the two bills as a political necessity in the present and a precursor for further expansions of employment protections in the future:

> The question facing us— the LGBT community and the tens of millions of others who are active supporters of our fight against prejudice— is whether we should pass up the chance to adopt a very good bill because it has one major gap. I believe that it would be a grave error to let this

opportunity to pass a sexual orientation nondiscrimination bill go forward, not simply because it is one of the most important advances we'll
have made in securing civil rights for Americans in decades, but because
moving forward on this bill now will also better serve the ultimate goal
of including people who are transgender than simply accepting total
defeat today.[45]

In an unabashed defense of incrementalism, Frank credited "a good
deal of work, education of the general public, and particularly the decision by tens of millions of gay and lesbian people over that time to be
honest about our sexual orientation" as the necessary and sufficient fac-
tors in garnering the support of the majority of his colleagues in the
House. Frank charged those desiring similar protections for gender
identity discrimination to channel their energies into educating legislators as to the importance of this provision. In his estimation, trans
people, the proper object of gender identity language, needed to work
harder. The use of "our sexual orientation" in the preceding statement
reflects Frank's overall framing of sexual orientation and gender identity as separate and distinct issues. This attitude, when followed up
with remarks such as "[gender identity] is a fairly recent addition to
the fight," is understandably frustrating to those who have been and
are engaged in these efforts and are troubled by the neat partitioning of
sexual orientation and gender identity into discrete and disparate categories. To be fair, Frank did end this sentence on a more collective note,
in stating that "our educational efforts regarding gender identity are
much less far along, and given the prejudices that exist, face a steeper
climb." Even so, the earlier chastising of trans advocates and allies for
what Frank understood as their failure to do the hard work of retail
politics undercut his attempts to position himself as a sympathetic supporter of trans rights. Similarly, Frank's later characterization of transgender advocates as politically naïve worked at cross-purposes with his
intention to demonstrate alliance with trans causes:

One of the problems I have found over the years of discussing this is an
unwillingness on the part of many, including leaders in the transgender
community, to acknowledge a fact: namely that there is more resistance
to protection for people who are transgender than for people who are

gay, lesbian and bisexual. This is not a good fact, but ignoring bad facts is
a bad way to get legislation passed. I have for some time been concerned
that people in the transgender leadership were underestimating the difficulty we faced in a broadly inclusive bill being adopted.

Positioning himself as the cool-headed pragmatist, Frank then moved
on to outline the specific legislative history of ENDA to that point and
how it necessitated the parsing of ENDA parts into two separate bills.

On Frank's recounting of ENDA's legislative history, the gender identity provisions would never survive into final passage and could do more
harm than good for gays, lesbians, and trans people alike. After intro-
ducing the threat of Republican amendments to strip the gender identity section from the bill or "severely restrict it in very obnoxious ways,"
Frank asked the interested parties to "accept facts" and not "deny this
unpleasant reality." With the Democrats in the majority in the House,
however, Frank could not solely blame the Republicans for denying the
passage of ENDA. Thus, he went on to detail Democratic opposition
to the inclusion of gender identity and to construct a scenario wherein
Democrats would vote with Republicans to ensure an anti-gender identity amendment. Working from this assumption, one he buttressed with
the results of whip count (although he did not provide the actual tallies), Frank proffered and then dismissed various legislative and parlia-
mentary tactics for stealthily inserting the gender identity section back
into the bill once out of committee.

Refusing to accept the complete failure of ENDA as an option, he
argued instead for a narrower bill because it would not force members
of the House to record a vote against the inclusion of gender identity.
Moreover, the weakened ENDA could be the springboard for future
action. In a comment underlined for emphasis, Frank stated, a failed
all-or-nothing strategy would "mak[e] it harder ultimately to win that
support" because persuadable House members would be on record
opposing the provisions. With equal force, Frank spurned the calls for
postponing the vote. With an all-but-certain presidential veto looming
over the situation, a number of LGBT organizations declared their preference to hold off on the legislation if it did not include gender identity
as a protected class. Frank summarily dismissed these suggestions as an
unwise reversal of strategy:

[I]t should be noted this is directly contradictory to the arguments that the LGBT community has been making for years. That is, we have been very critical of arguments that we should not push for votes on anti-discrimination legislation simply because it wasn't going to win. People have correctly pointed to the value of getting people used to voting for this, of the moral force of having majorities in either the House or the Senate or both go on record favorably even if the President is going to veto it, and have in fact been getting Members ready so that if and when we get a president ready to sign this, we are closer to passage.

Of course, this line of argument could cut both ways and support an argument for a redoubled campaign to include gender identity within the purview of ENDA, but Frank intended it to reinforce the urgency of striking while the iron was hot.

To insulate himself from charges of pure political expediency, Frank concluded his statement with a commitment to extending ENDA's protective reach in the near future. Summoning a history of linear, cumulative progress in previous civil rights struggles, Frank emphasized that

In no case has any of those bills ever covered everybody or everything. Antidiscrimination legislation is always partial. It improves coverage either to some group or some subject matter, but never achieves everything at once. And insistence on achieving everything at once would be a prescription for achieving nothing ever.

The implicit assumption behind this proposition relies on a watered-down ENDA paving an easier and smoother path for gender identity protections in the future. As Frank saw it, "Even from the standpoint of ultimately including transgender people, it makes far more sense to go forward in a partial way if that is all we can do. Part of the objection to any antidiscrimination legislation is fear of consequences, which fears are always proven to be incorrect." Intended to temper objections to an incremental approach, the preceding line of argument did more to stoke the fears and ire of trans advocates and allies, especially given its explicit ranking of sexual orientation discrimination as more politically palatable. For them, Frank's promise that LGBs would return to fight for trans rights in the future was a promise with a poor track record, as well. Indeed, many read it as a self-congratulatory, preemptive missive absolving LGBs of any responsibility in the future because they had already labored long and hard for their own rights.

Blindsided by Frank's unexpected announcement, LGBT advocacy groups scrambled to develop a unified response. Although they had heard rumors of such a change in strategy, they had not expected it to surface the week before the bill's markup in committee. The HRC issued press releases declaring their support for a gender-identity-inclusive bill, but they stopped short of withdrawing their support for ENDA if it included sexual orientation as the sole protected class. Other groups, such as National Gay and Lesbian Task Force (NGLTF) and Lambda Legal (LL), renounced Frank's decision and its presentation as a *fait accompli* to those who had agitated to include gender identity in the bill. They also began building a consensus that LGBTs should operate from the perspective of wholeness, not oneness. Thus, for example, Matt Foreman, the executive director of NGLTF, stated that "In this defining and morally transformative moment, our community has come together in an unprecedented way and said once and for all that we will leave no part of it behind." Unwilling to submit to Frank's proposed incrementalism, Foreman concluded his remarks by declaring: "We are one community and we demand protections for all of us. Nothing else will suffice." [46]

As word of Frank's actions zipped through LGBT publications, websites, blogs, and message boards, opposition solidified against ENDA in its proposed form. Widespread dissatisfaction, if not anger and rage, surfaced in statements from local and state-based LGBT organizations, culminating in the formation of United ENDA, a coalition of hundreds of organizations and advocacy groups dedicated to passing a fully inclusive bill. [47] United ENDA's first act was to produce a letter for distribution to congressional members outlining their resistance to Frank's strategy. The text is as follows:

October 1, 2007

Dear Madam Speaker and Representatives:
The undersigned represent the vast and celebrated diversity of the LGBT community in this country. Some of us are national leaders of organizations with tens of thousands of members and constituents, some of us run the only local organization in our state. But we are united in a

common cause: We ask you to keep working with us on an Employment Non-Discrimination Act that protects everyone in our community, and to oppose any substitute legislation that leaves some of us behind.

We ask and hope that in this moment of truth, you will stand for the courage real leadership sometimes demands. You each command enormous respect from all of us and we do appreciate the difficulty of balancing a variety of competing demands. But the correct course in this case and on this legislation is strikingly clear. We oppose legislation that leaves part of our community without protections and basic security that the rest of us are provided.

You told us you supported a fully inclusive ENDA and would bring it up for a vote this year. We expect that you will honor that commitment and we look forward to working together to pass a bill that we can all be proud to support.[48]

The repeated construction of LGBTs as an indivisible community, as an "us," with collective interests in comprehensive legislation, not political expediency, announced a repudiation of politics as usual wherein LGBs were willing to sacrifice trans people for their own gains. By taking gender identity protections off the table as a bargaining chip, United ENDA demonstrated the changing political consciousness of some LGBTs—a shift that is no doubt linked to the growth of local and state LGBT groups that may not share the values and priorities of institutionally entrenched national organizations such as the HRC. While Frank's sudden reversal of course took many local and state organizations by surprise and prevented them from engaging their representatives in time, United ENDA enabled these disparate groups to position themselves as a counterbalance to the HRC's influence in Congress.[49] This is not to say that local and state groups are intrinsically prone to the perspective of wholeness and national organizations to oneness, but the immediate outpouring of support for the inclusion of gender identity in ENDA from local and state groups indicated a surprising predisposition toward solidarity and a common willingness to sacrifice the bill for a larger principle. While not all LGBTs signed on to or agreed with this position, at least one hundred national organizations did eventually affiliate themselves with United ENDA.

Prompted by United ENDA's campaign, a number of commentators followed Frank's lead and talking points and asserted (wrongly) that trans people had only recently interjected themselves into this legislative struggle and were coming in at the last moment to profit off of the work of others. Underlying these claims is a severe case of historical amnesia regarding the collective work of LGBTs, as well as the similarity in sources of discrimination directed at them. Conservative gay blogger Chris Crain used the phrase *trans-jacked* to express his anger about the delay of ENDA, even going so far as to suggest "it would be a remarkable betrayal of gays across the U.S., who have been waiting for more than 30 years to pass a basic civil rights bill through Congress."[50] Susan Ryan-Vollmar, the editor-in-chief of *Bay Windows*, an influential LGBT news outlet, wrote a scathing editorial declaring the all-or-nothing approach of United ENDA "madness," the criticism of the HRC's continued support of ENDA "ignorant of reality," and the coalition's "petulant insistence on purity, principle and perfection" anything but a virtue.[51] After starting off with the all-too-familiar "I support full transgender rights," Robin Tyler, an outspoken lesbian activist, expressed dismay at the call for transgender inclusion in ENDA, citing her transgender friends' lack of reciprocal sacrifice with regard to marriage rights: "They did not sacrifice their legal rights on the alter [*sic*] of political correctness to give up the State and Federal benefits of marriage."[52] And no doubt similar strains of argument circulated in casual conversations of LGBs who were skeptical of their connection to trans people.

John Aravosis's widely circulated blog posts represented these positions well, for they were the most fully developed vernacular discourse on the subject and generated significant blowback from trans advocates and allies. In a post first published on his own blog and then in a revised version on *Salon*, Aravosis claimed to speak for the silent majority of LGBs opposed to delaying the vote on ENDA. Outright denying any common past with trans people, his original version of "The Transgender Fiasco" claimed they had joined this political effort only in the last five months. Comparing trans inclusion in the LGB community to a failed revolution imposed by one nation on another, employing the United States' occupation of Iraq as the analogy, and suggesting that the people "have no ownership" in the success of an externally imposed solution, Aravosis questioned whether LGBT politics evolved organically or followed orders of leaders of national organizations.[53] The perverse inversion of trans people as the superpower unjustly invading the helpless LGB community—and for Aravosis it is one community— is laughable, as well as disheartening because of the unacknowledged tone of privilege Aravosis assumes as he masquerades as the victim. When Aravosis elaborated on his position—"I'm just saying that I don't think the T was added because there was a groundswell of demand in the gay community that we add T to LGB. I think it happened through pressure, organizational fiat, shame, and osmosis"—he expressed a sentiment shared by some LGBs. He also invoked the suspicious Nixonian trope of the silent majority in asserting that "gay people . . . simply sat back and shut up about their questions and concerns and doubts out of a sense of shame that it was somehow impolite to even question what was happening, and fear that if they did ask questions they'd be marked as bigots." Acting as the voice for the voiceless, Aravosis demanded an explicit conversation about "the fear and confusion and doubt about the transgender issue in the gay community." Given the tone of Aravosis's post, this imagined conversation probably resembled more of an excommunication than a sincere plea for an exchange of ideas.

In the extended version of this post on *Salon* entitled "How Did the T Get in LGBT?" Aravosis ramped up his snarkiness and paranoia. Attributing the relative tolerance of trans people and their issues to a manufactured consent secured through the actions of national LGBT organizations and leaders, Aravosis claimed to speak for the LGBs "who weren't running national organizations, weren't activists, or weren't living in liberal gay enclaves like San Francisco and New York." Even as he conceded nominal alliances between LGBs and Ts over the last decade, Aravosis judged them to be only begrudgingly accepted by LGBs and "only because our leaders kept telling us it was so."[54] He then asked, as his gay friends had been in the previous decade, "what they have in common with transsexuals, or at the very least why transgendered people qualify as our siblings rather than our cousins." Here we need not resort to a critique of reproductive heteronormativity to ask a simpler question: what does it matter if the imagined relationship is one of siblings or cousins? Should we not want the same for both of them? Obviously for Aravosis, the familial distance makes a difference and speaks to an underlying assumption of scarcity and an unwillingness to sacrifice for others, especially his cousins. "It's a fair question,"

Aravosis continued, "but one we know we dare not ask. It is simply not p.c. in the gay community to question how and why the T got added on to the LGB, let alone ask what I as a gay man have in common with a man who wants to cut off his penis, surgically construct a vagina, and become a woman." In addition to the haunting echoes of conservative critiques of identity politics (we were one but those with differences unjustly want us to accept those differences and act accordingly), the juxtaposition of a supposedly preformed coherent whole with the assumed lack represented by the emasculated transwoman is startling in its vitriolic blame for the problems with LGBT politics. Aravosis tried to insulate himself from just this line of critique: "I'm not passing judgment, I respect transgendered people and sympathize with their cause, but I simply don't get how I am just as closely related to a transsexual (who is often not gay) as I am to a lesbian (who is). Is it wrong for me to simply ask why?" Of course, as Aravosis knew well, it matters how you ask the question, and the setup for the question prefigured the basis for community in sexual object choice; it also relied on an undifferentiated equivalence where all sexualities are understood as equally abjected, as long as they are not trans sexualities. That a trans person might also identify as gay or lesbian is not even a possibility in Aravosis's discourses. In conclusion, Aravosis resorted to the pragmatic position involved in the politics of ENDA. "We're not talking right and wrong here," he said; "we're talking political reality." It took Congress "30 years to embrace a gay ENDA," he reminded readers; one could not reasonably expect this same body to "welcome the T's [*sic*] into the bill in only five months." For these reasons, Aravosis felt forced to choose between something and nothing, and he chose the former—"I'll take that half-a-loaf any day"— as long as he did not have to share it with his cousin.

Transgender historian and public intellectual Susan Stryker crafted a stinging response, also published on *Salon*, to dispel the conspiracy theory forwarded by Aravosis and to give presence to another view of LGBT history. Appropriately caustic, Stryker's retelling of Aravosis's tale likened trans inclusion in ENDA to a trans individual crashing a swank dinner party before it begins, with Aravosis and his ilk pushing others out of the way to grab the only food to actually make it on to the table before this disturbance: one half of a loaf of civil rights. This narrative

reframed the resistance to trans inclusion in LGBT politics as one motivated by greediness and expediency, in a marked contrast to Aravosis's
Iraqi democracy analogy, thus allowing Stryker to define this form of
antagonism as "homocentric," or when "gay is the term around which
the GLBT universe revolves."[55] Stryker recontextualized further the
scapegoating of trans people as complicit, in form and in content, with
conservative rhetorics opposing the Equal Rights Amendment, the use
of the racially charged Willie Horton ads as a scare tactic, and the fear
of gay sex in barrack showers used to scuttle the open service of LGBT
members of the military. Correctly identifying Aravosis's and Frank's
willingness to let transphobic arguments circulate unchallenged, if not
perpetuating a few of their own, Stryker lamented this strategy as presenting "a false issue that panders to the basest and most ignorant of
fears."

Not just bad form in its complicity with transphobia, the failure
to defend gender identity protections would also result in bad policy,
according to Stryker, who cited analyses of the "gender identity loophole"—an issue that became importance in establishing why the addition of gender considerations into the bill mattered to everyone, not
just those who identified as trans. Upon Frank's proposal to split ENDA
into two pieces of legislation, Lambda Legal (LL), TLC, the American
Civil Liberties Union, the National Center for Lesbian Rights, and Gay
& Lesbian Advocates & Defenders (GLAD) issued a report detailing
how sexual orientation protections would be narrowly construed so as
to allow employers to circumvent ENDA and fire LGBTs for violating
gender norms, not for their sexual orientations. If the courts read the
legislative history of the bill and inferred an explicit choice to exclude
gender identity as a cause of action, these groups reasoned, "the courts
could rule that the law does not cover discrimination because a person is seen as not meeting others' expectations of how a 'real' man or
woman should look and act"; this meant that employers could legally
fire LGBs because of their atypical gender performances, not their
sexuality.[56] Aware of the skepticism this may stir in the lay public, they
underscored the point: "If this sounds unlikely, it isn't. We have already
seen very similar, super technical interpretations of what is prohibited under laws that ban discrimination based on marital status, sex or
disability." In light of the inability of many trans litigants to gain legal

traction with Title VII's prohibition on employment discrimination due to one's sex, there was ample precedent for just this kind of jurisprudential gymnastics.[57] In their experience, the LGBT legal advocates found that "discrimination based on sex, sexual orientation and gender identity at some level are *all* discrimination based on stereotypes about what is or is not appropriate for men and women"; hence, "trying to split them apart makes little sense and invites the kind of legal hairsplitting that has made so many civil rights laws less effective." In their estimation, dividing LGBTs would mean that the resulting legislation would effectively fail to protect any of the interested parties.

Frank took exception to this critique of ENDA, and posted on the *Bilerico Report* to dismiss the effect of the gender identity loophole on LGB discrimination. Citing the eight states that protect LGBs but not trans people, Frank stated, "I am not aware of any instances where anti-gay discrimination, even based to some degree on gender non-conformity, was not covered."[58] Not content to leave it at that, Frank warned the bill's critics that the airing of such scenarios was "an invitation to bigots to try to get around the law," and that any qualified lawyer "would easily defeat such an attempted end-run around the sexual orientation language." In response, LL reiterated the historical precedent of similar statutes wherein courts had not been willing to read into the law an unexpressed intent; in this instance, the explicit record of Congress's choice not to include gender identity into ENDA would be damning: "we are very concerned that employers may argue that a law that prohibits sexual orientation discrimination but that intentionally *eliminated* the protections against discrimination based on gender nonconformity would provide no protection to employees judged by an employer to be non-conforming."[59] Pursuing the issue in another direction, LL condemned Frank's "me first" approach to the process: "It is simply wrong for lesbians, gay men and bisexuals to seek protections for themselves and leave transgender people in the dust. Transgender individuals have fought against discrimination along with gay people years before Stonewall and were prime actors at that epic moment in our joint civil rights history." Emphasizing the paradigm of wholeness, LL invoked previous civil rights struggles as supporting their approach to the situation: "Imagine if the proponents of the 1964 Civil Rights Act had decided that the prohibition against race discrimination included only some racial groups but not others. For gay people to sacrifice transgender people to get protection only for themselves would be wrong." Keeping in mind the fact that ENDA would not become law at this point because of Bush's promised veto, this statement about how LGBTs should work together and not against each other properly re-situated the actual stakes of this issue as one of "what I want for us is justice."

Returning to Stryker's essay—after reviewing the importance of closing up the gender identity loophole and refuting Aravosis's conspiratorial accusations about national LGBT leaders, Stryker shifts to reviewing the historical record of LGBT and queer coalitional politics to undercut the notion that the LGBT communities are convenient modern fictions. Locating the impetus for LGBT collective action in responses to the HIV/AIDS epidemic and queer configurations of identity evolving from this period, Stryker credited the rhetorical refusal to allow HIV/AIDS to be understood as a gay disease as a means for enabling these sometimes disparate groups to get "past the squabble of homosexual identity politics left over from the 1960s, '70s and '80s." Here, then, was another example of wholeness trumping oneness. The shared enemy of cultural indifference to HIV/AIDS, in Stryker's words, "fostered political alliances between lots of different kinds of people who all shared the common goal of ending the epidemic—and sometimes precious little else." In this way, Stryker narrated transgender demands for inclusion in ENDA as an act of reciprocity in a time of need to deflect Aravosis's accusation of trans piggybacking on the success of another, separate movement. After tracing a brief history of transgender activism from 1895 to the present, Stryker presented the concept of LGBT unity as a byproduct, in part, of the thinking of "a new generation of queer kids" who were charting alternative configurations of community which were different in composition and political sensibilities from the nostalgic community Aravosis imagined to have been present in the past. These ideas of community, Stryker made clear, were not imposed by some outside force, but instead came "from below, and from within." In stark contrast to Aravosis's vision of what LGBT meant and means, Stryker reminded those who were willing to listen that we have been before and can be again whole, not one.[60]

As we already know, the stripped down version of ENDA would eventually pass the House but fail to reach the Senate floor. Thus, the

importance of reviewing the rhetorical responses of those who emphasized the perspective of the wholeness of the LGBT community rests
not in whether or not they succeeded in blocking the House vote—this
is only one measure of this constitution of community. We should not
extrapolate from the legislative outcome in this one instance to its guaranteed failure as a strategy for uniting persons together in sacrificing
for others to make the people whole, not one. This short-sighted metric
omits the consideration of how the internal contestation of identity can
be a valuable form of politics in and of itself, latent with potential to
transform attitudes in a more profound manner than the passage of a
law. Obviously United ENDA's arguments did not persuade Frank, who
continued to attack their efforts all the way to the House floor: "I say
to my colleagues in the gay community, maybe I will do a little stereo-
typing, maybe they have seen the Wizard of Oz too often. They seem
to have Speaker Pelosi, a wonderful dedicated, committed supporter
of human rights, confused with Glenda the good witch. They think if
she waved her magic wand she could somehow change things."[61] Even
so, United ENDA remained undeterred in pressing for a fully inclusive
ENDA in the future.

Take, for example, GLAD's press release after the passage of the
sexual-orientation-only ENDA, which emphasized the progress for
trans inclusion: "the conversation around this legislation has demonstrated unprecedented community support for civil rights protections
for all lesbian, gay, bisexual and transgender people."[62] Recognizing the
opportunities offered by the occasion, GLAD further noted, "we have
had a tremendous opportunity to educate our political leaders and the
public on the importance of an inclusive bill, to show that we are united
as a community, and that excluding gender identity is unacceptable not
only because it abandons transgender people, it ignores the reality that
gender identity and expression are at the root of much anti-gay discrimination." With more than a little optimism, GLAD looked forward
to a "substantial shift in the commitment of a growing number of legislators to support an inclusive ENDA in the future." The efforts of United
ENDA paid off because the most recent version of ENDA restored the
gender identity protections, and we can hope that the past is not a pro-
logue to the efforts of those who agitate for a bill reflecting the idea of
wholeness.

Identity, Politics, Action

In this chapter, I have emphasized the importance of public debates about identity and its relationship to the law to highlight productive strategies for negotiating queer identity politics. If we were to restrict ourselves to reading the statutes' text alone to pass judgments about its effectivities in public cultures, we would miss out on its circulation as a site of controversy. By placing the law within larger cultural contexts and attending to public contestations of legislation, we are likely to discover different interpretations and investments in the law, both in terms of its procedural legislative path and its meaning for those whom it is meant to protect. That is not to say that legal analyses of statutory language fail to provide worthwhile critiques. Patrick McCreery's insightful reading of a previous version of ENDA, which is still applicable to the legislation in its present form, identifies the normative limits of sexual orientation protections if this category does not also include sexual practices—meaning, for example, that someone could be fired for having sex in public regardless of their sexual orientation.[63] This line of analysis reminds us that calls for more generous legislation, such as the inclusion of gender identity in ENDA, generates its own constitutive exclusions. At the same time, from such a removed vantage point, we cannot assume the only political attachment to identity and the law available to LGBT advocates and allies is a self-centered, self-serving wounded attachment incapable of fostering effective political action. The practice of identity politics need not always result in self-pity and inescapable loops of understanding one's self as a victim unable to transform the conditions of one's own possibility. If we survey the discursive field with a more agentic ear, as Bickford implores us to do, we can interpret the articulation of one's identity vis-à-vis the law not as "automatically an assertion of powerlessness or innocence," but as "an assertion about the exercise of unjust power" to convey the message that "I am a peer, a rightful participant in the argument about the just and the unjust, in the collective exercise of power."[64] This attitude may not be present in every case, but it is likely operative in many cases, and we need to account for this kind of collective identity formation and action.

At this point, it is not enough to trumpet the call for coalitional politics and labor under the pretense that the self-evident truth of the

issues involved in a controversy can or will forge persuasive or enduring bonds between similarly situated individuals. As Janet Jakobsen's
work demonstrates, even in favorable conditions for collective political
action, "alliance politics" is "often a matter of invocation rather than,
say, of enactment."[65] If we cannot assume any necessary correspondence
between one's identity and political commitments, either in form or
content, then we will have to learn from and develop specific communicative strategies for accomplishing coalitional identity politics. What
this controversy offers us is a model of how to speak from the perspective of "What I want for us" as opposed to "I want," thereby foreground-
ing one's commitment to communal interests and a better future for
those involved in struggling together. What this perspective of community and self promises are greater opportunities to make the people
whole, with differences being accounted for and valued as resources
for collective problem-solving, and in a way that is not reducible to a
utilitarian or communitarian construction of the self and others, but
instead allows for, and maybe even requires, sacrifice to build trust
among members of a coalition. The setting aside of self-interested discourses is more than a stylistic consideration—the rhetorical posture of
"What I want for us" can constitute the communities it articulates. Even
as the conclusions about the importance of imagining effective identity politics matter more than the particular articulations involved in
this controversy, since these rhetorical strategies will have be adapted to
address specific exigencies, the marking of gender as a common identity and the revision of LGBT history to include trans people as valuable
members of this community require further unpacking before we move
from the particular to the universal.

LGBT and queer coalitions have always been fragile, provisional, and
fraught with disputes about what unites them in common cause, and
fault lines continue to inform the current state of LGBT and queer politics. In spite of tremendous progress over the last two decades, when
major organizations and events have slowly and sometimes begrudgingly included trans people in their mission statements, advocacy
efforts, and fundraising, the persistent issue is the relative importance
of sexuality in defining the core of LGBT identities. Without completely
sidestepping this issue, the supporters of the fully inclusive ENDA
shifted this discussion to the importance of gender normativities,

which include but are not subsumed under the rubric of sexuality. By focusing on the shared ways in which LGBTs can be read as violating gender norms, trans advocates and allies did not assert an essential sameness or an equivalence of all discrimination based on gender, but they were able to redefine the gender identity provisions in ENDA as relevant to the whole populations of LGBTs to move it out of the realm of self-interest and homonormativity. For this reason, I find the actions of United ENDA and others like them to be beneficial models for queer identity politics, in which ontological questions about who one is and the transcendent meanings attached to this category of identity are not central. In their place, communities are constituted by more fluid senses of identity, in which performative embodiments of nonnormativity circulate in public cultures and generate shared interests. At the same time, the focus on gender nonnormativity is not a panacea. On the whole, LGBT and queer organizations do not have a particularly strong record of negotiating racial or class diversity, among other intersecting axes of identity, and it would be foolish to assume that isolating gender as a common site of alliance will adequately address all of these issues.[66] Gender can calcify in the same manner as sexual orientation, and we will be back to square one. But, if we can build from the productive responses to the ENDA controversy and allow gender to become implicated in and responsive to other identity categories, we may be closer to whole LGBT and queer communities.

Finally, the disputes over the historical roots of LGBT and queer communities that arose in the ENDA controversy are instructive about the continued importance of historical memory to our present and in the futures ahead of us. The ability to articulate narratives emphasizing histories of trans activism and LGBT cooperation and community countered many of the objections of LGBs opposed to postponing the passage of ENDA. Without a doubt, these narratives could not persuade LGB ideologues who were vehemently against aligning themselves with trans people, but we should not underestimate how these arguments strengthened the sense of communal identity necessary to create the conditions for LGB reciprocity and sacrifice in the present and the future. Undoubtedly history can be used to many ends, and not all of them are beneficial for the subjects of that history. But the work of Stryker and others to excavate trans history to motivate action in the present and the future, and its repetition by transgender advocates and allies in their public statements refuted the selfishly motivated "me first" rhetoric of LGBs unwilling to wait for more inclusive legislation. We might cynically suggest that the promised veto of ENDA by Bush never really forced the issue, and LGBs may not have been so willing to voice their opposition to ENDA if it was assured passage. Both are entirely possible. At the same time, the sense of community created by this shared past set into motion rhetorical resources to militate against future backsliding by LGBs, and it is to the future we now set our sights on as we consider the trajectories of transgender identities and politics in new regimes of visibility.

5

In Defense of an Impure Transgender Politics

Up to this point we have engaged how trans people employ legal discourses and redeploy the terms of these rhetorical cultures across a variety of domains. In addition to efforts to gain official state recognition, trans people negotiate the legal regulation of their bodies, the spaces in which they work and live, and others' understandings of their claims to citizenship. Far from uncritically adopting the normativities undergirding legal discourses, the trans people featured thus far demonstrate a dynamic relationship with these norms as they rework them in their activism and everyday lives. By privileging the law as an everyday practice of managing stranger-relationalities rather than an external set of rules and regulations created by legislatures and courts, we gain a more expansive view of how the law operates in and through cultural flows of meaning-making. If we avoid the reductionist logics of representation, wherein legal texts are accepted as deterministic discursive arrangements of culture, and aim instead to account for how it is that the law is a lived experience facilitated, but not foreclosed, by these conditions of possibility, a different evaluation of legal agencies becomes available to us.

In these concluding pages, I will revisit some of the themes and concepts from previous chapters to lay the foundation for some speculative comments on the prospects of trans identities and politics. My muse is a magazine cover image and the associated feature story in the *New Republic* (*TNR*) on the future of transgender rights advocacy. On the one hand, the image and story can be read as somewhat normative, from the trans person featured on the cover to the linking together of transgender and previous civil rights movements to the rehearsal of expected narratives about transgender life experiences. On the other hand, the image and story enact a radical demand for equal treatment before the law. We need to contextualize properly this demand for equality, justice, and freedom, and by reading the cover and cover story as a text, as well as attending to its circulation in an unexpected venue, we can discern how articulations of equal citizenship initiate a productive performative contradiction by both doing and undoing legal discourses.

These arguments take place in an ongoing conversation about the overall state of transgender politics, both internal and external. We are two decades removed from Sandy Stone's manifesto declaring the need for posttranssexuality, or transsexuals who would not pass and choose to mark themselves publicly as transsexuals, to make an invisible minority visible to the general public. As a result of the relative advances enabled by the form of visibility Stone named, I want to ask, "Are we post-posttranssexuality"? Here, the modifier "post-" is not meant to signal the irrelevance of this identity category, as it does for those who claim that we live in a post-racial America where race is no longer a significant concern or a source of discrimination. Rather, the "post-" in *post-posttranssexuality* signifies the need to account for contexts where trans people are increasingly recognized in culture, maybe not at the pace we would hope for, but recognized nonetheless, and where this new visibility instigates its own promises and perils. Examining how resorting to legal discourses can help to sustain these newly visible communities, I will conclude with a consideration of how we might think of what has been developed across these pages as a worthwhile form of impure politics, invested in but not complicit with its authorizing gestures.

Contextualizing the Contingency of Queerness

A recent cover story for *TNR* declared the push for transgender rights to be "AMERICA'S NEXT GREAT CIVIL RIGHTS STRUGGLE." In a departure from the magazine's usual cover design aesthetic featuring caricatures of politicians or appropriations of iconic cultural objects, this issue featured a simple portrait of Sam Berkley seated on an old metal stool against a brown backdrop, dressed in dark blue denim and a lighter blue military-inspired shirt with the sleeves rolled up. Berkley's image takes up the entire cover except for a small text box in the right-hand corner identifying this issue as the summer books issue of the magazine. Berkley's hair is styled so as to give the appearance of being disheveled, although we know from the sheen of styling products the hair has been pushed forward purposefully, and the noticeable stubble above the lip completes the look of what would be an otherwise unremarkable photograph of a trendy, young, svelte, light-olive skinned man, were it not for the block lettered caption: "HE WAS BORN IN A WOMAN'S BODY. NOW HE IS A SECOND-CLASS CITIZEN." This caption intends to shock the reader in at least two ways—first, by revealing Berkley's trans identification through the trope of "being born in the wrong body," and second, by announcing Berkley's vexed legal status, a fact made all the more shocking because of the assumed privilege men of a certain race and class tend to enjoy. Framing Berkley's face, the cover encourages the assumed cisgender viewer to read the straightforward stare as a demand for equality and recognition—I say "assumed cisgender viewer" because the tone implied by the subsequent phrase on the cover "Welcome to America's Next Great Civil Rights Struggle" presumes a lack of familiarity with the topic. The intended juxtaposition between text and photo dislodges the visual as a transparent truth about sex and gender as it crudely reminds us Berkley was a woman and is now a man. (Berkley is not the focus of the essay so it is not clear if Berkley would narrate identity within this linear logic of female to male.) Berkley's image is not threatening in the usual sense of the word: he appears to be a typical man, not the conservative fantasy of the mentally ill sexual pervert who preys on children or women in bathrooms; nor is Berkley projecting anger or rage. For precisely these reasons, then, we might read the image as threatening due the ways in which it asks uninformed or unsupportive cisgender viewers to question their own investments in denying their fellow transgender citizens full and equal treatment under the law. On what basis and to what ends could one justify looking Berkley in the eyes and arguing against access to legal protections from discrimination and violence?

There are, of course, other possible readings of this cover and the accompanying article. For some, Berkley's image may appear to be not queer enough to sustain an important intervention into public culture. His dress, pose, and overall appearance do not necessarily initiate a sustained critique of gender norms or markers. Without reading the caption identifying Berkley as transgender, one could interpret this image

Figure 5.1. Cover of the *New Republic* featuring Sam Berkley, July 14, 2011.

as a photograph of an ordinary, middle-class man sitting for a portrait divorced from any explicit political consideration. Along this line of antinormative critique, some may wish for a more transgressive image to trouble the normative codes of gender. That is, some may infer a certain politics of respectability operating through this choice of a cover photo over other possible options. Likewise, Berkley is identified by the editors as a female-to-male trans person, which can be construed as reinforcing the stability of binary sexual categories in the assumption that one can move from one discreet and distinct sex to the other. In this same vein, the choice to showcase a transman as opposed to a transwoman traffics in its own politics about the relative acceptability of different gender identifications. We could continue on down this road, but let it stand for now that this image and story would not qualify as queer enough for some readers.

Without shutting down this mode of critique, I want to interject a concern about the somewhat unattainable goal of satisfying the noun and adjectival forms of *queer* and *queerness* associated with their more dogmatic renderings as visible resistance to norms and normativities. Far too often, modes of recognition are mistaken for one's acceptance of the norms and normativities underwriting the logics of legibility associated with these cultural formations. As a result, the deployment of queer and queerness as a heuristic can rely upon its own critical insatiability such that these concepts are almost always mirages, available to us only in the world of representations, such as films or novels, and even then only rarely and fleetingly. For this reason, it is not an accident or simply a matter of rote memory that our work continues to be identified primarily as *queer theory* and not *queer studies* when the metrics of queer and queerness prefigure their impossibility in our quotidian practices and politics. I am not suggesting that we can finally attain a permanent state of queerness in the last instance or that this should be our goal. Instead, I am suggesting that we undersell the potential, even if it is only momentary and in small ways, for practices to queer existing cultural formations and initiate dialectical renegotiations of norms and normativities, which may settle back into previously received relations of meaning but not without some disturbance and accommodation.

In this way, queer critique often installs its own mythic norms from the outset in a ironic move that mimics the very habits of thought it is meant to denaturalize. I am not alone in this appraisal of the state of queer studies and how it would preposition us to approach *TNR*'s image and essay. Robyn Wiegman's meditation on queer studies' peculiar and paradoxical fixation with antinormativity as the "precondition for the field's self-constitution and managed incoherence" confirms this troubling state of affairs.[1] "With antinormativity as the highest critical value," Wiegman contends, "the field must cultivate, often to the point of idealization, the most resolutely alternative—that is, the most radically perverse and socially unassimilable—in order to do justice to the project of alterity and difference invested in the sign of the queer."[2] This ever-narrowing semiotics of queer, driven by an outflanking of one practice by an even more antinormative one, unnecessarily banishes from its imaginary a whole host of practices and subjectivities which cannot be accurately depicted as normative. More than an academic quibble over analytical categories, this policing of queerness, intentionally or not, disavows the rich and varied motivations animating demands for equality.

When these expectations of queerness are saddled onto trans bodies and identities, a double burden emerges as these bodies and identities are assumed to be exemplars of queerness, often appearing as exotic props supported only by the most superficial depictions, and only if their appearance is transgressive. Thus, trans queerness is ensconced primarily in a visual economy and only at the pleasure of the other's eye. In effect, then, dominant modes of queer critique get us only so far, especially when they operate at the level of an isolated representation divorced from more complex forms of contextualization.

In that spirit, and in order to establish the context for engaging *TNR*'s image's contingent potential for queer culture, I should note that the editors chose Berkley's image from a photo shoot of ten trans activists who form the subject of an accompanying online photo essay entitled "Breaking Boundaries."[3] Along the side of each photograph, a lengthy caption explains who the pictured person is and the forms of activism in which they participate. In the print version, the photographs and truncated versions of these captions fill the bottom of the pages of Eliza Gray's cover story on "Transitions." On the whole, the trans people featured in "Breaking Boundaries" represent a relatively diverse group of activists in terms of race, ethnicity, class, gender presentation, and age.

Some, such as Pauline Park, Jillian Weiss, and Laverne Cox, are more recognizable trans activists on the national stage, while the others are known more for their local efforts. I mention this not to insulate the cover image from all criticism; these circumstances do, however, alleviate some of the pressure placed on any one image to represent the entirety of trans activism and experiences since the photo essay does acknowledge the breadth of trans identities. Are there queerer images than Berkley's that would satisfy those wedded to visibly jarring images as a precondition of queerness? Maybe. I guess it depends on what one means by "queer" and "queerer." But, again, this mode of critique would read the image against an imagined standard of queerness at the expense of actually existing challenges to cultural normativities. While I will return to this issue, I want first to call attention to the appropriation of the cover in an unlikely place and examine one way in which it can be read as queering culture.

TNR's cover story caught the eyes of the Weekly Standard's (TWS) editor, William Kristol, who deemed it worthy of the weekly "Parody" page of the print version of the magazine. Each week, this influential conservative magazine publishes a cartoon or a photograph to highlight the excesses of the so-called liberal agenda. Draped in humor, but often just mean-spirited hate that denigrates differences and trades in tired stereotypes, the "Parody" pages are reproduced as regular fixtures on numerous blogs, talk radio, and other conservative media outlets. Starting with the inauguration of Barack Obama, the magazine chose to publish from time to time a "Not a Parody" page, the first one being a reproduction of a headline announcing Obama's Nobel Peace Prize Award.[4] For the edition in question for our purposes, TWS reprinted TNR's cover, slightly cocked to the left and made to look torn along the bottom, with a caption at the top identifying it as "Not a Parody."[5]

Although it is presented as a self-evidently ludicrous image and idea, we should not underestimate the various arguments at work in TWS's re-presentation of the image. Even as we are told the image is an actual cover of another magazine because it is not a parody, that this image graces the page normally reserved for a good conservative laugh instructs us to scrutinize it as an example of the discrepancy between the imagined reader's traditional values and the radical politics of liberals. Are we supposed to chuckle at trans people in general, their demand for civil rights, the idea that trans people can or should have civil rights, the idea that what they desire is even mentioned in the same sentence as civil rights, all of this at once, or maybe something else? Without direct guidance as to where we should direct our incredulity, it seems the entire package of image, text, and their combined meaning is put forth as being so ridiculous as to need no further comment. In fact, when Gray, the author of *TNR* essay, contacted Kristol to ask why he chose to reprint the cover, he replied, "I've found over the years that it's best not to try to explain jokes or parodies—and I think it makes sense to extend this rule to a 'not a parody.' It stands (or falls) on its own."

Politico picked up this story and offered Gray the chance to reply to Kristol's non-responsive quip: "The lack of any argument whatsoever in the Standard's 'parody' is telling. It's the 'philosophy' of a junior high school bully, for whom pointing and laughing is the only argument required. The joke here is that political magazines are supposed to be able to make intellectual arguments." When given the opportunity to further comment on this issue, Kristol demurred: "We simply designated the New Republic's cover as that week's Not a Parody. It speaks for itself, and others are free to comment as they wish."[6] With this response, which substitutes unreflexive privilege for reason, Kristol trusts like-minded bigots to fill in the enthymeme, without the need for him to construct a logical argument opposing equal treatment under the law for trans people.

Before we dismiss *TWS*'s text as a trivial example of conservative humor, we must not underestimate its indexing of the threat posed by Berkley's image to accepted understandings of sex, gender, and citizenship. In contrast to a reading of this text as not queer enough and thus employing a standard judged against a mythic queerness, might we read the controversy involving *TNR*'s cover as an indication of its latent potential to queer cultural assumptions about bodies and identities. Of all of the possible topics available for conservative scorn during the production of that issue, *TWS*'s editors selected this image. We don't need to hazard some guess at deep-seeded psychological motives to distill a defensive response to the unsettling of a host of norms and normativities in the disdain directed at the image and idea of trans equality. Without question, those exposed to *TWS*'s reproduction of the image interpreted it in any number of ways. And I doubt seriously

Figure 5.2. The "Parody" page from the *Weekly Standard*'s July 4–July 11, 2011, issue, reproducing the cover of the *New Republic* and labeling it "*Not* a Parody."

many readers of *TWS* were persuaded by *TNR*'s cover to the point that they would rethink their biases and support transgender rights. Persuasion is not the most important question or answer for our argument. Instead, if we can employ *TWS*'s non-parody parody as an indication of the violation of expected norms, we may want to revisit the knee-jerk reaction to images like Berkley's as inherently normative and thus not able to queer existing epistemologies of sex, gender, sexualities, bodies, and citizenship.

Within the context of dominant cultures in the United States, Berkley's image exposes several regimes of normativity as tenuous and malleable. Although *TWS*'s parody tries to banish the consideration of trans people as frivolous folly, by addressing the topic at all, the magazine gives presence to trans people even as it excludes them from what the editors perceive to be the hallowed grounds of Constitutional rights and obligations. What may be meant as a sign of liberal excess also expresses some defensiveness and apprehension about the permeability of bodies, gender, and the letter of the law. In this case, *TWS*'s parody does a lot of rhetorical work to try to secure normative conceptions of bodies and the law in its curt dismissal of transgender citizens. If transgender demands for equal rights carried no plausible chance for greater traction with American publics, they would not require any response at all from conservative voices like *TWS*.

These contextual arguments may seem to some to set the bar too low, not only because the magazine cover probably did not shift the opinions of many *TWS* readers, but also because we should not measure queer potential against the arguments of conservative magazines since the field of non-normativity is so large for them. But it bears repeating that we should not confuse the effectivities of these images with successful persuasion (an almost impossibe to discern metric for any utterance), and so images such as the cover of *TNR* must not read against a mythic standard of queerness when evidence exists to suggest the textual disruption of common sense. When undertaken within larger discursive currents circulating within cultures, a reparative reading of this cover and its parody unearths insight into the capability of the image to contest conventional wisdom about bodies, genders, sexualities, the reliability of visual observations, and the scope of the law.

If we move across the political spectrum, from right to left, Gray's article detailing transgender activism may not find much safer harbor. *TNR*'s underlying faith in left legalism with its announcement of transgender rights advocacy efforts as "AMERICA'S NEXT GREAT CIVIL RIGHTS STRUGGLE" no doubt betrays the spirit of antinormative politics espoused by some on the Left. Left legalism, as understood by Wendy Brown and Janet Halley, is the unfortunate practice of articulating "broad-based, locally, and culturally rich 'movement' politics to demands for state-enforced rights," thereby translating "wide-ranging political questions into more narrowly framed legal questions" and prematurely foreclosing the possibilities for "open-ended discursive contestation" about the sources of injury and the appropriateness of legal protections for remedying these unjust conditions.[7] On Brown and Halley's reading, left legalism is sustained as a rhetorical resource in the present by the memory of landmark judicial victories for racial civil rights movements in cases such as *Brown v. Board of Education* and the forgetting of the multifaceted forms of activism beyond legal reforms that challenged the cultural conditions complicit with racial animus. As a result, Brown and Halley conclude, when "the available range of legal remedies preempts exploration of the deep constitutive causes of an injury," an unintended consequence of such habits of thoughts is the sacrificing of "our chance to be deliberative, inventive political beings who create our collective life form."[8] Thus, for critics of left legalism, preemptive recourse to an expanded discourse of rights incapacitates us from envisioning other cultural arrangements more amenable to justice.

For Brown and Halley, transgender rights advocacy serves as an example of the tight grip that left legalism has on our political imaginaries. In their words,

> As a language and strategy for seeking justice for the historically subordinated, the civil rights discourse coined for racial justice has become almost hegemonic. More recent emancipatory and egalitarian efforts model themselves explicitly and seemingly inevitably on the black civil rights movement remembered only in its liberal and legalistic modalities: the women's movement, the disabled movement, even transsexual

and transgendered activists have turned to the vocabulary of civil rights
as to an ineluctable fund of justice claims.[9]

In isolating transsexual and transgender activism as "even" guilty of
these discursive formations, Brown and Halley may be registering a
startled reaction to a perceived turning away from queerer political
projects. Or, perhaps they mean to mark how nascent movements trying to gain greater visibility cannot help but gravitate toward these rhetorical strategies. Another possible message conveyed by this phrasing is
the perceived difficulty of translating the strategies associated with one
social movement into a generic, transhistorical template for all social
movements. It could be also some combination of these views. Whatever the case may be, what we want to challenge about these indictments of left legalism is the expectation that rights assertion necessarily short-circuits cultural pedagogies of sex, gender, sexualities, and
citizenship as well as other modes of democratic engagement among
family, friends, co-workers, and strangers. Gray's essay in *TNR* points
toward the generative conditions of more modest forms of left legalism.

In "Transitions," a titular play on words referring to moving from a
sex medically assigned at birth to another category of identity as well as
to the evolution of transgender activism, Gray intersperses her interactions with a transgender interviewee, Caroline Temmermand, with
informative blocks of prose outlining the precarious legal position of
transgender Americans and their efforts to gain equality. After intro-
ducing the reader to various forms of discrimination and violence trans
people contend with in their lives, Gray distinguishes the success of
transgender activism from gay and lesbian activism by comparing their
relative visibility within culture and the resulting tolerance enabled by
the growing numbers of Americans who have contact with gays and
lesbians, whether directly or through mediated representations. Esti-
mating the U.S. trans population to be about 700,000, as compared to
8 million gays, lesbians, and bisexuals, Gray highlights how trans people are "invisible in a way that other minorities are not." For this reason, Gray surmises, trans people face an uphill battle against prejudice
since "civil rights movements have prevailed when they have convinced
enough people that a minority is being treated in a way that is fundamentally un-American." "For this to happen," Gray concludes, "people

need to see members of a disadvantaged group as human beings before anything else."[10] Gray's humanizing story about trans activists serves, then, as a way for her to speed up the process.

In one way, Gray's description of Temmermand's life journey is complicit with the tendency of cisgender-crafted and -oriented mediations of transgender experiences to focus on appearance, mannerisms, and stereotypical behaviors. For example, on the first page, Gray notes Temmermand's tall frame, her choice to wear a pants suit, that her "voice and manner were effortlessly feminine," how she is more outwardly emotional since starting hormonal therapy, and how she finds humor in the gendered expectations of women. For the most part, rather than exoticizing trans people, Gray's observations offer a more compassionate understanding. As she states, "After our first hour together, I couldn't think of [Temmermand] as anything but a woman." Gray goes on to weave together Temmermand's struggle to accept her identity after a failed marriage and difficult family life, bouts of depression, and another failed relationship, and then, her eventual realization of her identity as a trans person with the help of a therapist. Situating this narrative within a larger history of transgender discrimination and activism, Gray contextualizes Temmermand's situation within the cultural pressures working on and through trans people. In the end, we learn that after some initial resistance, Temmermand's family generally accepts her identification as transgender and her activism.

After a review of different court cases involving trans litigants and the controversy over excluding gender identity protections from the Employment Non-Discrimination Act, Gray concludes the essay by returning to Temmermand to emphasize the importance of transgender activism beyond the scope of national organizations and their litigation efforts. While recovering from a facial surgery, Temmermand watched a widely circulated YouTube video of an attack of a transwoman, Chrissy Lee Polis, in a nearby McDonald's in Baltimore County, Maryland. As the video shows, patrons did not intervene, but they did laugh at the situation, as a fourteen-year-old and an eighteen-year-old woman savagely beat Polis after she used the women's bathroom. One of the assailants dragged Polis around the restaurant by her hair, stopping only after Polis started to have a seizure.[11] Despite her own impaired condition, Temmermand immediately organized a protest outside of the McDonald's where the attack happened. Word spread quickly, hundreds of people joined Temmermand, and the McDonald's had to close for the night. In addition to this direct action protest, Temmermand would later lobby the Maryland legislature for gender identity protections in housing and employment.

In the second to last paragraph, Gray restates the need for cisgender readers to interrogate their own investment in the legal and cultural regulations of bodies, genders, and sexualities. "For people to feel safe, our society will need to build a series of legal and cultural protections for transgender people. And, at a broader level, it will need to reevaluate just how necessary it really is to define people according to what's between their legs. This would clearly help the transgender community, but it might be healthy for the rest of us, too." This statement is immediately followed by the recounting of Temmermand's coming out to her coworkers in a government administrative office. In a meeting with approximately eighty coworkers, Temmermand addressed rumors about her longer hair and earrings to confirm her plans to, in her words, "switch genders" (18). In contrast to Gray's initial pessimism about the future of transgender equality, she found "cause for hope" when Temmermand informed Gray that her coworkers ended the meeting with a standing ovation. Through a mix of activities, at least in Gray's telling of the tale, Temmermand found a way to move through time and space and land in a more comfortable, tolerant world than when we first meet her in the opening pages of the essay.

Temmermand's actions, as depicted in Gray's article, may not mollify all of the concerns of critics of left legalism, but I want to suggest that we reconsider this critique in light of Gray's essay. In the narrative reconstruction of Temmermand's activism, we find no evidence that engaging the law, say in the form of lobbying, necessarily results in the total usurpation of advocate energy in litigation and legislative lobbying. Temmermand participated in these efforts, but she also organized the McDonald's protest to directly confront a community and business guilty of indifference with regard to transgender safety. Transgender advocacy takes many forms, all the way from the lobbying of Congress to enact legal protections to the everyday negotiations of the law and legal notions of equality, fairness, and the scope and the acceptability of the regulation of one's body. Here, we should not conflate the work of legal advocacy organizations with the entirety of transgender advocacy efforts. Critics of left legalism may respond by noting that the preemptive translation of cultural contestations of norms into legally inflected rhetorics, even in the employ of progressive politics, already narrows the range of our imagination to the point where the eventual reinscription of existing norms is the only possible outcome. Yet, this presumed result occurs only if we arrest the mobility of legal rhetorics and underestimate the radical potential of performative contradictions to instantiate an injustice and work against the conditions enabling that injustice. As a performative enactment, the law is a diachronic resource invoked by individuals, and in its invocation, the law is synchronically interpreted, redeployed, and modified. Viewed in this light, legal cultures must not be understood as hegemonically solidified cultural formations that inhibit agentic practices upon one's entrance into these discursive regimes. Rather, the dialectical negotiation of historically saturated legal principles against their contingent context by individuals with competing motives underscores the need to approach legal cultures from the perspective of undoing rather than domination and subordination. This shift in perspective, without denying or understating the state's power to create, interpret, and enforce its own meaning of the law, provides an important supplement to institutionally based analysis of the law with studies of how the law is actually employed as a way to manage stranger-relationalities in liberal-democratic polities.

Undoing Left Legalism

As I have noted throughout *Transforming Citizenships*, legal rhetorical cultures evolve in their recirculation as the law and culture do and undo each other through the articulation of unexpected elements into demands for citizenship. Even if these demands do not result in the radical restructuring of the normative architectures of culture, they must be accounted for. In the process, these discourses reshape the logics of intelligibility underwriting the discursive formations put under pressure by the performative contradiction. That is to say, the general thrust of demands for equality operates in relation to the idea of fairness, whether in opportunity or outcome. While critics of left legalism would have us do away with these tainted concepts in the hopes of crafting discursive systems of meaning free from already contaminated liberalisms, their critique relies on a fundamental misperception of the rhetoricity of the law in that it assumes the discursive relationship between law and culture runs only in one direction wherein the former circumscribes the latter. As a result, the critique of left legalism cannot explain the how it is that dissident subjectivities develop vis-à-vis the law in the first place. With a rich history of fugitive articulations of the law upon which we can draw, from women demanding suffrage to trans people petitioning for employment protections, it is difficult to cede such deterministic power to the law. Although it may be possible that other cultural formations could flourish and provide more responsive forms of justice than what is currently understood as legal discourse in American cultures, I remain unconvinced that disadvantaged groups must remain oppressed to formulate superior cultural arrangements. As we have already seen, legal discourses available to citizens in the here and now are capacious enough to allow for similar, if not better, results than a nebulous future free from liberalism.

The perspective of undoing mitigates many of the concerns associated with left legalism, and it operates in two related registers. The first explicates the dynamic relationships of identities, institutions, cultural formations, and agency. Agency, especially after post-structuralist critique, is an inherently slippery concept complicated by its tethering to political programs. For some, an agentic subject is one who acts rationally and publicly within the boundaries of cultural norms to achieve some goal. For others, agency is impossible once one invokes dominant discourses as they are irrevocably tainted by hegemonic norms. What I have demonstrated throughout this work is that neither of these perspectives provides a productive framework for examining how subjects operate in rhetorical cultures if the only choices available to agentic subjects are wholly within or outside of cultural norms. If agency is defined as action in accordance to one's recognition within dominant norms, conformity trumps invention when norms are understood as external forces constraining individuals to a narrow range of preapproved subjectivities. Conversely, if agency is dependent upon one's rejection of all institutions and norms due to their ideological saturation, individuals experience agency only if they make themselves unintelligible to others. Where the first view of agency accepts normalization in exchange for recognition, the later incorrectly assumes that we can somehow stand at an instrumental distance from power and critique it from outside, which underestimates the importance of legibility in the cultural field. Illegibility is not an option for most trans people as it creates the conditions for discrimination and violence. In response to this dualism, agency is best thought of as a process of doing and undoing to allow the latitude needed to navigate the problematics of recognition.

As developed in previous chapters, this sense of agency relies on real or imagined recognition that challenges the normativities underwriting this recognition. Recognition must not be conflated with Althusserian understandings of interpellation as a unilateral hailing of subjects into dominant ideologies and norms. Norms, according to Butler, "provide the framework and the point of reference for any set of decisions we subsequently make," yet "this does not mean that a given regime of truth sets an invariable framework for recognition; it means only that it is in relation to this framework that recognition takes place or the norms that govern recognition are challenged and transformed."[12] Given these enabling and constraining conditions of possibility, an agentic subject is not "fully determined nor radically free" as "its struggle or primary dilemma is to be produced by a world, even as one must produce oneself in some way."[13] Thus, as one is performatively produced or undone by norms beyond one's control, one also undoes the norms in performatively producing one's own identity within and against these norms. On this view, agency is not found in heroic actions within or outside cultural formations but rather in performative repertoires, or the everyday contestations of identity informed by one's experiences but not determined in advance by these same experiences. In Butler's words, agency is achieved when "a certain self is risked in its intelligibility and recognizability in a bid to expose and account for the inhuman ways in which 'the human' continues to be done and undone."[14] When trans people such as Temmermand articulate themselves as transgender citizens entitled to equal treatment before the law, they transform the law as they work within and stretch its limits. Concurrently, the law transforms, which is not the same as normalizes, individuals in ways great and small, in both constraining and enabling ways.

If we are willing to forego ontological and epistemological certainties about norms, institutions, and identity, we may come to different conclusions about the discursivity of legal norms and recognition. This uncertainty can create concerns for those who rely on stable identities for political mobilization, for those who want to focus their energies primarily on reforming institutions or rejecting their legitimacy, and for those who benefit from unquestioned norms. These concerns can lead to charges of nihilism, defeatism, individuating politics, or identity politics. As should be clear, however, promoting a sense of agency that embraces the generative fissures, contradictions, and limits of our cultural logics of recognition does not necessarily signal a retreat into a privatized politics unconcerned with the material conditions of existence, nor does it condemn us to left legalism. Instead, this understanding of agency, which is not determined by official state recognition or faithfulness to dominant norms and institutions, reminds us that the important work of politics takes place in our everyday interactions as much as, if not more than, it does in exerting influence on state actors; at the same time, this everyday politics also requires a certain level of intelligibility available through means such as legal discourses before one can engage others. Rather than fear this conception of politics and stranger-relationality, we need to learn how to negotiate its paradoxical form of subjectivity and recognize that our "willingness to become undone in relation to others constitutes our chance of becoming human." Butler established the stakes in the following manner: "To be undone by another is a primary necessity, an anguish, to be sure, but also a chance—to be addressed, claimed, bound to what is not me, but also to be moved, to be prompted to act, to address myself elsewhere, and so to vacate the self-sufficient 'I' as a kind of possession."[15] If we allow ourselves to be undone and to undo the interpellative gestures meant to contain and constrain our living of meaningful lives, non-state-centered forms of agency are more likely to emerge, even if they begin with an invocation of an articulation generally associated with the logics of the state.

The trans people discussed throughout this book demonstrate how the performativity of identity and the perspective of undoing is not a new radical theory of being or acting in the world; rather, it is always already the condition of our possibilities. For example, Debbie Mayne wanted to be known as a woman and to be free to move about in the world as one. In occupying this identity position, Mayne adopted stereotypically feminine mannerisms, sought out and finally found a doctor willing to perform sex-reassignment surgeries, and, at the same time, challenged the immutability of bodies and the authority of medical, psychiatric, and legal officials to control her body. The discrepancy between Mayne's public and hidden transcripts reveals an agentic subject capable of exposing the limits of recognition, albeit in a tactical and localized manner, to reconfigure the modalities of domination she faced in her daily life. Similarly, INTRAA advocates working to gain formal equality in Indiana expressed a desire to be explicitly recognized as a protected class of citizens, which can be read cynically as an inescapably normalizing form of citizenship. Yet, the interviews informing that chapter evidence a critical engagement with norms. INTRAA is working both within and outside of the law to create a more hospitable climate for trans people in Indiana. This two-track strategy refutes the claim that norms hegemonically seduce and thereby contain individuals through the internalization of the regulatory intentions of norms. In this way, it stresses the need for us to remember that "theory is an activity that does not remain restricted to the academy," for it "takes place every time a possibility is imagined, a collective self-reflection takes place, a dispute over values, priorities, and language emerges."[16] Rather than a call to abandon politics, this is a call to recognize the ways in which norms, recognition, identity, and agency operate in our everyday lives.

In summary, a perspective of agency that recognizes its constraints as an enabling set of possibilities does not necessarily subscribe to a deterministic politics that strengthens the grip of hegemonic norms. By allowing ourselves to be undone by these norms and while also undoing them at the same time, agential pathways are opened rather than closed. In comparison to the alternatives, complete acceptance or rejection of all norms, this paradoxical vision of agency more accurately describes how it is that we survive the pressures of normalizing regimes. In this way, what some understand as left legalism does not play out like a stable script due to the multifarious embodiments of the law in the performative relationships of family, friends, and strangers.

The first register of undoing complements the second as it explains how law and culture productively destabilize each other. In framing law and everyday life as cultural elements that continually implicate and modify the other, we recognize this rich site of cultural contestation as constituted in and by the mutual instability that each causes the other. Following Austin Sarat's and Thomas Kearns's lead, we need to recognize the ways in which "the everyday defines its own rules and knows its own law," for the "law does not descend on the everyday as an all-powerful outsider without encountering a lively resistance."[17] Of course, this resistance is rhetorically negotiated. As Rosemary Coombe argues, the law relies on and produces discursive resources, which are inherently unstable foundations in that they are themselves performatively produced phenomena, in a process that in turn "invites and shapes (although it does not determine) activities that legitimate, resist, and potentially rework" the norms of one's rhetorical culture.[18] Rather than read this framing of law and culture as a retreat into the politics of textual play, Coombe asks us instead to "recognize both the signifying power of the law and law's power of signification as evidenced in concrete struggles over meaning and their political consequence" as a way to capture the materialities of legal cultures more fully.[19]

PISSAR's coalitional politics are an exemplary case of how the law inaugurates resistant subjectivities who can appropriate the law to their own ends. The synergistic energy created by the fusion of seemingly disparate genderqueer and disabled individuals allowed PISSAR to articulate their different struggles through similar and shared rhetorics. Using the bathroom as a site of politics, PISSAR members overcame the shame associated with bathroom use and politics through the language of accessibility and safety. Even as the Americans with Disabilities Act expressly prohibits accommodations for trans people, the genderqueer members latched onto the legal concept of accessibility to justify their claims. This appropriation of accessibility solidified their coalition with disabled members as they realized they shared sources of spatial oppression. Moreover, the PISSAR patrols afforded the disabled members an opportunity to see that the design of sex-specific bathrooms, predicated on the assumption that it provides a relative amount of safety from sexual violence, may actually cause more harassment and violence than it prevents. With these insights, PISSAR successfully lobbied for improvements to existing bathrooms and the conversion and construction of more gender-neutral bathrooms. PISSAR's redeployment of legal principles may not have fit squarely within strict readings of the law. Nonetheless, they tactically employed legal rhetorics to strengthen their coalition and challenge the pissing privilege that so many people enjoy.

Through the enactment of performative repertoires, wherein subjects operate through logics of recognition but are not subservient to them, individuals employ a reservoir of corporeal knowledges to navigate the discursive circuitries of hegemonic norms. Therefore, as trans people performatively do and undo the law through their quotidian practices, the law is revealed to be a set of unstable signifiers continually modified through their invocation. Debbie Mayne's performative repertoires allowed her to be recognized first as an unruly legal subject who then used this initial sign of recognition to undo the law's power to circumscribe her movement in public places. Similarly, INTRAA advocates' embodied interactions with others enabled them to create moments of identification to set the groundwork for greater legal protections. Together, these sites of cultural contestation speak to the need not only to engage the state, but also to demonstrate how trans people find agential avenues outside of official legal recognition.

The perspectives of undoing advanced here may not lead us to correctives that are easily translated into discrete legal reform programs. To suggest that agency is the undoing of identity and its authorizing norms or that law and culture undo each other does not provide any universalizable principles beyond the need to sharpen our critical awareness of our relationship to normativities, legal and otherwise. Might trading in teleology for the rhetorical conditions of contingency and context be understood as resulting in a strength instead of a liability? If legal critique is always already operating within a culture, how does that alter the locations of legal and cultural change? Most importantly, is it possible that this shift in perspective might activate new avenues of agency that escape the lure of left legalism? Gray's essay does not ask or answer all of these questions, but before we transition into another set of concerns, I want to suggest it unwittingly proffers a host of responses to those opposed to left legalism. As Temmermand's actions show, queer critique must take into account context and contingency to get past *a priori* rejections of the law as inherently normative and normalizing. Critical sensitivity to the rhetoricity of the law in actually existing articulations of the law may undermine the prevailing assumptions and suspicions of queer critique. To elaborate on the effectivities of doing and undoing, I will now attend to contemporary forms of legal, medical, and cultural recognition to further explore the contours of transgender civil rights movements.

Post-Posttranssexualities

A recent conference hosted by Susan Stryker to honor the twentieth anniversary of the publication of Sandy Stone's essay "A Posttranssexual Manifesto" provides the subtitle for this section and asks us to consider the histories and trajectories of trans activism. Even though attendees were there to celebrate the interventions enabled by Stone's essay, the conference title, "postposttranssexual: Transgender Studies and Feminism," posed a provocative proposition by positing the possibility that we may be post-posttransexuality. In the opening keynote conversation, Stone, Stryker, and Kate Bornstein covered a great many topics as they reviewed the importance of this essay to themselves and others, their own struggles to gain legitimacy in their professional lives, and the importance of their friendship. The most moving part of the evening came at the end when Stone read aloud the final paragraphs of the essay. Recalling the motivations that compelled the writing of the essay and noting the continued resonance of the words with the audience, Stone triumphantly exclaimed the last lines, held her fist up in the air, and drank in the thunderous applause. I found the conference to be an invigorating experience, but I still wanted more. I wanted an answer to the question posed by the conference title. The speakers on the stage never directly addressed what the inclusion of *post-* in the conference title meant, rightly deferring to it as an open signifier available for unanticipated articulations. Upon reflection, however, the opening session and the conference as a whole did provide a provisional answer that I see more clearly now. On my reading, the *post-* indicated not a moving past or beyond the essay in question, but an evolution, albeit not always a linear progression, of the term *posttranssexuality* in response to changing cultural conditions. As with any conference theme, the goal was to provide provocations and to unsettle established patterns of thought, not to supply definitive answers about the relationships between transgender studies and feminisms. In what follows, I want to wrestle with the importance of Stone's essay and the idea of post-postranssexuality, or what we might call post-transgender, as a form of internal and external politics in a time when trans people are gaining the forms of recognition Stone called for. But first, a brief review of the essay is warranted.

In 1991, Sandy Stone gave academic voice to transsexuals living openly as transsexuals, or those who wanted to be, asking them to participate in a project of "post-transsexuality." Stone explicitly challenged the medically enforced notion that transsexuals should remain invisible and assimilate into traditional sexual and gender roles, colloquially known as "'stealth,' 'woodwork,' or into 'the closet at the end of the rainbow.'"[20] Written against medical/psychological protocols requiring transsexuals to repeat tropes such as feeling as if one was "trapped in the wrong body," as well as the common practice of "constructing a plausible history" (a therapeutic tool that forces transsexuals to rewrite their sexual past to erase any traces of their experiences as the sex they were assigned at birth), Stone challenged transsexuals to create a "counterdiscourse" that refused such erasures of unique and individual experiences. As Stone put it, "what is gained" by the recitation of a plausible history "is acceptability in society," while "what is lost is the ability to authentically represent the complexities and ambiguities of lived experiences" by denying the emergence of stories "disruptive to the accepted discourses of gender, which originate from within the gender minority itself and which can make common cause with other oppositional discourses."[21] Citing Butler's work on cultural intelligibility and the potential for non-normative bodies to dislodge the epistemic certainty undergirding hegemonic cultural formations, Stone suggested that "the transsexuals for whom gender identity is something different from *and perhaps irrelevant to* physical genitalia are occulted by those for whom the power of the medical/psychological establishments, and their ability to act as gatekeepers for cultural norms, is the final authority for what counts as a culturally intelligible body." Yet, Stone predicted, the accumulation of visible, loud, and polyvocal trans voices would reveal that "the identities of individual, embodied subjectivity [are] far less implicated in physical norms, and far more diversely spread across a rich and complex structuration of identity and desire, than it is now possible to express."[22] In the conclusion of this essay, Stone stated bluntly:

"I could not ask a transsexual for anything more inconceivable than to forgo passing, to be consciously 'read,' to read oneself aloud—and by this troubling and productive reading, to begin to write oneself into the discourses by which one has been written—in effect, then, to become a (look out—dare I say it again?) posttranssexual."[23]

More than just a personal practice, Stone envisioned posttranssexuality as a necessary precursor to trans mobilization and advocacy. Comparing the practice of plausible histories to racial and gay and lesbian passing, Stone framed these medically mandated narratives as "an imperfect solution to personal dissonance" that "foreclose[s] the possibility of authentic relationships," given the relationships "begin as lies."[24] Stone's call for post-transsexuality understood how invisibility prevented the formation of political alliances. Thus, "visible transsexuals" needed to swell the ranks by "recruiting members from the class of invisible ones, from those who have disappeared into their 'plausible histories.'"[25] Speaking directly to transsexuals, Stone beckoned them to forego the personal privilege afforded by their invisibility in exchange for a stronger and more effective trans politics capable of challenging medicalized models of trans genders, sexes, bodies, and sexualities. Shifting the focus from the individual to the community, Stone stated: "I know that you feel that most of the work is behind you and that the price of invisibility is not great. But, although *individual* change is the foundation of all things, it is not the end of all things. Perhaps it's time to begin laying the groundwork for the next transformation."[26] The open-ended conclusion excitedly anticipates a different discursive universe than the one available to Stone and others at the time, and from the reception of the conference audience, Stone's words were both prescient and still needed.

Stone's investment in visibility politics must be understood within a set of competing and complementary cultural exigencies, some of which are still operative today and others that are not. First, her essay directly engaged feminists who were skeptical of, if not explicitly hostile to, transsexuals. In an effort to refute charges of gender essentialism, Stone's theory of post-transsexuality asked transwomen to challenge explicitly the medicalized public transcripts that required them to perform hyper-femininity. Although Stone did not use this language in the essay itself, we can translate the theory into one of exposing the previously hidden transcripts of transsexuals to dislodge the supposed stability and uniformity of the public transcripts of transsexual experience. Stone spoke from personal experience here as she had been attacked by Janice Raymond in *The Transsexual Empire*, probably the most popular and widely read feminist attack on transsexuals, because of her work at Olivia Records, a female music collective. An experienced sound engineer who had previously worked with Jimi Hendrix, David Crosby, and Van Morrison, Stone was the subject of an intense and nasty campaign to force Olivia Records to fire her after it was revealed that she was a male-to-female transsexual.[27] Raymond recounted this episode in her work, and it is worth noting that one of Raymond's most famous and criticized phrases, "All transsexuals rape women's bodies by reducing the real female form to an artifact, appropriating this body for themselves," is a direct reference to Stone's employment at Olivia Records.[28] It is within this context that Stone's suggestion that transsexuals expose the complexity of their corporeal practices and investments in gender norms must be understood.

Second, the availability and quality of mass-mediated representations entrenched a very limited range of legibility associated with transsexual subjectivity. Transsexual autobiographies followed a stale generic form replicating the fixed epistemic frame of the medicalized models of transsexuality that emphasized essentialized gender roles and presentation. As for visual media, the representations of trans people in documentaries and talk shows were offensive, degrading, and exploitative. When not focusing on surgeries, before and after shots, and the application of make-up and doing one's hair, audiences and hosts fixated on questions about sex.[29] Those who did not comply with the producers' wishes and refused to exaggerate gender stereotypes would either be cut from the show or misrepresented against their wishes.[30] In order to make it onto the small screen, transsexuals had to enact public transcripts that reproduced the medicalized model of transsexuality to be recognizable as transsexual subjects for mediated audiences. This vicious cycle limited the range of representations available for audiences and failed to portray adequately the diversity of sexual and gender projects undertaken by transsexuals. It is not surprising, then, that before 1991, male-to-female transsexuals dominated the transsexual imaginary; female-to-male transsexuals did not generate the same cultural gaze as "only one autobiography existed on the topic, in addition to two biographies and one psychological study."[31]

Finally, many out transsexuals were often older because of the resources needed to achieve corporeal modifications. At the time of Stone's writing, transsexual identity was still defined primarily in terms of surgery and hormones, a situation that is changing as trans people have continued, with greater degrees of success, to challenge medicalized models of transsexuality. As a result, Stone's understandable concern about the negation of one's entire life history and the resulting psychic damage must be taken into account. Indeed, the counter-discourses that Stone called for have been surprisingly successful at challenging transsexual treatment protocols. Of course, in presenting these cultural conditions as an exigency for Stone, I do not mean to suggest that today's situation is radically different—it is better put as a matter of degree than difference as trans medical and psychological care increasingly responds to these challenges to their authority.

As stated earlier, Stone did not inaugurate posttranssexuality so much as name a subcultural phenomenon. Stone's neologism overlaps to a significant degree with the emergence of transgender as a subcultural discourse.[32] In a postscript on Stone's version of the essay on her website, one that has been amended over time, Stone provided the following endorsement of *transgender* as encompassing the identities hailed by the essay: "Note on the nomenclature: 'Posttranssexual' was an ironic term, since when this essay was first published everything in theory was post-something-or-other. I was looking for a way forward. 'Transgender' is way better."[33] With that said, the nomenclature of transgender does not resolve all political questions about what forms of engagement are most useful for those who lay claim to this sign.

Much like queers and gays and lesbians, trans communities have become increasingly fragmented over the issue of whether or not those who exhibit characteristics and mannerisms that may be in accord with dominant sexual and gender codes should be considered trans. As Julia Serano describes, some trans communities privilege "subversivism," which is "the practice of extolling certain gender and sexual expressions and identities simply because they are unconventional or nonconforming. In the parlance of subversivism, these atypical genders and sexualities are 'good' because they 'transgress' or 'subvert' oppressive binary gender norms."[34] As a corollary, then, hierarchies develop around the subversion of gender which brand those who choose not to radically challenge gender norms as "conservative, even 'hegemonic,' because they are seen as reinforcing or naturalizing the binary gender system."[35] Serano takes this unfortunate form of gender border policing as "an early sign that more outward-looking, changing-the-world-focused transgender and queer movements of the 1990s are shifting into a more insular and exclusionary queer/trans community, one that favors only a select group of queers and trans folks, rather than all people who fall under those umbrella terms."[36] In an odd turn of events, the queer impulse to explode hegemonic sexual and gender binaries has been neutralized somewhat by those who want to circumscribe the boundaries of trans identity. In many ways, the lessons of trans engagements with exclusionary versions of feminisms have been forgotten as gender non-normativity becomes the new norm that authorizes an exclusionary politics. And now we return to the concept of post-postranssexuality to engage what comes after the initial moves to gain cultural visibility and recognition—that is, how recognition functions within and outside of trans communities.

In 1997, Pat Califia presciently predicted the persistence of these competing agendas in *Sex Changes: The Politics of Transgenderism*. However, Califia asked us to see this conflict as a generative antagonism instead of an impasse:

> Although it would seem that the goals of these two aspects of trans activism are mutually exclusive, in fact, both are important components of the struggle for a gender-sane society. If the concept of gender freedom is to have any meaning, it must be possible for some of us to cling to our biological sex and the gender we were assigned at birth while others wish to adapt the body to their gender of preferences, and still others to question the very concept of polarized sexes.[37]

For Califia, transgender individuals lose their claim to queerness when the purchase of their identity trades in rigidly reconstructed gender hierarchies. Moreover, the emphasis on visible gender transgression relies on a number of assumptions that require further interrogation. As Butler suggests, practitioners of visibility politics must be self-reflexive

about their own complicity in the creation and maintenance of hegemonic formations:

> As much as identity must be used, as much as "outness" is to be affirmed,
> these same notions must become subject to a critique of exclusionary
> operations of their own production: For whom is outness a historically
> available and affordable option? Is there an unmarked class character
> to the demand for universal "outness"? Who is represented by *which*
> use of the term, and who is excluded? For whom does the term pres-
> ent an impossible conflict between racial, ethnic, or religious affiliation
> and sexual politics? What kinds of policies are enabled by what kinds of
> usages, and which are backgrounded or erased from view?[38]

Thus, the management of visibility and outness remains a concern we
need to address.

In light of this concern, I want to caution against the idea that creating a counter-discourse in and of itself is the only acceptable model
of transgender identity. What troubles me about the creation of this
counter-discourse is that while it is intended to dislodge the hegemonic
force of medicalized trans identities, it also has the potential to recreate
another limiting hegemonic formation in its place. In other words, if
the only acceptable model of trans identity is preconditioned on one's
willingness to lay bare all of one's life's history to be read by others, then
there is only one acceptable model of trans identity. The end result of
this move is to reconsolidate gender norms. I am not suggesting that all
trans people should remain invisible or that, in and of itself, visibility
politics is always problematic. Moreover, I am not arguing that Stone's
specific understanding of posttranssexuality is necessarily predestined
to recreate the gender hierarchies that it is intended to undermine.
Instead, my concern is motivated by Butler's arguments about cultural
intelligibility that asks us to be vigilant about how gender and sexual
norms, even ones that are meant to be progressive, can ironically solidify another set of restrictive norms. That is to say, can we understand
those who choose to remain invisible or unmarked as participating in
an equally valuable project of corporeal politics? Rather than reading
them as liars or fakes or people who are simply trying to take advantage
of sexual privilege, we might better understand them as participating in

a project of disidentification that allows them to survive tactically in a world that often violently disapproves of trans people.

Although these intracommunity contestations of identity may seem far removed from the considerations of citizenship that we have taken up so far, the advocacy work aimed at gaining legal prohibitions against discrimination based upon gender identity may work against these divisive pressures. Of course, subversivism takes place in support groups, bars, and other social spaces, as well as in activist groups, and not every trans person participates in political advocacy. Still, gender identity protections, both the struggle to get them into law and their effects in culture, may continue to provide a center of gravity to unite trans people in common cause. As we have noted in this chapter and the two previous ones, gender identity protections often employ language against discrimination based on one's actual or perceived gender identity. In our investigation of INTRAA's advocacy work and United ENDA's refusal to sacrifice gender identity protections, we saw how the law can serve as a site of coalitional politics. And we might find a similar phenomenon at work within trans communities. Visibility begets its own issues about respectability and who counts as a legitimate member of an identity category. So, in this post-posttransexual era, what remains to be seen is whether disputes about subversivism will divide the community or present opportunities to rethink the bases of that community. Legal recognition may just initiate productive discussions towards these ends. What I want to stress most about post-posttransseuxality is the future of trans political action, if it is to be successful, cannot be guided by an orthodox commitment to any one philosophy about how best to enable more livable cultural conditions. Instead, in the final pages I want to outline the importance of approaching transgender advocacy as a matter of impure politics.

Impure Politics

In the end, the political commitments of *Transforming Citizenships* may be characterized best as a defense of an "impure politics" for they are the only politics available to those who want to engage strangers in the quest for recognition and justice.[39] If we telescope out into the future, we may find the topics we have covered thus far are useful maps for how to think through advocacy as it both engages and critiques the state's ability to regulate bodies, genders, and sexualities, if not other identity categories. Originally introduced by cultural studies scholar Lawrence Grossberg, the the idea of impure politics was meant to open a way to move past the paralyzing impasse of programmatic theories of how the Left should respond to the growing threat posed by burgeoning hegemony of conservative thought and policies. We can profitably translate Grossberg's concerns to transgender politics to advance an argument about the need to think of political advocacy within the frame of context and contingency in order to develop increasingly effective responses to the attempts to thwart the progress of transgender advocates and allies.

The enactments of citizenship presented in this book remind progressive advocates that they need to attend to dominant logics as opportunities instead of impediments. As we have demonstrated in various ways throughout the preceding pages, critics and advocates have differing outlooks on how best to achieve equality. Whatever perspective one takes, at the end of the day, interacting with and in publics requires an acute awareness of the probable and the possible. Contrary to a view that assumes institutional discourses preemptively disable creative appropriations of the law, advocates must "find reasonably democratic structures of institutionalization," as Grossberg argues, "even if they are impure and compromised."[40] Opposition to institutions in and of itself provides some worthwhile subject positions from which to operate, but it does not follow that these efforts are mutually exclusive with engaging the state or are contrary to them. An impure politics accepts from the outset the need for "both intellectual and political progress by movement within the fragile and contradictory realities of people's lives, desires, fears and commitments, and not by some idealized utopia nor by its own theoretical criteria."[41] As a consequence, an impure politics is a "politics for people who are never innocent and whose hopes are always partly defined by the very powers and inequalities they oppose," as well as a "modest politics that struggles to effect real change, that enters into the often boring challenges of strategy and compromise."[42] For some, an impure politics may promise too little or mistakenly sell itself short. In the absence of any plausible political position free from the contamination of normativities, institutions for collective governance, and power more generally, we will have to learn how to tactically appropriate what is already available in the name of equality.

By way of comparison, we might juxtapose impure politics with Dean Spade's proposed critical trans politics. From the start, I want to be clear about my admiration of Spade's activist and academic work. As the founder of the Sylvia Rivera Law Project and a prolific author on transgender legal issues, Spade has furthered the cause of trans justice in numerous ways. And Spade's recent defense of critical trans politics as one remedy for the violence perpetrated by administrative law (e.g., state agencies tasked with issuing identity documents, prison regulations, or immigration decisions) focuses much-needed attention to the implementation of abstract legal principles. As Spade describes it, critical trans politics "must move beyond the politics of recognition and inclusion" because "meaningful transformation will not occur through pronouncements of equality from various government institutions" since "transformative change can only arise through mass mobilization led by populations most directly impacted by the harmful systems that distribute vulnerability and security."[43] It follows, then, that the agenda of critical trans politics requires "building a political context for massive redistribution" and "imagin[ing] and demandi[ng] an end to prisons, homelessness, landlords, bosses, immigration enforcement, poverty, and wealth."[44] Spade's repeated use of the phrase "distribution of vulnerability" sticks with me as one frame for remembering that the injustices trans people face are not isolated or accidental. Likewise, the overall thrust of critical trans politics reminds us that trans justice involves a commitment to addressing related forms of inequalities.

As much as I am moved by Spade's work, I want to engage it as one option among many in the development of an impure politics. For me, an impure transgender politics is preferable because it is more than vulgar strategic essentialism or unreconstructed pragmatism; instead, it involves faith in the inventive capabilities of individuals to navigate the complicated discursive terrains of recognition. Transgender advocates and allies may find coalitional opportunities with other activist communities beyond lesbian, gay, and bisexual groups, such as public health advocates, abortion rights activists, and others concerned with social justice. These efforts will transform the understanding of equality, justice, and freedom as they are deployed. They are also likely to frustrate the law's ability to regulate bodies, genders, and sexualities. At times, demands for recognition may be complicit with prevailing norms and normativities, but we should also listen to them as public transcripts supported by hidden transcripts that may not invest themselves in these norms and normativities. As these discourses are circulated, they will both do and undo those who initiate and consume them. Understood in this manner, the future holds out hope because it is yet to be articulated.

NOTES

NOTES TO THE INTRODUCTION

1. As John Howard details, Piedmont Park has long been a popular destination for all sorts of sexual activities, and this wave of sex panic is not first of its kind. "The Library, the Park, and the Pervert: Public Space and Homosexual Encounter in Post–World War II Atlanta," *Radical History Review* 62 (1995): 166–87.

2. Given the subject matter of this book, I considered rearranging the acronym "LGBT" to place the "T" at the front of it, but I ultimately decided to use "LGBT" for two reasons. First, I wanted to decenter gay men as the primary consideration of this identity category—hence "LGBT" over "GLBT." With that said, I understand that switching the order of gay men and lesbians could be read as my tacit agreement with the assumption that the order of the letters indicates a descending order of importance wherein sexual orientation trumps gender identity. To be clear, then, the second reason for using "LGBT" is to highlight not my own investment in prioritizing who counts more or less; rather, it is an indication of how trans people are often the last consideration of the general populace, LGBs included, when they lump together these related but potentially disparate subjectivities. The issues in play here are addressed more fully in the chapter on "GENDA Trouble."

3. Qtd. in Eric Ervin, "Atlanta Police, Trans Activists Try to 'Build Bridges,'" *Southern Voice*, October 13, 2006, 7.

4. Qtd. in Ervin, "Atlanta Police," 7.

5. Ryan Lee, "Gay Group Hopes to Counter Midtown Security Tactics," *Southern Voice*, August 17, 2007, 8.

6. After the negative press, Gower later claimed that some of the text in the newsletter had been copied from an email from the president of the Piedmont Park Conservancy. However, in its original form, the text is attributed to Gower, and the quotations I cull from the newsletter appear to have been written by Gower. See Ryan Lee, "Conservancy Raised Concerns First About Park's Sunday Night Crowd," *Southern Voice*, August 3, 2007, 5.

7. Qtd in Ryan Lee, "Midtown Security Tactics Questioned," *Southern Voice*, July 20, 2007, 1. All of the quotations attributed to Gower come from a reprinted version of the original text associated with this article.

8. Andrew Belonsky, "Birdbrained Gays Chirp About Black, Trans, Voguers," *Queerty.com*, July 20, 2007.

9. No author, "Midtown Security Group Deserves Praise for Efforts," *Southern Voice*, July 27, 2007, 19.

10. Anonymous comment qtd. in Laura Douglas-Brown, "YouTube vs. Midtown Sex Workers," *Southern Voice*, July 20, 2007, 12.

11. Douglas-Brown, "YouTube" 12.

12. Tracee McDaniel, "Banning Trans Job Bias Would Help End Sex Work," *Southern Voice*, 17 August 2007, 3.

13. . Dyana Bagby, "Police: Despite TV Reports, No Increased Violence Among Midtown Crossdressing Prostitutes," *GA Voice*, May 17, 2012.

14. In using the phrase "not not me," I mean something along the lines of Richard Schechner's schema in *Between Theater and Anthropology* (Philadelphia: University of Pennsylvania Press, 1985), esp. 109–13. Here I want to mark an interpersonal relationship whereby subjects recognize themselves as mutually implicated in one another.

15. Robert Asen, "A Discourse Theory of Citizenship," *Quarterly Journal of Speech* 90 (2004): 191, emphasis in original.

16. My understanding of effectivities is indebted to Lawrence Grossberg's meditation on the subject in *We Gotta Get Out of This Place: Popular Conservatism and Postmodern Culture* (New York: Routledge, 1992). As Grossberg defines "effectivities," the term "describes an event's place in a complex network of effect—its effects elsewhere on other events, as well as their effects on it; it describes the possibilities of the practice for effectuating changes or differences in the world" (50). Refusing the linear logic of discernable and discrete causes and effects, Grossberg further elaborates: "effectivity points to the multidimensionality of effects, to the connections that exist between disparate points as they traverse different planes or realms of effects" (50–51). I find it a useful conceptual tool for thinking through the anticipated and unexpected radiance of forces across cultural fields of meaning and action.

17. The distinction between articulation as a method and a perspective is the subject of Jennifer Daryl Slack's "The Theory and Method of Articulation in Cultural Studies," in *Stuart Hall: Critical Dialogues in Cultural Studies*, ed. David Morley and Kuan-Hising Chen (London: Routledge, 1996), 112–27.

18. Qtd. in Grossberg, "On Postmodernism and Articulation: An Interview with Stuart Hall," in *Stuart Hall: Critical Dialogues*, 141, emphasis in original. In this interview, Hall expresses his debt to Ernesto Laclau's earlier work on subject formation as well as Laclau's co-authored elaboration of articulation with Chantal Mouffe in *Hegemony and Socialist Strategy: Towards a Radical Democratic Politics* (London: Verso, 1985).

19. For the most definitive treatment of this idea, see Lawrence Grossberg, *Cultural Studies in the Future Tense* (Durham, NC: Duke University Press, 2010), 21–23.

20. Qtd. in Grossberg, "On Postmodernism," 142.

21. Sally Hines's critique of the tendency of queer studies scholarship to describe trans identities and trans people as if they are homogenous experiences informs my cautious deference to the particular over the universal. "What's the Difference? Bringing Particularity to Queer Studies of Transgender," *Journal of Gender Studies* 15 (2006): 49–66.

22. Cressida Hayes's admonition against the careless and callous use of trans people in academic arguments to extrapolate larger principles beyond trans concerns deserves further consideration: "Whether appropriated to bolster queer theoretical claims, represented as the acid test of constructionism, or attacked for suspect political commitments," she observes, "transgender has been colonized as a feminist theoretical testing ground" ("Feminist Solidarity after Queer Theory: The Case of Transgender," *Signs* 28 [2003]: 1098).

23. Vivian Namaste, *Invisible Lives: The Erasure of Transsexual and Transgendered People* (Chicago: University of Chicago Press, 2000), 15.

24. Genny Beemyn and Susan Rankin's cataloguing of the identity markers used by gender-variant and gender non-conforming individuals, compiled from an extensive survey of more than three thousand participants responding to a call for transgender volunteers, provides rich qualitative data to substantiate this claim. *The Lives of Transgender People* (New York: Columbia University Press, 2011), 15–36.

25. Academic references to the use of *transgender* as an "umbrella term" are too numerous to list fully. Some of the more influential texts to use adopt this frame include: Susan Stryker, "My Words to Victor Frankenstein above the Village of Chamounix: Performing Transgender Rage," *GLQ* 1 (1994): 251n2; Leslie Feinberg, *Transgender Warriors: Making History from Joan of Arc to Dennis Rodman* (Boston: Beacon Press, 1996), x; and, Henry S. Rubin, *Self-Made Men: Identity and Embodiment among Transsexual Men* (Nashville, TN: Vanderbilt University Press, 2003), 19. Megan Davidson's ethnographic study of the conditions of possibility created by the umbrella metaphor, including its limitations, captures wonderfully the complicated discursive terrain of transgender identity politics ("Seeking Refuge Under the Umbrella: Inclusion, Exclusion, and Organizing Within the Category *Transgender*," *Sexuality Research & Social Policy* 4, no. 4 [2007]: 60–80).

Here, Adrienne Rich's "compulsory heterosexuality" is another critical concept, and one that deserves further explanation for readers unfamiliar with her work. Rich first proposed "compulsory heterosexuality" to denaturalize heterosexuality, to underscore the patriarchal roots and effectivities of heterosexuality, and to expose the vast range of rewards associated with the practice of heterosexuality ("Compulsory Heterosexuality and the Lesbian Continuum," *Signs* 5 [1980]: 631–60). In this article, Rich wrote primarily about the erasure of lesbianism, and I do not mean to further erase lesbian subjectivities by appropriating Rich's ideas in a different context. Rather, extending the concept of "compulsory heterosexuality" to trans people exposes the ways in which other identities are similarly erased and denied privileges because of their failure to follow neatly the mythic dictates of hegemonic heterosexualities. Without equivocating lesbian and transgender identities, "compulsory heterosexuality" is a useful term for capturing the complex circuitry of discursive networks constraining and enabling sexual and gender identities. C. L. Cole and Shannon L. C. Cate draw a similar conclusion in "Compulsory Gender and Transgender Experience: Adrienne Rich's Queer Possibilities," *Women's Studies Quarterly* 36, no. 3/4 (2008), 277–85. Finally, I am aware of Rich's contested legacy and the potential problems with employing her work in a transgender context given her relationship with Janice Raymond. In addition to my own concerns about rejecting someone's entire corpus of work because of an assumed guilt by association, I do not read any inherent anti-trans subtext in her discussion of this particular concept, thus rendering it available for an articulation that may or may not comport with Rich's own politics.

26. In contrast to many forms of identity that rely on a stable sense of identity, Paisley Currah notes the paradoxical position of some transgender rights advocates when they participate in an "identity politics movement that seeks the dissolution of the very category under which it is organized" ("Gender Pluralisms under the Transgender Umbrella," in *Transgender Rights*, ed. Paisley Currah, Richard Juang, and Shannon Minter [Minneapolis: University of Minnesota Press, 2006], 24).

27. I borrow the term "necessary error of identity" from Judith Butler, who appropriates it from Gayatri Spivak, to remind us of the inability of identity categories to fully capture all that one is and does. Identity claims are always, in some sense, a form of misrecognition, even when they are employed in the service of a communal politics as a site of unity (*Bodies That Matter: On the Discursive Limits of "Sex"* [New York: Routledge, 1993], 229).

28. Susan Stryker, *Transgender History* (Berkeley, CA.: Seal Press, 2008), 1, emphasis in original.

29. Gayle Salamon, *Assuming a Body: Transgender and Rhetorics of Materiality* (New York: Columbia University Press, 2010), 101.

30. On the vernacular roots of "transgender," see, Jamison Green, *Becoming a Visible Man* (Nashville, TN: Vanderbilt University Press, 2004), 14; and, Judith Halberstam, *Female Masculinity* (Durham, NC: Duke University Press, 1998), 53–54.

31. David Valentine, *Imagining Transgender: An Ethnography of a Category* (Durham, NC: Duke University Press, 2007), 33. Others locate the widespread usage of "transgender" as occurring in 1995 (Currah, Juang, and Minter, Introduction, *Transgender Rights*, xiv).

32. Riki Anne Wilchins, *Queer Theory, Gender Theory: An Instant Primer* (Los Angeles, CA: Alyson Books, 2004), 26.

33. The ability of *transgender* to serve as a source of coalitional politics has been documented by scholars and activists. Currah argues that it comes with risks of erasing the diversity and differences between trans people, but it should be

used nonetheless as a way to organize disparate identities under a common sign (Currah, Juang, and Minter, Introduction, xv). Valentine describes the ways in which *transgender* can be used to identify a distinct minority and hence motivate institutional action on issues such as health care and public safety (*Imagining Transgender*, 119, 227). Finally, Pauline Park warns against the dissolution of the category of *transgender* if it is replaced by a universal term such as *gender rights*. ("GenderPAC, the Transgender Rights Movement, and the Perils of a Post-Identity Politics Paradigm," *Georgetown Journal of Gender and the Law* 4 [2003]: 758–59).

34. Judith Halberstam, *In a Queer Time and Place: Transgender Bodies, Subcultural Lives* (New York: New York University Press, 2005), 49.

35. Although *transgender* can be a useful category, some worry about its potential to deny the differences among the wide-ranging identities compromising the category. For example, Vivian Namaste is concerned with the erasure of transsexuals from the category by trans advocates who exclude them because of their assumed gender essentialism (*Invisible Lives*). Similarly, Wilchins reminds us that *transgender* can recreate gender hierarchies by privileging only those who visibly challenge gender and sexual codes (*Queer Theory*, 29). Finally, Valentine expresses reservations about the ability of *transgender* to authorize intersectional reflection on issues such as race and class (*Imagining Transgender*, 17–20, 242). On my reading, each of these concerns justifies an introspective review of one's investments and blind spots when using the term; that is, they do not expose any inherent flaw in the concept, only the need to be careful when it is used.

36. For more on the genealogy of *transsexual*, see Joanne Meyerowitz, *How Sex Changed: A History of Transsexuality in the United States* (Cambridge, MA: Harvard University Press, 2002), 15–50.

37. Halberstam's reading of the colonialist undertones in some articulations of trans identities as travel narratives or border crossings reminds us of the complex interlocking exchanges of meaning in otherwise well-intentioned attempts to offer strangers a metaphorical access point to one's sense of self (*Female Masculinity*, 162–73).

38. Halberstam, *In a Queer Time*, 54.

39. Judith Butler, *Gender Trouble: Feminism and the Subversion of Identity*, 10th Anniversary ed. (New York: Routledge, 1990; reprint, 1999), 11.

40. Butler, *Gender Trouble*, 10–11.

41. Alissa Quart, "When Girls Will Be Boys," *New York Times*, March 16, 2008.

42. Transgender Law and Policy Institute, "Transgender Issues: A Fact Sheet," http://www.transgenderlaw.org/resources/transfactsheet.pdf. One of the most thoughtful meditations on the difficulty of quantifying and surveying trans populations is B. R. Simon Rosser, J. Michael Oakes, Walter O. Bockting, and Michael Minter, "Capturing the Social Demographics of Hidden Sexual Minorities: An Internet Study of the Transgender Population in the United States," *Sexuality Research & Social Policy* 4, no. 2 (2007): 50–64.

43. William Van Meter, "Cold Crossings of the Gender Line," *New York Times*, December 8, 2010.

44. Transgender Law Center, *State of Transgender California* (San Francisco, CA: Transgender Law Center, 2009). The definitions of *cisgender* and *cissexual* come from Stryker, *Transgender History*, 22. Although I recognize the problematic freighting of identities and politics generated by the prefix *cis-*, at the same time, it is an increasingly popular nomenclature that I use in this work to name particular relations. It is, however, worth noting that A. Finn Enke's cautionary critique of the evolution and circulation of these terms informs my reluctant usage of these *cis-* terms. "The Education of Little Cis: Cisgender and the Discipline of Opposing Bodies," in *Transfeminist Perspectives: In and Beyond Transgender and Gender Studies*, ed. Anne Enke (Philadelphia, PA: Temple University Press, 2012), 60–77. I am not trying to avoid the thornier issues of this terminology, yet, as should be clear from the other modes of theorizing in this introduction, it is a convenient, even if problematic, way to name modes of interaction between those who would and would not identify with trans-. Indeed, all of the identity markers employed here involve necessary errors of identity open to further interrogation and revision.

45. Gwendolyn Ann Smith, "Stand Against Trans Violence," *Southern Voice*, November 11, 2006, 20. Researchers and advocates debate among themselves about the accuracy of these statistics, but even the conservative end of these estimates is shocking and sobering.

46. Richard M. Juang, "Transgendering the Politics of Recognition," in *Transgender Rights*, ed. Paisley Currah, Richard M. Juang, and Shannon Price Minter (Minneapolis: University of Minnesota Press, 2006), 254.

47. Jerome Hunt, "A State-by-State Examination of Nondiscrimination Laws and Policies: State Nondiscrimination Policies Fill the Void but Federal Protections Are Still Needed," (Washington, DC: Center for American Progress Action Fund, June 2012), 5.

48. National Gay and Lesbian Task Force, "2002 Year in Review, State and Local Trans-Inclusive Legislation," http://www.thetaskforce.org/downloads/reports/fact_sheets/transgender_year_in_review.pdf.

49. These totals can be found by aggregating the vote tallies from the National Gay and Lesbian Task Force Transgender Civil Rights Project's annual reviews. They are available on the "Transgender Issues" page of the website: http://www.thetaskforce.org/issues/transgender.

50. Transgender Law and Policy Institute and National Gay and Lesbian Task Force, "Scope of Explicitly Transgender-Inclusive Anti-Discrimination Laws," http://www.transgenderlaw.org/ndlaws/ngltftlpichart.pdf

51. Currah, "Gender Pluralisms," 21.

52. Kylar Broadus, "The Evolution of Employment Discrimination Protections for Transgender People," in *Transgender Rights*, ed. Paisley Currah, Richard M.

Juang, and Shannon Price Minter (Minneapolis: University of Minnesota Press, 2006), 99.
53. Pat Califia, *Sex Changes: The Politics of Transgenderism* (San Francisco: Cleis Press, 1997), xv.
54. Currah, Juang, and Minter, Introduction, xxii–xxiii, emphasis in original.
55. Currah, Juang, and Minter, Introduction, xxiii.
56. Stryker, *Transgender History*, 51.
57. For the most developed example of the latter with regard to trans people, see Andrew Gilden, "Toward a More Transformative Approach: The Limits of Transgender Formal Equality," *Berkeley Journal of Gender, Law & Justice* 23 (2008): 83–144.
58. Currah, Juang, and Minter, Introduction, xxii.
59. Paisley Currah, "The Transgender Rights Imaginary," *Georgetown Journal of Gender and the Law* 4 (2003): 712.
60. Janet Halley, "The Construction of Heterosexuality," in *Fear of a Queer Planet: Queer Politics and Social Theory*, ed. Michael Warner (Minneapolis: University of Minnesota Press, 1993), 98.
61. Currah, "Rights Imaginary," 712.
62. Robert Cover, "*Nomos* and Narrative," *Harvard Law Review* 97 (1983): 68.
63. Thomas Farrell, *Norms of Rhetorical Culture* (New Haven, CT: Yale University Press, 1993), 94.
64. Naomi Mezey makes a similar argument in "Law as Culture," in *Cultural Analysis, Cultural Studies, and the Law: Moving Beyond Legal Realism*, ed. Austin Sarat and Jonathan Simon (Durham, NC: Duke University Press, 2003), 37–72.
65. Paul Kahn, *The Cultural Study of Law: Reconstructing Legal Scholarship* (Chicago: University of Chicago Press, 1999), 6, 30.
66. Grossberg, *Cultural Studies*, 8.
67. Grossberg, *Cultural Studies*, 8
68. Eve Kosofsky Sedgwick, *Touching Feeling: Affect, Pedagogy, Performativity* (Durham, NC: Duke University Press, 2003), 124.
69. Sedgwick revisits the contextualized evolution of paranoid readings from the initial emergence and emergency of HIV/AIDS, wherein institutional refusals to acknowledge or address the epidemic produced no small amount of paranoia. Without arguing that we are no longer in an HIV/AIDS crisis, Sedgwick sees a disconnect between the continued mobilization of paranoia and its connection to contemporary queer lives and politics (*The Weather in Proust* [Durham, NC: Duke University Press, 2011], 139). At the same time, I want to clarify that paranoid readings still have a place and a time, and that they share a dialectical relationship with reparative readings. Heather Love advances a version of this argument in "Truth and Consequences: On Paranoid Reading and Reparative Reading," *Criticism* 52 (2010): 235–41.
70. Grossberg, *Cultural Studies*, 17.

71. John Nguyet Erni, "Reframing Cultural Studies: Human Rights as a Site of Legal-Cultural Struggles," *Communication and Critical/Cultural Studies* 7 (2010): 224.

72. Taylor Flynn, "The Ties That Don't Bind: Transgender Family Law and the Unmaking of Families," in *Transgender Rights*, ed. Paisley Currah, Richard Juang, and Shannon Minter (Minneapolis: University of Minnesota Press, 2006), 36. Empirically speaking, even in states where such discrimination is prohibited, plaintiffs have a difficult time finding lawyers familiar with relevant case law or who are supportive of their claims, never mind securing the thousands of dollars needed for a retainer. See, for example, Jon Davidson, "Lambda Legal's Analysis of H.B. 3685: Narrow Version of ENDA Provides Weaker Protections for Everyone," October 16, 2007, http://data.lambdalegal.org/pdf/enda_llanalysis_20071016.pdf. In a California survey, where antidiscrimination laws have been in place since 2004, "only 15% of those who reported some form of discrimination or harassment filed a complaint. Of those who did not file any complaint, 44% did not think they could get the assistance they needed or prove their case. Thirty percent did not know if transgender people have any legal protections against discrimination. Of those who did not file a complaint, 27% did not know how or where to file a complaint and 26% were afraid to lose their job. Thirteen percent of those persons were afraid to come out in order to file a complaint" (Transgender Law Center, "State of Transgender California," March 2009, np).

73. Paisley Currah and Shannon Minter, "Unprincipled Exclusions: The Struggle to Achieve Judicial and Legislative Equality for Transgender People," *William and Mary Journal of Women and the Law* 7 (2000): 39.

74. Austin Sarat and Thomas Kearns, "Editorial Introduction," in *Law in Everyday Life*, ed. Sarat and Kearns (Ann Arbor: University of Michigan Press, 1993), 7.

75. Rosemary Coombe, "Contingent Articulations: A Critical Cultural Studies of Law," in *Law in the Domains of Culture*, ed. Austin Sarat and Thomas Kearns (Ann Arbor: University of Michigan Press, 1998), 21. Here Coombe writes against James Boyd White's understanding of the law as a constitutive force in everyday life. For more on White's understanding of the constitutive character of rhetoric, law, and culture, see *When Words Lose Their Meaning: Constitutions and Reconstitutions of Language, Character, and Community* (Chicago: University of Chicago Press, 1983), 6–20.

76. John Louis Lucaites, "Between Rhetoric and 'The Law': Power, Legitimacy, and Social Change," *Quarterly Journal of Speech* 76 (1990): 447, emphasis in original.

77. Michael Warner, *Publics and Counterpublics* (New York: Zone Books, 2002), 66, emphasis in original.

78. Warner, *Publics*, 76

79. Meyerowitz, *How Sex Changed*, 51.

80. Danielle Allen, *Talking to Strangers: Anxieties of Citizenship since Brown v. Board of Education* (Chicago: University of Chicago Press, 2004), 10.

81. Allen, *Talking to Strangers*, 12, emphasis in original.
82. Allen, *Talking to Strangers*, 30.
83. Allen, *Talking to Strangers*, 17.
84. Allen, *Talking to Strangers*, 88.
85. Biddy Martin addresses the pitfalls of defaulting to radical antinormativity as the only modality of queerness in "Extraordinary Homosexuals and the Fear of Being Ordinary," *differences* 6, no. 2/3 (1994): 100–25.
86. Janet Jakobsen, "Queer Is? Queer Does? Normativity and the Problem of Resistance," *GLQ* 4 (1998): 520.
87. Jakobsen, "Queer Is," 526.
88. Karen Zivi, "Rights and the Politics of Performativity," in *Judith Butler's Precarious Politics: Critical Encounters*, ed. Terrell Carver and Samuel Chambers (London: Routledge, 2008), 165.
89. Judith Butler and Gayatri Chakravorty Spivak, *Who Sings the Nation-State?* (Oxford: Seagull Books, 2007), 68–69.
90. Michael Cobb, *God Hates Fags: The Rhetorics of Religious Violence* (New York: New York University Press, 2006), 55–56.
91. Currah, Juang, and Minter, Introduction, xviii.
92. Eve Kosofsky Sedgwick, *Tendencies* (Durham, NC: Duke University Press, 1993), 8.
93. Brenda Cossman, "Sexing Citizenship, Privatizing Sex," *Citizenship Studies* 6 (2002): 484.
94. Cossman, "Sexing Citizenship," 484.
95. Steven Seidman, "From Identity to Queer Politics: Shifts in Normative Heterosexuality and the Meaning of Citizenship," *Citizenship Studies* 5 (2001): 323.
96. Michael Warner, *The Trouble with Normal: Sex, Politics, and the Ethics of Queer Life* (Cambridge, MA: Harvard University Press, 1999), 25.
97. Warner, *The Trouble with Normal*, 105.
98. Amy Brandzel, "Queering Citizenship? Same-Sex Marriage and the State," *GLQ* 11 (2005): 198.
99. David Eng, *The Feelings of Kinship: Queer Liberalism and the Racialization of Intimacy* (Durham, NC: Duke University Press, 2010), 25.

NOTES TO CHAPTER 1

1. I borrow Debbie Mayne's pseudonym from Joanne Meyerowitz, *How Sex Changed: A History of Transsexuality in the United States* (Cambridge, MA: Harvard University Press, 2002). Even though Mayne's name is part of the public record, the use of archival materials located in the Kinsey Institute for Research in Sex, Gender, and Reproduction (KI) necessitates the use of pseudonyms.
2. "What They Say About [Debbie]! Man Has Sex-Switch Operation, Flaunts Finery at Sad Cops," *Keyhole*, March 2, 1956, np., and, "Man-Woman Cleared," file: Debbie Mayne (D.M.), ONE/International Gay and Lesbian Archives (ONE), University of Southern California, Los Angeles, Calif. (USC). See also "Office

Clerk Cleared of Charge of Masquerading," *Los Angeles Times*, February 15, 1956, np., box 2/4 clippings, Virginia Prince Collection (VPC), Oviatt Library, California State University at Northridge (CSUN). Professor Meyerowitz shared some of her archival research with me when I drafted the first version of this chapter, and her act of generosity provided important contextual clues for my reading of Mayne's actions.

3. "What They Say."

4. "Well, Is It [Debbie] Belle or [Debbie] Bill?" and "[Debbie]'s He or She as Case May Be." These clippings lack any source information but they can be found in box 2/4 clippings, VPC, CSUN. A legal brief filed by the city attorney and Mayne's lawyer confirms these facts of the case; see "Stipulation of Facts" (SOF), Debbie Mayne (D.M.) Folder, box 6, Series IIC, Harry Benjamin Collection (HBC), KI.

5. "Well, Is It?"

6. "Office Clerk."

7. "Man-Woman Cleared."

8. In 1941, Barbara Richards convinced a judge that she had experienced a "spontaneous sexual metamorphosis" and received a legal order to change her legal name and sex. Joanne Meyerowitz, "Sex Change and the Popular Press: Historical Notes on Transsexuality in the United States, 1930–1955," *GLQ* 4 (1998): 167.

9. The SOF lists the date of her legal name and sex change as "on or about November 30" while one newspaper account lists the date as November 18 ("What They Say"). Regardless, by the time of her trial, Mayne was already legally recognized as a woman.

10. John Louis Lucaites, "Between Rhetoric and 'The Law': Power, Legitimacy, and Social Change," *Quarterly Journal of Speech* 76 (1990): 445.

11. James Scott, *Domination and the Arts of Resistance: Hidden Transcripts* (New Haven, CT: Yale University Press, 1990), 2.

12. Scott, *Domination*, 199, emphasis in original.

13. Scott, *Domination*, 4. In many ways, the concept of hidden transcripts complements our understanding of vernacular rhetorics and discourses. In terms of vernacular rhetorics, Gerald Hauser asks us to pay more critical attention to the ways in which individuals publicly engage issues through their everyday activities in *Vernacular Voices: The Rhetoric of Publics and Public Spheres* (Columbia, SC: University of South Carolina Press, 1999). In a different key, Kent Ono and John Sloop offer the concept of "vernacular discourses" to mark everyday forms of "communication that [are] assumed to be for the direct purposes of supplying information to more limited demographic groups within" a polity; see *Shifting Borders: Rhetoric, Immigration, and California's Proposition 187* (Philadelphia: Temple University Press, 2002), 13. The importance of studying the often ignored texts and practices of the marginalized groups was originally developed in Kent A. Ono and John M. Sloop, "The Critique of Vernacular Discourse," *Communication Monographs* 62 (1995): 19–46. The study of hidden transcripts

thus extends the critique of everyday interactions to understand the multiple discursive agendas operating in these public exchanges.

14. Scott, *Domination*, 199. Although Scott's work is not concerned with the interactions of those living in liberal-democratic polities, public and hidden transcripts are present in them. Without equivocating different modalities of domination, the dynamic relationships between domination and resistance are a constant condition of any culture. As a result, Scott's work can be easily translated to contexts beyond his own work.

15. Here I use the phrase "repertoire" in a manner similar to Diana Taylor to signify "embodied memory: performances, gestures, orality, movement, dance, singing—in short, all those acts usually thought of as ephemeral, nonreproducible knowledge" (*The Archive and the Repertoire: Performing Cultural Memory in the Americas* [Durham, NC: Duke University Press, 2003], 20).

16. Dwight Conquergood, "Ethnography, Rhetoric, and Performance," *Quarterly Journal of Speech* 78 (1992): 82–83. In this review of Scott and de Certeau, Conquergood does not define the phrase "performative repertoire," but I appropriate it here in a manner consistent with his usage of the phrase.

17. Charles Morris, "Archival Queer," *Rhetoric & Public Affairs* 9 (2006): 147.

18. While scholarship in the vein of Janice Raymond's transphobia and Bernice Hausman's skepticism of trans agency is less common today, these arguments still circulate in the work of psychologists such as Michael Bailey; see Raymond, *The Transsexual Empire: The Making of the She-Male* (Boston: Beacon Press, 1979; reprint, 1994); Hausman, *Changing Sex: Transsexualism, Technology, and the Idea of Gender* (Durham, NC: Duke University Press, 1995); and Bailey, *The Man Who Would Be Queen: The Science of Gender-Bending and Transsexualism* (Washington, DC: Joseph Henry Press, 2003). Readers familiar with Hausman's work might ask how my project differs from her reading of transsexual narratives. The simple answer is the methodology that informs our perspectives on discourse, identity, and agency. In her preface, Hausman explicitly states her reliance on "'official discourses' of transsexualism—those produced both by medical personnel and by transsexuals" (viii). As should be clear from my attitudinizing frame, official discourses or public transcripts provide a distorted and/or incomplete picture of intersubjective exchanges. Thus, when Hausman claims that we can best discern transsexual agency (meaning a "compulsive relation to technology" and medical interventions [140]) by reading medical discourses about and by transsexuals (3–4, 110), I am skeptical of the reliability of such a tautological perspective. To be fair, Hausman concedes, on several occasions (110, 129, 131, 143), the influence transsexuals have had in crafting trans medical standards and care. However, Hausman's concessions have to be tempered against her suspicion of transsexuals as "dupes of gender" (140) who reinforce the stability of sexual and gender identities. For me, such claims are difficult to accept, given my readings of the hidden transcripts of trans people. Moreover, in a recent review of Meyerowitz's *How*

Sex Changed, Hausman maintains that academic "politics" designed "to put transsexual and transgender people on the map as the authors of their histori-cal identities" runs counter to "many feminist writers on the topic, including myself, who have tended to see transsexuals' social emergence as an effect of historical transformations in technology, in meanings of sex and gender, and in social mechanisms to subordinate women" (Book Review, *Journal of Medical Humanities* 26 [2005]: 197). Setting aside the obvious political implications of Hausman's own reading of transsexuality, her continued suspicion of trans people is all the more peculiar given her professed interest in a Foucaultian reading of transsexual narratives (*Changing Sex*, vii). On my reading, one that is influenced in important ways by Butler, the more faithfully Foucaultian approach is to ask how trans people resist the modalities of their domina-tion.

19. Joel Handler's 1991 presidential address to the Law and Society Association ignited the resistance debates in legal studies. In an all-out assault on the "politics of postmodernism," Handler stated: "The contemporary stories are about *individuals*, in the most marginalized spaces, engaging in very small acts of defiance, and, for the most part, very little if anything happens. . . . The con-temporary stories are stories of resistance, but they are also stories of despair" ("Postmodernism, Protest, and the New Social Movements," *Law & Society Review* 26 [1992]: 724, emphasis in original).

20. Michael McCann and Tracey March, "Law and Everyday Forms of Resistance: A Socio-Political Assessment," *Studies in Law, Politics, and Society* 15 (1996): 225.

21. McCann and March, "Law and Everyday Forms," 226.

22. McCann and March, "Law and Everyday Forms," 231. Mariana Valverde makes similar arguments against the romanticization of micropractices of legal resis-tance in "'Which Side Are You On?': Uses of the Everyday in Sociolegal Schol-arship," *Political and Legal Anthropology Review* 26 (2003): 86–98. From a more sympathetic position, Susan Silbey warns that the idea of "the everyday" is used as an unmediated truth by scholars who often fail to link their work back up to larger systemic issues such as ideology and hegemony ("After Legal Conscious-ness," *Annual Review of Law and Social Science* 1 [2005]: 323–68).

23. Jeffrey Rubin, "Defining Resistance: Contested Interpretations of Everyday Acts," *Studies in Law, Politics, and Society* 15 (1996): 245.

24. A fuller account of this debate and its stakes can be found in Patricia Ewick and Susan Silbey, "Narrating Social Structure: Stories of Resistance to Legal Author-ity," *American Journal of Sociology* 108 (2003): 1328–72.

25. Despite critiques to the contrary, Butler's interrogation of the materializations of sex, gender, and bodies had a decidedly political purpose. *Gender Trouble* and *Bodies That Matter* were, after all, immanent critiques of feminisms as well as feminist and gay and lesbian studies to make them more inclusive and hence responsive to the needs of those who might want to lay claim to them in an agentic fashion.

26. Judith Butler, *The Psychic Life of Power: Theories in Subjection* (Stanford, CA: Stanford University Press, 1997), 15.

27. Judith Butler, *Excitable Speech: A Politics of the Performative* (New York: Routledge, 1997), 40. Gayle Salamon's defense of the quotidian qualities of performativity runs throughout *Assuming a Body: Transgender and Rhetorics of Materiality* (New York: Columbia University Press, 2010), but it is most explicitly argued in a reading of a "Boys of the Lex" calendar, which was a calendar sold by the Lexington Club in San Francisco. In one rebuttal of the misreadings of Butler's basic premises of performativity, Salamon responds to those who mistake Butler's association with social construction as a dismissal of these subjectivities, that is, as a valuation of abstract and dense theory over lived experience. Salamon offers another take on this critique, suggesting instead that "social construction must not be construed oppositionally to a 'felt sense' of bodily being, for one can contend both that a body is socially constructed and that its felt sense is undeniable. What social construction offers is a way to understand *how* that felt sense arises, in all its historical and cultural variations, with all its urgency and immediacy, and to ask what it is, finally, that is delivered by that felt sense" (77). As a result, to understand the body and its sensations as materialized in and through discourse is not to discount one's experience, but, as Salamon concludes, "Claiming that the body *feels* natural is not the same as claiming that it is natural" (77). To dislodge sex and gender from an ontological foundation and think through how bodies and identities are performatively produced is not to dismiss them; instead, doing so asks us to understand how we come to matter through lived experiences. As Salamon states:

> How we embody gender *is* how we theorize gender and to suggest otherwise is to misunderstand both theorization and embodiment. To offer the category of real gender in an attempt to discipline what are perceived as the excesses of theoretical gender is to domesticate gender as it is lived and to deny its considerable complexity, which often outpaces our language to describe it. It is undeniable that queering gender is not only theoretical work. But it is also surely the case that those everyday instances of embodying transgressive gender that might at first seem far removed from academic discourse are performed with a complexity and a self-awareness that are rendered invisible if we understand them as simply opposed to a theorizing that is unnecessarily complicated and complicating. What the boys of the Lex demonstrate is that gender as it is lived and embodied is, in some powerful sense, always already theorized. When a distinction is made between the theorizing and the performance of gender expression, we might do well to ask who or what such a distinction serves (71–72).

28. Judith Butler, *Bodies That Matter: On the Discursive Limits Of "Sex"* (New York: Routledge, 1993), 30.

29. Louis Althusser, "Ideology and Ideological State Apparatuses (Notes Towards an Investigation)," in *Mapping Ideology*, ed. Slavoj Žižek (London: Verso, 1994), 130.

My recuperation of Althusser is also influenced by the fusing of rhetoric and psychoanalysis offered up in the work of Joshua Gunn and Shaun Treat, who recuperate fantasy as an enabling moment of subjectivity in "Zombie Trouble: A Propaedeutic on Ideological Subjectification and the Unconscious," *Quarterly Journal of Speech* 91 (2005): 144–74. In their words, ideological subjectification "provid[es] limits" (164) but also "generates the very agential maps that enable us to locate its contradictions and constructedness" (163).

30. Butler, *Excitable Speech*, 5.
31. Butler, *Excitable Speech*, 32.
32. Butler, *Excitable Speech*, 33.
33. Butler, *Excitable Speech*, 26.
34. Butler, *Excitable Speech*, 15–16.
35. See Michel Foucault, *The History of Sexuality*, trans. Robert Hurley (New York: Vintage Books, 1978), as well as *Discipline and Punish: The Birth of the Prison*, trans. Alan Sheridan (New York: Vintage Books, 1977), esp. 194.
36. Butler, *Bodies That Matter*, 2.
37. Butler, *Excitable Speech*, 16.
38. Judith Butler, "What Is Critique? An Essay on Foucault's Virtue," in *The Judith Butler Reader*, ed. Sara Salih (Malden, MA.: Blackwell, 2004), 317.
39. Judith Butler, *Undoing Gender* (New York: Routledge, 2004), 8.
40. Butler, *Psychic Life*, 10.
41. Judith Butler, *Giving an Account of Oneself* (New York: Fordham University Press, 2005), 20.
42. See Meyerowitz, *How Sex Changed*, esp. 102–104. Benjamin used the word "transvestite" as an analytical category, although today we may be more likely to use a term like cross-dressing to describe similar acts.
43. D. M. to H. B., December 10, 1955. In these letters I have chosen not to correct the spelling or grammatical errors or annotate with "*sic*"; such interventions in the letters' numerous errors would disrupt their flow.
44. Meyerowitz, *How Sex Changed*, 46.
45. D. M. to H. B., November 13, 1953.
46. D. M. to H. B., December 29, 1954.
47. H. B. to D. M., December 30, 1954.
48. C. E. to H. B., March 15, 1954.
49. H. B. to D. M., March 15, 1954.
50. D. M. to H. B., March 17, 1954.
51. Benjamin used intermediaries, including a transwoman scheduled for surgery with Mayne in Mexico, to counsel Mayne in this period. Although he would not provide Mayne with a definitive course of action, Benjamin remained skeptical of the Mexican doctor, Dr. [F.]. See H. B. to C. S., February 14, 1955; C. S. to H. B., March 2, 1955; H. B. to C. S., March 10, 1955, and April 1, 1955.
52. D. M. to H. B, April 17, 1955. It is worth noting here that I do not understand transsexuality as a purely medicalized identity that is complete or finished

with hormonal or surgical intervention. As Kate Bornstein explains in *Gender Outlaw: On Men, Women, and the Rest of Us* (New York: Routledge, 1994), trans identities, like all identities, are better understood as a process of becoming without any predetermined or final destination.

53. D. M. to H. B., October 6, 1955.
54. H. B. to D. M., October 10, 1955.
55. D. M. to H. B., December 10, 1955.
56. D. M. to H. B., December 12, 1955.
57. C. S. to H. B., August 14, 1955; C. S. to H. B., September 9, 1955; A. D. to H. B., November 11, 1955; and A. D. to H. B., November 16, 1955.
58. H. B. to A. D., November 14, 1955.
59. A. D. to H. B., November 21, 1955.
60. H. B. to A. D., December 2, 1955.
61. H. B. to D. M., December 12, 1955.
62. Steve Pile, "Opposition, Political Identities, and Spaces of Resistance," in *Geographies of Resistance*, ed. Steve Pile and Michael Keith (London: Routledge, 1997), 23.
63. D. M. to H. B., December 13, 1955. Despite the date, it seems clear that Mayne is responding to Benjamin's December 12, 1955, letter.
64. H. B. to D. M., December 22, 1955.
65. H. B. to D. M., February 11, 1956.
66. D. M. to H. B., February 14, 1956.
67. See D. M. to H. B., April 9, 1956; H. B. to D. M., April 9, 1956; and D. M. to H. B., April 18, 1957. Dan Irving has criticized Benjamin, as well as other pioneers in trans medical care, for fusing trans identity with exploitative capitalist relations In his "Normalized Transgressions: Legitimizing the Transsexual Body as Productive," *Radical History Review*, no. 100 (2008): 45–46. Although I cannot speak to Benjamin's thoughts about labor and trans identity, I would characterize Benjamin's concern about his patients' and acquaintances' ability to find a job as being motivated not by an ignorance of the exploitative nature of labor but by concerns for their immediate welfare post-transition.
68. Butler, *Undoing Gender*, 29.
69. Patricia Ewick and Susan Silbey, *The Common Place of Law: Stories from Everyday Life* (Chicago: University of Chicago Press, 1998), 14.
70. Butler, *Undoing Gender*, 20.
71. Butler, *Undoing Gender*, 4. Kathleen Lennon makes a similar argument when clarifying what she sees as Butler's vague use of terms such as "livability" and "livable life." Lennon proposes that we think of livability and intelligibility in the following manner: "intelligibility consists of people being able to 'find their feet' with each other in everyday interactions. It is this kind of making sense to ourselves and others which I would suggest is necessary if life is to be livable" ("Making Life Livable: Transsexuality and Bodily Transformation," *Radical Philosophy* 140 [2006]: 28).

72. Austin Sarat, et al., "Ideas of the 'Everyday' and the 'Trouble Case' in Law and Society Scholarship: An Introduction," in *Everyday Practices and Trouble Cases*, ed. Austin Sarat, et al. (Evanston, IL: Northwestern University Press, 1998), 3, emphasis in original.

73. Butler, *Undoing Gender*, 101.

74. Butler, *Undoing Gender*, 8.

75. Bulter, *Undoing Gender*, 101.

NOTES TO CHAPTER 2

1. Importantly, there are some exceptions even to this rule when we consider other axes of identity such as religious identities. For example, Islamic custom dictates the use of water to cleanse one's body after urination or defecation, which is not likely to be readily available in many public bathrooms in Western cultures.

2. Barbara Penner, "A World of Unmentionable Suffering: Women's Public Conveniences in Victorian London," *Journal of Design History* 14, no. 2 (2001): 36–37.

3. Penner, "World," 36.

4. For a poignant reminder of the racially motivated hegemonic functions of "Whites Only" signs, see Kimberle Williams Crenshaw, "Race, Reform, and Retrenchment: Transformation and Legitimation in Antidiscrimination Law," *Harvard Law Review* 101 (1988): 1377–84.

5. Taunya Lovell Banks, "Toilets as a Feminist Issue: A True Story," *Berkeley Women's Law Journal* 6 (1990): 285. The case to which Banks refers here is *Turner v. Randolph*, 195 F Supp 677.

6. Patricia Cooper and Ruth Oldenziel, "Cherished Classifications: Bathrooms and the Construction of Gender/Race on the Pennsylvania Railroad During World War II," *Feminist Studies* 25 (1999): 17.

7. Jane Sherron De Hart, "Gender on the Right: Meanings Behind the Existential Scream," *Gender & History* 3 (1991): 258.

8. Jane Mansbridge, *Why We Lost the Era* (Chicago: University of Chicago Press, 1986), 114.

9. Ruth Barcan, "Dirty Spaces: Separation, Containment, and Shame in the Public Toilet," in *Toilet: Public Restrooms and the Politics of Sharing*, ed. Harvey Molotch and Laura Norén (New York: New York University Press, 2010), 26, emphasis in original. For a provocative reading of the public trafficking of shame and shitting, see Wayne Koestenbaum, *Humiliation* (New York: Picador, 2011).

10. Here I have consciously chosen to employ the language of "people with disabilities" and "disability" over other terms because these are the terms preferred by the majority, if not all, of the authors that I cite in this chapter. As with all identity categories, we must be attentive to linguistic self-determination as well as to the cultural-political work performed by these identity markers. Unfortunately, according to Simi Linton, many of the terms meant to mark the agency of people with disabilities (such as "differently-abled" and "physically challenged") "may be considered well-meaning attempts to inflate the value of

people with disabilities," yet they also "convey the boosterism and do-gooder mentality endemic to the paternalistic agencies that control many disabled people's lives" (*Claiming Disability: Knowledge and Identity* [New York: New York University Press, 1998], 14). Shelley Tremain rejects the term "differently-abled" because "it is an especially condescending, and pejorative euphemism, one with which disabled persons repeatedly, and consistently, refuse to identify." Using her own compilation of the work of disabled dykes as proof for her claim, Tremain continues, "as a matter of fact, none of the more than 50 disabled dykes from whom I received over 150 submissions for this anthology referred to herself in that way, nor even mentioned the term" ("Introduction: We're Here. We're Disabled and Queer. Get Used to It.," in *Pushing the Limits: Disabled Dykes Produce Culture*, ed. Shelley Tremain [Toronto: Women's Press, 1996], 20).

Linton similarly critiques the term "physically challenged," saying, "This phrase does not make much sense to me. To say that I am physically challenged is to state that the obstacle to my participation is physical, not social, and that the barrier is my own disability. Further, it separates those of us with mobility impairments from other disabled people, not a valid or useful partition for those interested in coalition building and social change. Various derivatives of the term *challenged* have been adopted as a description used in jokes. For instance, 'vertically challenged' is considered a humorous way to say short, and 'calorically challenged' to say fat. A review of a Broadway musical *Big* in the New Yorker said that the score is 'melodically challenged'" (*Claiming*, 14).

Eli Clare objects to the these terms on the grounds that "nondisabled people, wanting to cushion us from the cruelty of language, invented these euphemisms. . . . *Differently abled* is simply easier to say, easier to think about than *disabled* or *handicapped* or *crippled*. . . . In the world as it should be, maybe disabled people would be *differently abled*: a world where Braille and audio-recorded editions of books and magazines were a matter of course, and hearing people signed ASL; a world where schools were fully integrated, health care, free and unrationed; a world where universal access meant exactly that; a world where disabled people were not locked up at home or in the nursing homes, relegated to sheltered employment and paid sweatshop wages. But, in the world as it is, *differently abled, physically challenged* tell a wishful lie" (*Exile and Pride: Disability, Queerness, and Liberation* [Cambridge, MA: South End, 1999], 70, emphases in original).

11. As Robert McRuer explains, LGBTs and people with disabilities often serve as metaphors for the other through "conflation and stereotype: people with disabilities are often understood as somehow queer (as paradoxical stereotypes of the asexual or oversexual person with disabilities would suggest), while queers are often understood as somehow disabled (as an ongoing medicalization of identity, similar to what people with disabilities more generally encounter, would suggest)" ("Compulsory Able-Bodiedness and Queer/Disabled Existence," in *Disability Studies: Enabling the Humanities*, ed. Sharon Snyder, Brenda

Jo Brueggemann, and Rosemarie Garland-Thomson [New York: Modern Language Association of America, 2002], 94). Thankfully, an emerging group of scholars are working against these negative articulations of one identity with the other to challenge our understanding of bodies, desires, and abilities. See, for example, Robert McRuer and Anna Mollow, ed., *Sex and Disability* (Durham, NC: Duke University Press, 2012).

12. Like Santiago Solis, I use "hetero-corporo-normativity" to highlight the inter-related logics of able-bodiedness and heterosexuality ("Snow White and the Seven 'Dwarfs'—Queercripped," *Hypatia* 22 [2007]: 129). I add "homo" to this term to mark the potential for sexual minorities to recirculate and reify these normativities.

13. The lack of legislative history makes it difficult to know the exact way the provision was included in the bill. In one account, "the genesis of Section 504 has been traced to James Pedley, a young legislative aide to Charles Vanik, an Ohio member of Congress. Vanik had become interested in the problems of employment discrimination and transportation accessibility faced by people with disabilities." After failing to get it as an amendment to the Civil Rights Act of 1964, the effort was revived in the final stages of the 1973 Rehabilitation Act (Thomas Burke, *Lawyers, Lawsuits, and Legal Rights: The Battle over Litigation in American Society* [Berkeley: University of California Press, 2004], 67). Others trace the inclusion of Section 504 to "legislative aides working for Senators Alan Cranston and Harrison Williams, among others," who included "this section during the last stage of the policymaking process, and, surprisingly, it almost went unnoticed" (Ruth Ann O'Brien, *Crippled Justice: The History of Modern Disability Policy in the Workplace* [Chicago: University of Chicago Press, 2001], 107).

14. Roberta Ann Johnson, "Mobilizing the Disabled" in *Waves of Protest: Social Movements since the Sixties*, ed. Jo Freeman and Victoria Johnson (Lanham, MD: Rowman & Littlefield, 1999), 30.

15. See Jonathan Young, *Equality of Opportunity: The Making of the Americans with Disabilities Act* (National Council on Disability, 1997).

16. Americans with Disabilities Act of 1990, 42 U.S.C. 12211 (2000).

17. Ruth Colker, "Homophobia, AIDS Hysteria, and the Americans with Disabilities Act," *The Journal of Gender, Race & Justice* 8 (2004): 39–40.

18. Colker, "Homophobia," 50.

19. This list is adapted from one generated by Carrie Sandahl, "Queering the Crip or Cripping the Queer? Intersections of Queer and Crip Identities in Solo Autobiographical Performances," *GLQ* 9 (2003): 26. There are, of course, important differences between these two populations. As Ellen Samuels notes, the commonalities are strained when issues such as visibility and coming out are factored into the analogy for there are a number of disabilities that are not optically obvious. "My Body, My Closet: Invisible Disability and the Limits of Coming-out Discourse," *GLQ* 9 (2003): 233–55. Thus, while many of the disability issues discussed here involve physical

impediments created by human-designed architecture, I understand "disability" as a category of identification that encompasses more than physical impairment.

20. Rob Kitchin and Robin Law, "The Socio-Spatial Construction of (In)Accessible Public Toilets," *Urban Studies* 38 (2001): 289.

21. Kyla Bender-Baird documents the difficulties trans people face when employers are not accommodating in the workplace in *Transgender Employment Practices: Gendered Perceptions and the Law* (Albany: State University of New York Press, 2011), 79–85.

22. Michel de Certeau, *The Practice of Everyday Life*, trans. Steven Rendall (Berkeley: University of California Press, 1984), 117, emphasis in original. Geographers tend to use these terms in an opposite fashion, but I want to remain faithful to Certeau's schema, given his interest in quotidian practices and their communicative functions.

23. Certeau, *The Practice of Everyday Life*, xix, emphasis in original.

24. Certeau, *The Practice of Everyday Life*, 36.

25. Certeau, *The Practice of Everyday Life*, 35.

26. Certeau, *The Practice of Everyday Life*, 35.

27. Steve Pile, "Introduction: Opposition, Political Identities and Spaces of Resistance," in *Geographies of Resistance*, ed. Steve Pile and Michael Keith (London: Routledge, 1997), 16.

28. Steve Pile and Michael Keith, Preface, in *Geographies of Resistance*, ed. Steve Pile and Michael Keith (London: Routledge, 1997), xi.

29. Raka Shome, "Space Matters: The Power and Practice of Space," *Communication Theory* 13 (2003): 40.

30. Shome, "Space Matters," 40.

31. Barcan, "Dirty Spaces," 28

32. Shome, "Space Matters," 43.

33. Michel Foucault, *Power/Knowledge: Selected Interviews & Other Writings, 1972–1977* (New York: Pantheon Books, 1980), 149, emphasis in original.

34. Michel Foucault, "Of Other Spaces," *diacritics* 16 (1986): 23.

35. David Sibley, *Geographies of Exclusion: Society and Difference in the West* (London: Routledge, 1995), 72.

36. Ruth Holliday and John Hassard, "Contested Bodies: An Introduction," in *Contested Bodies*, ed. Ruth Holliday and John Hassard (London: Routledge, 2001), 13.

37. Jodie Marksamer and Dylan Vade, *Gender Neutral Bathroom Survey* (San Francisco: San Francisco Human Rights Commission, 2002), np.

38. Judith Halberstam, *Female Masculinity* (Durham, NC: Duke University Press, 1998), 22.

39. Halberstam, *Female Masculinity*, 20. Alkeline Van Lenning elaborates on the flexibility of sex and gender codes in "The Body as Crowbar: Transcending or Stretching Sex?" *Feminist Theory* 5 (2004): 25–47.

40. Richard M. Juang, "Transgendering the Politics of Recognition," in *Transgender Rights*, ed. Paisley Currah, Richard Juang, and Shannon Price Minter (Minneapolis: University of Minnesota Press, 2006), 247.

41. Kath Browne, "Genderism and the Bathroom Problem: (Re)Materialising Sexed Sites, (Re)Creating Sexed Bodies," *Gender, Place and Culture* 11 (2004): 338.

42. Cooper and Oldenziel, "Cherished Classifications," 15.

43. Halberstam, *Female Masculinity*, 24.

44. Tim Cresswell, *In Place/Out of Place: Geography, Ideology, and Transgression* (Minneapolis: University of Minnesota Press, 1996), 149.

45. Doreen Massey, "Entanglements of Power: Reflections," in *Entaglements of Power: Geographies of Domination/Resistance*, ed. Joanne Sharp, Paul Routledge, Chris Philo, and Ronan Paddison (London: Routledge, 2000), 282. See also, Massey, *For Space* (London: Sage, 2005), 25–30, 45–8.

46. Doreen Massey, *Space, Place, and Gender* (Minneapolis: University of Minnesota Press, 1994), 7.

47. Lise Nelson, "Bodies (and Spaces) Do Matter: The Limits of Performativity," *Gender, Place and Culture* 6 (1999): 331–53.

48. Robyn Longhurst, *Bodies: Exploring Fluid Boundaries* (London: Routledge, 2001), 5.

49. Lynn Stewart, "Bodies, Visions, and Spatial Politics: A Review Essay on Henri Lefebvre's *The Production of Space*," *Environment and Planning D: Society and Space* 13 (1995): 610, emphases in original.

50. Brett Genny Beemyn, "Making Campuses More Inclusive of Transgender Students," *Journal of Gay & Lesbian Issues in Education* 3 (2005): 81–82.

51. Simone Chess, et al., "Calling All Bathroom Revolutionaries," in *That's Revolting: Queer Strategies for Resisting Assimilation*, ed. Mattilda (Brooklyn, NY: Soft Skull Press, 2004), 190.

52. Chess, et al., "Calling," 189.

53. Chess, et al., "Calling," 192.

54. Twyla Ilyne Johnson, "Aunt Flo Faces Unending Flow," *Daily Nexus*, January 23, 2003, http://www.dailynexus.com/article.php?a=4255.

55. Chess, et al., "Calling," 191.

56. Chess, et al., "Calling," 193.

57. "PISSAR Mission and Goals," http://www.uweb.ucsb.edu/~schess/organizations/pissar/mission.html.

58. Janice Irvine, "Shame Comes Out of the Closet," *Sexuality Research and Social Policy* 6, no. 1 (2009): 75.

59. David Serlin, "Pissing without Pity: Disability, Gender, and the Public Toilet," in *Toilet: Public Restrooms and the Politics of Sharing*, ed. Harvey Molotch and Laura Norén (New York: New York University Press, 2010), 169.

60. Serlin, "Pissing without Pity," 169, 184

61. Chess, et al., "Calling," 194.

62. Olga Gershenson, "The Restroom Revolution: Unisex Toilets and Campus Politics," in *Toilet: Public Restrooms and the Politics of Sharing*, ed. Harvey Molotch
and Laura Norén (New York: New York University Press, 2010), 192.

63. Chess, et al., "Calling," 194.

64. Chess, et al., "Calling," 193.

65. Chess, et al., "Calling," 193, emphasis in original.

66. Chess, et al., "Calling," 194.

67. Chess, et al., "Calling," 194.

68. "PISSAR Patrol Checklist," http://www.uweb.ucsb.edu/~schess/organizations/
pissar/checklist.htm.

69. Chess, et al., "Calling," 196, emphasis in original.

70. Alison Kafer, "Compulsory Bodies: Reflections on Heterosexuality and Able-
Bodiedness," *Journal of Women's History* 15, no. 3 (2003): 82–83.

71. Chess, et al., "Calling," 197.

72. Kenneth Burke, *A Rhetoric of Motives* (Berkeley: University of California Press,
1950), 25.

73. Burke, *A Rhetoric of Motives*, 21.

74. Burke, *A Rhetoric of Motives*, 21, emphasis in original.

75. Chess, et al., "Calling," 197.

76. Chess, et al., "Calling," 201.

77. Chess, et al., "Calling," 201.

78. Chess, et al., "Calling," 200.

79. Chess, et al., "Calling," 200.

80. Michael Warner, *The Trouble with Normal: Sex, Politics, and the Ethics of Queer
Life* (Cambridge, MA: Harvard University Press, 1999), 28.

81. Warner, *Trouble with Normal*, 33.

82. Warner, *Trouble with Normal*, 31.

83. Warner, *Trouble with Normal*, 35.

84. "PISSAR Mission and Goals."

85. Chess, et al., "Calling," 197, emphasis in original.

86. Judith Butler, *Bodies That Matter: On the Discursive Limits Of "Sex"* (New York:
Routledge, 1993), 228.

87. Butler, *Bodies That Matter*, 230.

88. Janet Jakobsen, "Queer Is? Queer Does? Normativity and the Problem of Resistance," *GLQ* 4 (1998): 511–36.

89. Robert McRuer, *Crip Theory: Cultural Signs of Queerness and Disability* (New
York: New York University Press, 2006), 30.

90. McRuer, *Crip Theory*, 30.

91. "PISSAR Mission and Goals."

92. Michael Brown, *Replacing Citizenship: AIDS Activism & Radical Democracy* (New
York: Guilford Press, 1997), 15, 14.

93. Brown, *Replacing Citizenship*, 184.

94. Chess, et al., "Calling," 192.

95. Chess, et al., "Calling," 191, 201.

96. "Minutes from Eucalyptus Meeting, July 23, 2003," http://www.uweb.ucsb.edu/~schess/organizations/pissar/Eucalyptus%20Meeting.htm , emphasis in original.

97. "Minutes."

98. Transgender Law and Policy Institute, "College/Universities and K–12 Schools," http://www.transgenderlaw.org/college/index.htm.

99. Patricia Leigh Brown, "A Quest for a Restroom That's Neither Men's Room or Female's Room," New York Times, March 4, 2005. http://www.nytimes.com/2005/03/04/national/04bathroom.html?ex=1184212800&en=80c1b6e99582ed3c&ei=5070.

100. For an informative view of how we might start transing the bathroom, see Lucas Crawford, "Transgender Movement(s) and Beating the Straight Flush: Building an Art of Trans Washrooms," in Transgender Migrations: The Bodies, Borders, and Politics of Transition, ed. Trystan T. Cotten (New York: Routledge, 2012), 59–75.

101. Lisa Mottet, "Access to Gender-Appropriate Bathrooms: A Frustrating Diversion on the Path to Transgender Equality," Georgetown Journal of Gender and the Law 4 (2003): 744.

102. Eve Kosofsky Sedgwick, "Queer Performativity: Henry James's The Art of the Novel," GLQ 1 (1993): 14.

103. Sally Munt, Queer Attachments: The Cultural Politics of Shame (Burlington, VT: Ashgate, 2007), 4.

104. Judith Halberstam, "Shame and White Gay Masculinity," Social Text 23 (2005): 220, 224.

105. Halberstam, "Shame," 224.

NOTES TO CHAPTER 3

1. Roy Maurer, "Gender Identity Ordinance Stirs Debate at Common Council," Indiana Daily Student, April 14, 2006, http://www.idsnews.com/news/story.aspx?id=35347&comview=1.

2. "Proposal Would Add 'Gender Identity' to Bloomington's Ordinance," Associated Press State & Local Wire, March 15, 2006.

3. John Clower, "HRC Recommends New Transgender Protections," Bloomington Alternative, October 30, 2005, http://www.bloomingtonalternative.com/articles/2005/10/30/7852.

4. Sarah Morin, "Should Gender Identity Be Part of Rights Ordinance? City's Human Rights Commission Votes Yes, Sending Issue to Council," Herald-TimesOnline.com, October 1, 2005, http://www.heraldtimesonline.com/stories/2005/10/01/news.1001-HT-A9_JLR27245.sto. I did not take detailed notes at this meeting, but the reporting and other official records match my memory of it.

5. Bloomington Human Rights Commission, "Minutes of September 26, 2005 Meeting," np.
6. Bloomington Human Rights Commission, "Minutes."
7. Maurer, "Gender Identity."
8. Clower, "HRC Recommends."
9. Clower, "HRC Recommends."
10. Susan Stryker's critique of "LGBT" as a suspect move meant to neutralize the more radical demands made by "queer" is taken up in the next chapter (*Transgender History* [Berkeley, CA: Seal Press, 2008], 137). I agree with Stryker's analysis of the material divisions constituted by GLBs who employ these terms to distinguish themselves as radically distinct from trans people, and therefore I want to make clear that when I use the term "LGBT politics," it is meant to call attention to precisely this kind of problematic conception of identity politics. At the same time, I should also clarify that I do not understand queer politics and those who march under its banner to be inherently trans-affirmative. Therefore, my use of "LGBT" and "queer" does not line up neatly and cleanly as a marker of hostility toward or acceptance of the concerns of trans people.
11. See, for example, Patrick Califia, *Sex Changes: Transgender Politics* (San Francisco: Cleis Press, 2003 [2nd ed.]); Viviane Namaste, *Invisible Lives: The Erasure of Transsexual and Transgendered People* (Chicago: University of Chicago Press, 2000) and *Sex Change, Social Change: Reflections on Identity, Institutions, and Imperialism* (Toronto: Women's Press, 2005); Deborah Rudacille, *The Riddle of Gender: Science, Activism, and Transgender Rights* (New York: Pantheon, 2005); David Valentine, *Imagining Transgender: An Ethnography of a Category* (Durham, NC: Duke University Press, 2007); and Jane Ward, *Respectably Queer: Diversity Culture in LGBT Activist Organizations* (Nashville, TN: Vanderbilt University Press, 2008).
12. Judith Halberstam, *In a Queer Time and Place: Transgender Bodies, Subcultural Lives* (New York: New York University Press, 2005), 37. Among the most interesting book-length projects in this area are Mary Gray, *Out in the Country: Youth, Media, and Queer Visibility in Rural America* (New York: New York University Press, 2009); and Scott Herring, *Another Country: Queer Anti-Urbanism* (New York: New York University Press, 2010).
13. David Eng, Judith Halberstam, and José Esteban Muñoz, "What's Queer About Queer Studies Now?" *Social Text* 23, no. 3–4 (2005): 10.
14. David Eng, *The Feeling of Kinship: Queer Liberalism and the Racialization of Intimacy* (Durham, NC: Duke University Press, 2010), 29.
15. Lisa Duggan, *The Twilight of Equality? Neoliberalism, Cultural Politics, and the Attack on Democracy* (Boston: Beacon Press, 2003), 50, 65–66.
16. Amy Brandzel, "Queering Citizenship? Same-Sex Marriage and the State," *GLQ* 11 (2005): 173, 197.
17. Brandzel, "Queering Citizenship," 174.

18. Lauren Berlant, *The Queen of America Goes to Washington City: Essays on Sex and Citizenship* (Durham, NC: Duke University Press, 1997), 10; and Shane Phelan, *Sexual Strangers: Gays, Lesbians, and Dilemmas of Citizenship* (Philadelphia, PA: Temple University Press, 2001).

19. Phelan, *Sexual Strangers*, 140–41.

20. For a succinct overview of the meaning and value of trashing, see Mark Kelman, "Trashing," *Stanford Law Review* 36 (1984): 293–348. Useful introductions to CLS include the "Critical Legal Studies Symposium" in the first two issues of the 1984 volume of the *Stanford Law Review*; Roberto Unger, *The Critical Legal Studies Movement* (Cambridge, MA: Harvard University Press, 1986); and Mark Kelman, *A Guide to Critical Legal Studies* (Cambridge, MA: Harvard University Press, 1987).

21. Jason Whitehead, "From Criticism to Critique: Preserving the Radical Potential of Critical Legal Studies through a Reexamination of Frankfurt School Critical Theory," *Florida State University Law Review* 26 (1999): 705.

22. Marouf Hasian has also argued against this form of "vulgar Marxis[m]" and its treatment of rhetoric as little more than "an epiphenomenal superstructure" supporting the interests of elites in "Legal Argumentation in the Godwin-Malthus Debates," *Argumentation and Advocacy* 37 (2001): 185.

23. Whitehead, "From Criticism," 708.

24. MacKinnon advances these theories in all of her work, but see the following two books for her most thorough treatments of this argument: *Feminism Unmodified: Discourses of Life and Law* (Cambridge, MA: Harvard University Press, 1987); and *Toward a Feminist Theory of the State* (Cambridge, MA: Harvard University Press, 1989).

25. Mary Joe Frug, "A Postmodern Feminist Legal Manifesto (an Unfinished Draft)," *Harvard Law Review* 105 (1992): 1045. See also Frug, *Postmodern Legal Feminism* (New York: Routledge, 1992).

26. A short list of their most important works would include: Derrick Bell, *And We Are Not Saved: The Elusive Quest for Racial Justice* (New York: Basic Books, 1987); Bell, *Faces at the Bottom of the Well: The Permanence of Racism* (New York: Basic Books, 1992); Kimberlé Williams Crenshaw, "Race, Reform, and Retrenchment: Transformation and Legitimation in Antidiscrimination Law," *Harvard Law Review* 101 (1988): 1331–87; Crenshaw, "Demarginalizing the Intersection of Race and Sex: A Black Feminist Critique of Antidiscrimination Doctrine, Feminist Theory and Antiracist Politics," *University of Chicago Legal Forum* 1989 (1989): 139–67; Crenshaw, "Mapping the Margins: Intersectionality, Identity Politics, and Violence against Women of Color," *Stanford Law Review* 43 (1991): 1241–99; Richard Delgado, "The Ethereal Scholar: Does Critical Legal Studies Have What Minorities Want?" *Harvard Civil Rights-Civil Liberties Law Review* 22 (1987): 301–22; Delgado, *The Rodrigo ChroNickles: Conversations About Race and America* (New York: New York University Press, 1995); Patricia Williams, "Alchemical Notes: Reconstructing Ideals from Deconstructed

Rights," *Harvard Civil Rights-Civil Liberties Law Review* 22 (1987): 401–33; and Williams, *The Alchemy of Race and Rights* (Cambridge, MA: Harvard University Press, 1991).

27. Williams, "Alchemical Notes," 424, emphasis in original.

28. Williams, "Alchemical Notes," 416.

29. Of course Gramsci's most famous work on the subject is *Selections from the Prison Notebooks*, trans. Quintin Hoare and Geoffrey Nowell Smith (New York: International Publishers, 1987).

30. Crenshaw, "Race, Reform, and Retrenchment," 1350–51.

31. Crenshaw, "Race, Reform, and Retrenchment," 1358.

32. Crenshaw, "Race, Reform, and Retrenchment," 1357n97.

33. Crenshaw, "Race, Reform, and Retrenchment," 1359, emphasis in original.

34. Bente Meyer, "Extraordinary Stories: Disability, Queerness and Feminism," *NORA: Nordic Journal of Women's Studies* 10 (2002): 245.

35. Harlon Dalton, "The Clouded Prism," *Harvard Civil Rights-Civil Liberties Law Review* 22 (1987): 436.

36. Paisley Currah, "Gender Pluralisms under the Transgender Umbrella," in *Transgender Rights*, ed. Currah, Richard Juang, and Shannon Price Minter (Minneapolis: University of Minnesota Press, 2006), 24.

37. Cianán Russell, interview with author, January 11, 2007. All of the interviews in this chapter were conducted in accordance and with the approval of the IRB at Indiana University (#06-11027). I asked my interviewees how they would like to be identified and have honored these requests.

38. Claire Dana, interview with author, March 4, 2007.

39. Nick Clarkson, interview with author, March 4, 2007.

40. Currah, Jamison Green, and Stryker qualify the persuasive limits of individual narratives to link together different forms of discrimination because these narratives rely on overly simplistic ideas of difference that tend to be unidimensional, meaning that officials tend to hear a compartmentalization of difference rather than a multidimensional claim to structural distributions of inequality (*The State of Transgender Rights in the United States of America* [San Francisco: National Sexuality Resource Center, 2008], 9).

41. Cianán Russell, interview with author, March 6, 2007. The remaining quotations of Cianán are taken from this interview.

42. *BloomingOUT* , January 12, 2006.

43. Clower, "HRC Recommends."

44. Clower, "HRC Recommends."

45. Deana Lahre, interview with author, March 5, 2007.

46. Bloomington Office of the Common Council, "Legislative Packet," April 5, 2006, np.

47. Bloomington Office of the Common Council, "Legislative Packet."

48. Bloomington Office of the Common Council, "Legislative Packet."

49. Bloomington Office of the Common Council, "Legislative Packet."

50. Marry Ann Glendon's *Rights Talk: The Impoverishment of Political Discourse* (New York: Free Press, 1991) issues an indictment against the circulation of many kinds of everyday rights claims, especially those reliant on a strong sense of individualism, such as the right to privacy. Without delving into the various critiques launched against Glendon's thesis, I would suggest for now that major disjunctions exist among Glendon's textual archive, court decisions and legal treatises, and her ability to make judgments about how citizens redeploy the law in their everyday lives. Other scholars, informed by participant observation and interviews with citizens, reach very different conclusions about how the general populace understands their legal subjectivities. See, for example, David Engel and Frank Munger, *Rights of Inclusion: Law and Disability in the Life Stories of Americans with Disabilities* (Chicago: University of Chicago Press, 2003); Patricia Ewick and Susan Silbey, *The Common Place of Law: Stories from Everyday Life* (Chicago: University of Chicago Press, 1998); Carol Greenhouse, Barbara Yngvesson, and David Engle, *Law and Community in Three American Towns* (Ithaca, NY: Cornell University Press, 1994); and, George Lovell, *This is Not Civil Rights: Discovering Rights Talk in 1939 America* (Chicago: University of Chicago Press, 2012).

NOTES TO CHAPTER 4

1. Mark Barabak, "Gays May Have the Fastest of All Civil Rights Movements," *Los Angeles Times*, May 20, 2012.
2. For more on the mutually constitutive relationships enabled by the religious right's fear-mongering and LGBT resistance to it, see Michael Cobb, *God Hates Fags: The Rhetorics of Religious Violence* (New York: New York University Press, 2006); Tina Fetner, *How the Religious Right Shaped Lesbian and Gay Activism* (Minneapolis: University of Minnesota Press, 2008); Janet Jakobsen and Ann Pellegrini, *Love the Sin: Sexual Regulation and the Limits of Religious Tolerance* (New York: New York University Press, 2003); and John Gallagher and Chris Bull, *Perfect Enemies: The Religious Right, the Gay Movement, and the Politics of the 1990s* (New York: Crown Publishers, 1996).
3. Jodi O'Brien, "Seeking Normal? Considering Same-Sex Marriage," *Seattle Journal for Social Justice* 2 (2003–2004): 463, emphasis in original.
4. A provocative exchange about the racial and class implications of LGBT civil marriage advocacy is found in Marlon Bailey, Priya Kandaswamy, and Mattie Udora Richardson, "Is Gay Marriage Racist?" in *That's Revolting: Queer Strategies for Resisting Assimilation*, ed. Mattilda Bernstein Sycamore (Brooklyn, NY: Soft Skull Press, 2008), 113–19.
5. To this day, the most trenchant critiques of same-sex civil marriage advocacy efforts are Paula Ettlebrick, "Since When is Marriage a Path to Liberation?" *OUT/LOOK* 9 (1989): 14–16; Michael Warner, *The Trouble with Normal: Sex, Politics, and the Ethics of Queer Life* (Cambridge, MA: Harvard University Press, 1999); and Judith Butler, "Is Kinship Always Already Heterosexual?" *differences*

13, no. 1 (2002): 14–44. The pessimism of this line of argument, which affords ideological and hegemonic determination to institutionally guaranteed subject positions without much hope for the performative embodiment of other futures, relies on a curious rendering of marriage as *the* institution impervious to insurrectionary invocations—a proposition I am not willing yet to concede. Ellen Lewin's research on lesbian and gay appropriations of public commitment rituals and alternative configurations of kinship networks cautions us against presuming marriage and the family are immune to subversive embodiments. See Lewin's *Lesbian Mothers: Accounts of Gender in American Culture* (Ithaca, NY: Cornell University Press, 1993); *Recognizing Ourselves: Ceremonies of Lesbian and Gay Commitment* (New York: Columbia University Press, 1998); and, *Gay Fatherhood: Narratives of Family and Citizenship in America* (Chicago: University of Chicago Press, 2009).

6. In light of favorable demographic trends, the overall trajectory for greater support of same-sex civil marriage rights seems likely. Nate Silver, "Gay Marriage Opponents Now in Minority," *New York Times*, April 20, 2011, http://fivethirtyeight.blogs.nytimes.com/2011/04/20/gay-marriage-opponents-now-in-minority.

7. Gallup Organization, "Gay and Lesbian Rights," http://www.gallup.com/poll/1651/gay-lesbian-rights.aspx.

8. Jeff Krehely, "Polls Show Huge Public Support for Gay and Transgender Workplace Protections," *Center for American Progress*, June 2, 2011, and Human Rights Campaign, "HRC's Recent Transgender-Related Work," http://www.hrc.org/issues/1502.htm. In the HRC poll cited here, "57 percent incorrectly believed that it was not legal to fire people just because they were transgender" and "61 percent of those polled believed the country needed laws to protect transgender people from discrimination." Another poll conducted by the National Gay and Lesbian Task Force in 2006 reported similar results with 59 percent supporting trans-inclusive antidiscrimination measures (Ethan Jacobs, "NGLTF Poll Shows Public Supports Trans-Inclusive Non-Discrimination Laws," *Bay Windows*, June 29, 2006).

9. While this chapter was in the drafting stage, three states (Hawaii, Nevada, and Connecticut) within two months of each other incorporated gender identity protections into their state laws. At least for now these developments indicate a growing awareness of the need for these measures.

10. Brad Sears, *Documenting Discrimination on the Basis of Sexual Orientation and Gender Identity in State Employment*, September 23, 2009, ch. 9, 1, http://www.law.ucla.edu/williamsinstitute/programs/EmploymentReports_ENDA.html. See also, Crosby Burns and Jeff Krehely, *Gay and Transgender People Face High Rates of Workplace Discrimination and Harassment* (Washington, DC: Center for American Progress, 2011).

11. Sears, *Documenting*, ch. 9, 28–29.

12. Jamie Grant, Lisa Mottet, Justin Tanis, Jack Harrison, Jody Herman, and Mara Keisling, *Injustice at Every Turn: A Report of the National Transgender*

Discrimination Survey (Washington, DC: National Center for Transgender Equality and National Gay and Lesbian Task Force, 2011), 56.

13. Transgender Law Center, *State of Transgender California*, March 2009, np, www.transgenderlawcenter.org/pdf/StateofTransCAFINAL.pdf .

14. Qtd. in Sears, *Documenting*, ch. 9, 25.

15. Human Rights Campaign, "Laws—Employment Non-Discrimination Act," April 7, 2011, http://www.hrc.org/laws_and_elections/enda.asp .

16. Abzug's bill covered a range of issues beyond employment discrimination, including public accommodations and housing. For a concise history, see Chai Feldblum, "The Federal Gay Rights Bill: From Bella to ENDA," in *Creating Change: Sexuality, Public Policy, and Civil Rights*, ed. John D'Emilio, William Turner, and Urvashi Vaid (New York: St. Martin's Press, 2000), 149–87.

17. Some might prefer to define LGBT and queer in relation to institutions so that queer marks resistance to institutions and LGBT as seeking recognition from institutions. As the previous chapters demonstrate, such binary schemes fail us.

18. Paisley Currah, "Stepping Back, Looking Outward: Situating Transgender Activism and Transgender Studies—Kris Hayashi, Matt Richardson, and Susan Stryker Frame Their Movement," *Sexuality Research & Social Policy* 5, no. 1 (2008): 96. See also, Susan Stryker, "Transgender History, Homonormativity, and Disciplinarity," *Radical History Review* no. 100 (2008): 145–57.

19. The references to minoritizing and universalizing logics are indebted to Eve Kosofsky Sedgwick's meditation on the subject in *Epistemology of the Closet* (Berkeley: University of California Press, 1990). A minoritizing perspective assumes issues of identity matter only to those who identify with the category, so that queer issues matter only to queers. Alternatively, universalizing perspectives seek to understand how all persons are subject to the effectivities of an identity category's production. For example, the normativities of homosexualities inform the normativities of heterosexuals and vice versa, and thus our identities are not as separate or immune from each other as some would like to imagine.

20. Amy Gutmann's treatise on the inescapability of identity politics in democratic cultures reminds us that we cannot wish away the fundamental importance of one's own sense of identity even as one understands one's self as a citizen of a common polity, whether in the past, present, or future. Gutmann deftly navigates one course for thinking through the possibilities of how identity groups can pursue justice claims without falling prey to the routine criticisms of identity politics (*Identity in Democracy* [Princeton, NJ: Princeton University Press, 2003]). Likewise, many of the contributions in Craig Calhoun, ed., *Social Theory and the Politics of Identity* (Oxford: Wiley-Blackwell, 1994) trace the varied routes of identity politics throughout history.

21. For a concise review of the New Left roots of identity politics, including its trans-Atlantic cross-fertilizations, see Grant Farred, "Endgame Identity? Mapping the New Left Roots of Identity Politics," *New Literary History* 31 (2000): 627–648.

22. The most comprehensive review of academic studies of identity politics is Mary Bernstein, "Identity Politics," *Annual Review of Sociology* 31 (2005): 47–74.

23. I should note here as well that this quick review of the history of identity politics runs the risk of complicity with liberal progress narratives, including the idea that liberal democracies are internally coherent and capable of seamlessly incorporating all citizens into the polity over time as minority groups persuade others to accept their rights claims. In one sense, this telling of the tale is somewhat unavoidable as many minority groups have gained greater liberty and freedom through appeals to these supposedly universal values. At the same time, not all liberal progress narratives are the same, and I am not suggesting that there is a finite point of actually achievable equality or that there is a linear path of cumulative progress. Instead, on the whole, life is better for many minorities because of their appeal to these constitutive values of American culture, even if substantial structural and material inequalities are still present today.

24. In spite of this conservative appropriation of the term, *identity politics* did not always have such a negative valence. Renee Anspach, a sociologist, first used identity politics to describe affirmatively the strategies employed by disability advocacy groups "wherein selves are continually created, dramatized, and enacted" and then "propagat[ed] . . . to attentive publics" ("From Stigma to Identity Politics: Political Activism Among the Physically Disabled and Former Mental Patients," *Social Science and Medicine* 13A [1979]: 766).

25. Lisa Duggan, "Commentary: Dreaming Democracy," *New Literary History* 31 (2000): 851, emphasis in original.

26. Here I am referencing Todd Gitlin, *The Twilight of Common Dreams: Why America Is Wracked By Culture Wars* (New York: Henry Holt, 1995); and, Arthur Schlesinger, *The Disuniting of America: Reflections on a Multicultural Society* (New York: W.W. Norton, 1992).

27. Schlesinger, *Disuniting*, 21. Gitlin, "The Rise of 'Identity Politics': An Examination and a Critique," *Dissent* (1993): 173.

28. For three classic pieces in this vein, see Arlene Stein, "Sisters and Queers," *Socialist Review* 22 (1992): 33–55; Rosemary Hennessy, "Queer Theory, Left Politics," in *Marxism Beyond Marxism*, ed. Saree Makdisi, Cesare Casarino, and Rebecca Karl (New York: Routledge, 1996), 214–42; and Donald Morton, "The Politics of Queer Theory in the (Post)Modern Moment," *Genders* no. 17 (1993): 121–50. These arguments also figure prominently in the following works: Dana Cloud, "Queer Theory and 'Family Values': Capitalism's Utopias of Self-Invention," *Transformation* 2 (2001): 71–114; Max Kirsch, *Queer Theory and Social Change* (London: Routledge, 2000); and Alan Sears, "Queer Anti-Capitalism: What's Left of Lesbian and Gay Liberation?" *Science & Society* 69 (2005): 92–112.

29. Walter Benn Michaels, *The Trouble with Diversity: How We Learned to Love Identity and Ignore Inequality* (New York: Henry Holt, 2006), 199–200. Amanda Anderson's *The Way We Argue Now: A Study in the Cultures of Theory* (Princeton: Princeton University Press, 2006) and Terry Eagleton's *After Theory* (New

York: Basic Books, 2003) also advance arguments along these lines, although not always with the polemical joy Michaels takes in chastising LGBT/queer individuals and scholarship.

30. Sherry Wolf, *Sexuality and Socialism: History, Politics, and Theory of LGBT Liberation* (Chicago. IL: Haymarket, 2009), 173, 195.

31. Judith Butler, "Merely Cultural," *Social Text*, no. 52/53 (1997): 270, emphasis in original. Similar discussions about the relationships between Butler's work and feminisms appear in Judith Butler and Joan Scott, ed., *Feminists Theorize the Political* (New York: Routledge, 1992); and, Seyla Benhabib, Judith Butler, Drucilla Cornell, and Nancy Fraser, *Feminist Contentions: A Philosophical Exchange* (New York: Routledge, 1995).

32. Nancy Fraser, "Heterosexism, Misrecognition, and Capitalism: A Response to Judith Butler," *Social Text*, no. 52/53 (1997): 279–89.

33. Butler, "Merely Cultural," 268–69.

34. David Valentine, *Imagining Transgender: An Ethnography of a Category* (Durham, NC: Duke University Press, 2007).

35. Amin Ghaziani, *The Dividends of Dissent: How Conflict and Culture Work in Lesbian and Gay Marches on Washington* (Chicago: University of Chicago Press, 2008).

36. Susan Stryker, *Transgender History* (Berkeley, CA: Seal Press, 2008), 137.

37. Valentine, *Imagining Transgender*, 64.

38. Wendy Brown, *States of Injury: Power and Freedom in Late Modernity* (Princeton, NJ: Princeton University Press, 1995), 51.

39. Susan Bickford, "Anti-Anti-Identity Politics: Feminism, Democracy, and the Complexities of Citizenship," *Hypatia* 12, no. 4 (1997): 123–24.

40. Danielle Allen, *Talking to Strangers: Anxieties of Citizenship since Brown v. Board of Education* (Chicago: University of Chicago Press, 2004), 17.

41. For a brief and accessible history of ENDA, see Edward Reeves and Lainie Decker, "Before ENDA: Sexual Orientation and Gender Identity Protections in the Workplace Under Federal Law," *Law & Sexuality* 20 (2011): 61–78.

42. Employment Nondiscrimination Act of 2007, H.R. 2015, Sec. 3(a)(6).

43. Phyllis Randolph Frye, "Facing Discrimination, Organizing for Freedom: The Transgender Community," in *Creating Change: Public Policy and Civil Rights*, ed. John D'Emilio, William Turner, and Urvashi Vaid (New York: St. Martin's Press, 2000), 462.

44. Paisley Currah, "Expecting Bodies: The Pregnant Man and Transgender Exclusion from the Employment Non-Discrimination Act," *Women's Studies Quarterly* 36, no. 3/4 (2008): 334.

45. Barney Frank, "Statement of Barney Frank on ENDA, the Employment Non-Discrimination Act," September 28, 2007, http://www.house.gov/frank/docs/2007/09-28-07-endastatement.html.

46. National Gay and Lesbian Task Force, "Task Force, Inc., Responds to Decision to Postpone Hearing on Substitute ENDA Aimed at Stripping Transgender

Protections," October 2, 2007, http://www.thetaskforce.org/press/releases/prMF_100207.

47. National Gay and Lesbian Task Force, "United ENDA Forms," October 3, 2007, http://www.thetaskforce.org/press/releases/prUENDA_100307.

48. United ENDA, "United Opposition to Sexual-Orientation-Only Nondiscrimination Legislation," October 1, 2007, http://www.thetaskforce.org/activist_center/ENDA_oct1_letter, emphasis in original.

49. Christopher Lisotta, "Does the 'T' Stand Alone?" *Nation*, October 17, 2007.

50. Chris Crain, "ENDA, Gay Rights Get Trans-Jacked," *Citizen Crain*, October 2, 2007, http://citizenchris.typepad.com/citizenchris/2007/10/enda-gay-rights.html.

51. Susan Ryan-Vollmar, "The Backlash Begins, Part I," *AmericaBlog*, October 4, 2007, http://www.americablog.com/2007/10/backlash-begins-part-i.html.

52. Robin Tyler, "The Backlash Begins, Part II," *AmericaBlog*, October 4, 2007, http://www.americablog.com/2007/10/backlash-begins-part-ii.html. Tyler would later serve as one of the plaintiffs in the California Supreme Court case legalizing same-sex civil marriage.

53. John Aravosis, "The Transgender Fiasco," *AmericaBlog*, October 3, 2007, http://www.americablog.com/2007/10/transgender-fiasco .

54. John Aravosis, "How Did the T Get in LGBT?" *Salon*, October 8, 2007, http://www.salon.com/opinion/feature /2007/10/08/lgbt.html .

55. Susan Stryker, "Why the T in LGBT is Here to Stay," *Salon.com*, October 11, 2007, http://www.salon.com/opinion/feature/2007/10/11/transgender.html.

56. Lambda Legal, "Weakened ENDA Means Less Protection for Everyone," October 4, 2007, http://www.lambdalegal.org/news/pr/ny_20071004_weakened-enda-means-less-protection.html. For an academic treatment of this issue, see Jill Weinberg, "Gender Nonconformity: An Analysis of Perceived Sexual Orientation and Gender Identity Protection Under the Employment Non-Discrimination Act," *University of San Francisco Law Review* 44 (2009): 1–31.

57. In April 2012, the Equal Employment Opportunity Commission issued an opinion declaring gender identity discrimination within the purview of Title VII's protected classes. Reading gender identity as a subset of sex, federal officials have been instructed to treat it as such in their litigation efforts. Whether or not this interpretation is upheld in federal courts in another matter with a mixed record thus far.

58. Barney Frank, "Barney Frank on Lambda Legal's Analysis," *Bilerico Report*, October 3, 2007, http://www.bilerico.com/2007/10/barney_frank_on_lambda_legals_analysis.html .

59. Kevin Cathcart, "Re: Your Press Release Dated October 3, 2007, Responding to Our Statement of October 1, 2007," http://data.lambdalegal.org/pdf/ltr_enda_frank.pdf, emphasis in original.

60. Susan Stryker also created a list of talking points to help those who wanted to counter the charge that trans people did not have enough of a history of

activism to warrant their inclusion in ENDA: "It's Your History—Use It! Talking Points for Trans-Inclusive ENDA Activists," October 2, 2007, http://www.equalityfederation.org/pdfs/enda/HistoryLessons.pdf.

61. Barney Frank, *Congressional Record* 153 (2007): 26920.

62. Gay & Lesbian Advocates & Defenders, "GLAD Statement on US House Passage of Limited ENDA," November 8, 2007, http://www.glad.org/uploads/docs/advocacy/2007-11-08-ENDApostvote.pdf.

63. Patrick McCreery, "Beyond Gay: 'Deviant' Sex and the Politics of the ENDA Workplace," *Social Text* no. 61 (1999): 39–58.

64. Bickford, "Anti-Anti-Identity Politics," 126.

65. Janet Jakobsen, "Queer Is? Queer Does?: Normativity and the Problem of Resistance," *GLQ* 4 (1998): 511.

66. For more on this topic, see Jane Ward, *Respectably Queer: Diversity Culture in LGBT Activist Organizations* (Nashville: Vanderbilt University Press, 2008).

NOTES TO CHAPTER 5

1. Robyn Wiegman, *Object Lessons* (Durham, NC: Duke University Press, 2012), 314.

2. Wiegman, *Object Lessons*, 339.

3. Eliza Gray, Margy Slattery, and Joe Heroun, "Breaking Boundaries," *New Republic*, June 23, 2011.

4. William Kristol, "Not a Parody," *Washington Post*, October 9, 2009.

5. "The Next Great Civil Rights Struggle: It's Not What You Think. Not a Parody." *Weekly Standard*, July 4–11, 2011.

6. Keach Hagey, "*TNR* vs. Weekly Standard," *Politico*, July 1, 2011.

7. Wendy Brown and Janet Halley, Introduction, in *Left Legalism/Left Critique*, ed. Brown and Halley (Durham, NC: Duke University Press, 2002), 8, 19. Although I find myself in agreement with the impulse of Brown and Halley's introduction and the volume as a whole, especially the suggestion that we need to allow for legal critique divorced from pragmatic considerations that would otherwise inhibit the posing of questions and answers challenging the normative foundations of legal thought, this chapter engages the assumed impenetrability and intractability of legal discourses as always already implicated in the reproduction of these modes of intelligibility.

8. Brown and Halley, Introduction, 19.

9. Brown and Halley, Introduction, 8.

10. Eliza Gray, "Transitions: What Will It Take for America to Accept Transgender People for Who They Really Are?" *New Republic*, July 14, 2011, 10.

11. For more on this despicable act of violence, see Jill Rosen, "Victim of McDonald's Beating Speaks Out," *Baltimore Sun*, April 24, 2011.

12. Judith Butler, *Giving an Account of Oneself* (New York: Fordham University Press, 2005), 22.

13. Butler, *Giving an Account*, 19.

14. Butler, *Giving an Account*, 133–34.
15. Butler, *Giving an Account*, 136.
16. Judith Butler, *Undoing Gender* (New York: Routledge, 2004), 175–76.
17. Austin Sarat and Thomas Kearns, "Beyond the Great Divide: Forms of Legal Scholarship and Everyday Life," in *Law in Everyday Life*, ed. Austin Sarat and Thomas Kearns (Ann Arbor: University of Michigan Press, 1993), 8.
18. Rosemary Coombe, "Contingent Articulations: A Critical Cultural Studies of Law," in *Law in the Domains of Culture*, ed. Austin Sarat and Thomas Kearns (Ann Arbor: University of Michigan Press, 1998), 37.
19. Coombe, "Contingent Articulations," 64.
20. Jason Cromwell, *Transmen & FTMs: Identities, Bodies, Genders & Sexualities* (Urbana: University of Illinois Press, 1999), 14.
21. Sandy Stone, "The Empire Strikes Back: A Posttranssexual Manifesto," in *Body Guards: The Cultural Politics of Gender Ambiguity*, ed. Julia Epstein and Kristina Straub (New York: Routledge, 1991), 295.
22. Stone, "The Empire Strikes Back," 298, emphasis in original.
23. Stone, "The Empire Strikes Back," 299.
24. Stone, "The Empire Strikes Back," 298.
25. Stone, "The Empire Strikes Back," 296.
26. Stone, "The Empire Strikes Back," 299, emphasis in original.
27. Thyrza Nichols Goodeve, "How Like a Goddess: An Interview with Artist Sandy Stone," *Artforum*, September 1995.
28. Janice Raymond, *The Transsexual Empire: The Making of the She-Male* (Boston: Beacon Press, 1979; reprint, 1994), 308.
29. Julie Serano, *Whipping Girl: A Transsexual Woman on Sexism and the Scapegoating of Femininity* (Emeryville, CA: Seal Press, 2007), 43. Serano further states: "Mass media images of 'biological males' dressing and acting in a feminine manner could potentially challenge mainstream notions of gender, but the way they are generally presented in these feminization scenes ensures that this never happens. The media neutralizes the potential threat that trans femininities pose to the category of 'woman' by playing to the audience's subconscious belief that femininity itself is artificial. . . . In fact, it's the assumption that femininity is inherently 'contrived,' 'frivolous,' and 'manipulative' that allows masculinity to always come off as 'natural,' 'practical,' and 'sincere' by comparison" (43; see also 53–64).
30. Joshua Gamson, *Freaks Talk Back: Tabloid Talk Shows and Sexual Nonconformity* (Chicago: University of Chicago Press, 1998), 138–69.
31. Cromwell, *Transmen & FTMs*, 137.
32. Jay Prosser credits Stone's work, along with the actions of similarly minded individuals, with the generation of a queer version of transsexuality: transgender. According to Prosser, "coming out; pride in marginality; a politics that deconstructs identity: many of transgender's tenets *are* queer." Prosser continues: "As transgendered or posttranssexual, the transsexual claims that queer place in the

borders: gender troubler now oppositional gender outlaw. . . . This is the significance of transgender's trade-in of passing for being read: the comfort of genetic-
sexed belonging for the platform of a political subjectivity" (*Second Skins: The
Body Narratives of Transsexuality* [New York: Columbia University Press, 1998],
173–74). To be clear, Prosser is also skeptical about posttranssexuality, advancing a politics of home that "would analyze the persistence of sexual difference
for organizing identity categories" (204). Of particular concern for Prosser is
the notion that "In pushing past a transsexual narrative ('post'), in ceding our
claims to sexed location, we relinquish what we do not yet have: the recognition
of our sexed realness; acceptance as men and women; fundamentally, the right
to gender homes" (204). As queer theory influenced queer politics and queer
actions informed queer theory, transgender individuals occupied this identity
category to signal their rejection of the norms established by medicalized transsexuality. According to Stryker, in a 1992 manifesto titled *Transgender Liberation: A Movement Whose Time has Come*, Leslie Feinberg presented the transgender subject position as "somebody who permanently changed social gender
through the public presentation of self, without recourse to genital transformation." More than just a repudiation of medicalized transsexuality, Feinberg's
usage of "transgender" hailed "a political alliance between all individuals who
were marginalized or oppressed due to their difference from social norms of
gendered embodiment, and who should therefore band together in a struggle
for social, political, and economic justice" ("(De)Subjugated Knowledges: An
Introduction to Transgender Studies," in *The Transgender Studies Reader*, ed.
Susan Stryker and Stephen Whittle [New York: Routledge, 2006], 4). Similarly,
Kate Bornstein, a performance artist and writer, challenged what she termed
"Gender Defenders" who "actively, or by knowing inaction, defends the status
quo of the existing gender system, and thus perpetuates the violence of male
privilege and all its social extensions." Explicitly addressing those who passed,
Bornstein wrote, "I agree that hiding, and not proclaiming one's transsexual status, is an unworthy stance, more heinous if one's invisible status is maintained
with the purpose of gaining power." Praising the creation of transgender subject
positions, Bornstein further declared: "Transsexuals are moving, however, in
the direction of openly embracing their borderline status—either willingly, or
by the probing eye of public interest—and the debate on being or not-being out
as a transsexual is, at this writing, heating up" (*Gender Outlaw: On Men, Women,
and the Rest of Us* [New York: Routledge, 1994], 74, 76–77).

33. Sandy Stone, "The Empire Strikes Back: A Posttranssexual Manifesto," 2004
    http://www.actlab.utexas.edu/~sandy/empire-strikes-back.

34. Serano, *Whipping Girl*, 346.

35. Serano, *Whipping Girl*, 347.

36. Serano, *Whipping Girl*, 351.

37. Pat Califia, *Sex Changes: The Politics of Transgenderism* (San Francisco: Cleis
    Press, 1997), 275.

38. Judith Butler, *Bodies That Matter: On the Discursive Limits Of "Sex"* (New York: Routledge, 1993), 227.

39. Phaedra Pezzullo provides an exemplary articulation of this imperfect practice of politics in "Contextualizing Boycotts and Buycotts: The Impure Politics of Consumer-Based Advocacy in an Age of Global Ecological Crisis," *Communication and Critical/Cultural Studies* 8 (2011): 124–45. Like so many other times before, her words, this time in the form of an essay, arrived at just the right time to help me make sense of this concluding chapter.

40. Lawrence Grossberg, *We Gotta Get Out of this Place: Popular Conservatism and Postmodern Culture* (New York: Routledge, 1992), 388.

41. Grossberg, *We Gotta Get Out*, 396.

42. Grossberg, *We Gotta Get Out*, 396.

43. Dean Spade, *Normal Life: Administrative Violence, Critical Trans Politics, and the Limits of Law* (Brooklyn, NY: South End Press, 2011), 28.

44. Spade, *Normal Life*, 68-9.

Agency, 28–29, 39–44; discursive theory of, 45; enabling constraints, 181, 183; legal, 24, 101, 163; limited view, 23; lived experience, 17, 39, 54, 180–181; non-state centered, 41, 57, 100, 180; and norms, 26, 97–98, 181; as performative, 71; and performative repertoires, 39–40, 54–55, 179; and publicity, 43; and recognition, 43, 97, 179; and resistance, 41; spaces and subjects, 71; trans, 205n18; undoing, 58, 179, 182

Allen, Danielle, 24–25, 144

Althusser, Louis, 42–44, 179, 207n29. *See also* Interpellation

Americans with Disabilities Act (ADA), 65–67, 77, 182

Aravosis, John, 152–155, 157

Articulation, 7–9, 126, 196n17, 196n18. *See also* Cultural studies

Asen, Robert, 6

Austin, J. L., 42, 44

Benjamin, Harry, 12, 23

Bornstein, Kate, 184, 209n52, 228n32

Brandzel, Amy, 31, 97–98

Brown, Wendy, 143–144, 173–174, 226n7

Burke, Kenneth, 79–80

Butler, Judith: agency as performative, 40–44; critical queerness, 82–83, 140–141; feminisms, 206n25; interpellation, 24; necessary error of identity, 198n27; norms, 179; performative contradictions, 27; performativity of identity, 56; sex and gender, 13; subjectivity, 45; trans agency, 206n18; undoing, 58, 179–180; visibility politics, 189–190

Califia, Patrick, 16, 189

Certeau, Michel de, 69–71, 87, 213n22

Cisgender, 14–15, 200n44

Citizenship, 5–7; acts of, 29; as articulation, 8, 17, 21; and bathrooms, 61; dominant

logics as opportunity, 192; habits of, 144; as lived experience, 16–18, 24; narrow definitions, 17, 97–100; and neoliberalism, 96–97, 118; as normative, 27–28, 31, 98–99, 126, 181; as performative contradiction, 27, 164, 177; performativity of, 28–29, 35, 126; and place and space, 30; queering, 31–33, 95, 98–100; and quotidian practices, 98; rhetoricity of, 7, 17, 178. *See also* Queer liberalism; Wholeness/ Oneness

Clarkson, Nick, 108–109, 112

Coalitional politics: bathrooms as site of, 76, 82; and communal interests, 64, 159–160; disability and genderqueer, 80; HIV advocates and disability advocates, 66–67; identity, 136, 144, 157; law as site of, 191; LGBT, 33; LGBT and queer, 157; opportunities beyond LGB, 193; queer, 64, 82; trans and disabled activists, 29, 86. *See also* People in Search of Safe and Accessible Restrooms (PISSAR); United ENDA

Cobb, Michael, 27

Compulsory heterosexuality, 9, 79, 197n25

Conquergood, Dwight, 39, 205n16

Consubstantiality, 68–69, 79–80

Contingency: and agency, 5, 41, 55, 183; and political advocacy, 192; and queerness, 55, 83, 183

Coombe, Rosemary, 21, 182, 202n75

Crenshaw, Kimberlé Williams, 102–104, 210n4

Critical Legal Studies (CLS): hegemony, 104; ideology thesis and indeterminacy thesis, 100–102; race and feminist critiques, 102–104; rights assertion, 16–17, 100, 103, 105, 109, 126, 174; trashing 100, 102–103, 218n20

Critical trans politics, 193

Cultural studies, 18–20, 97

Currah, Paisley, 16, 18, 28, 106, 198n26

Left legalism, 34–35, 174, 180, 183. *See also*
  Brown, Wendy; Halley, Janet
Legal Cultural Studies (LCS), 18–19
Legal incrementalism, 56, 97
Legibility, 58, 72, 178–179
Lesbian, Gay, Bisexual, Transgender (LGBT):
  employment discrimination, 131–136; and
  "gay" as umbrella, 141; and normativities,
  32–33, 126; and people with disabilities, 64,
  67, 211n11; politics of naming, 195n2; politics
  of respectability and, 77–78; and relationship to queer, 142, 217n10, 222n17; stigma
  and pride, 81–82, 87–88; unity, 157–158,
  160–161
Lewin, Ellen, 221n5
Livability, 45, 58, 209n71
Lucaites, John, 21, 38

Marriage: critiques of, 96, 220n5; race and
  class implications, 220n4; same-sex civil,
  129–131; as subversive, 221n5; as tension for
  coalitional politics, 32, 112, 115, 134
Massey, Doreen, 74
Mayne, Debbie, 22–24; and agency, 42–43,
  45–46, 56; correspondence with Harry Ben-
  jamin, 46–54; performative repertoires, 183;
  public and hidden transcripts, 39–40, 55
McRuer, Robert, 83, 211n11
Metronormativity, 94
Meyerowitz, Joanne, 22, 199n36, 203n1, 205n18
Michaels, Walter Benn, 140, 224n29
Morris, Charles, 40
Muñoz, José Esteban, 96

Namaste, Vivian, 9, 199n35
National Center for Lesbian Rights, 116, 155
National Center for Transgender Equality
  (NCTE), 14, 132
National Gay and Lesbian Task Force
  (NGLTF), 132, 150
The New Republic (*TNR*), 163–176
Nietzsche, Friedrich, 45, 143
Norms, 25–26; distinguishing among, 58;
  dynamic relationship with, 163; invocation
  and critique, 27–28; mythic, 86; as produc-
  tive, 178–179; and queer, 167; as regulatory
  force, 98. *See also* Impure politics; Law:
  two-track approach to; Undoing

Paranoid readings, 20, 201n69. *See also*
  Reparative readings
People in Search of Safe and Accessible Restrooms (PISSAR): and coalitional politics,
  29–30, 68, 82; and queer politics, 69, 83;
  resistant subjectivities, 182; and shame,
  77–79, 82; and spatial politics, 80–81, 87;
  theory and praxis, 84

Performative repertoires, 23, 39, 40, 46, 54–55,
  179, 183, 205n15
Performativity, 39, 42; invention and agency,
  55; politics of, 57; and quotidian qualities,
  207n27. *See also* Agency: as performative;
  Citizenship: performativity of; Identity:
  performativity of
Pezzullo, Phaedra, 229n39
Phelan, Shane, 98
Place/Space, 213n22; and citizenship, 30; place
  as space, 70, 72; and power, 71; rhetorical
  productions in, 68, 86–87; space as practiced place, 69; space and bodies, 74
Posttranssexuality, 164, 184, 186, 188, 190,
  228n32
Prosser, Jay, 227n32
Public bathrooms: and accessibility, 31; and
  cultural norms, 64, 73, 83; harassment and
  violence, 38, 75; and making a public, 61,
  63, 72; men's, 73; racial segregation, 62–63,
  210n4; regulation of, 59, 72–73; and religion, 210n11; and shame, 76–77, 86; women's,
  73
Public transcripts, 23, 38, 52, 186; awareness
  of, 109; incompleteness of, 205n18; instability of, 187; underwritten by hidden transcripts, 53, 194. *See also* Hidden transcripts;
  Scott, James
Publicity, 27, 38, 43

Queer: citizenship, 31–33, 95, 98; critically
  queer, 82–83; and disability, 211n11; and
  LGBT, 217n10, 222n17; and mythic norms,
  25–26, 170, 172, 203n85; as open mesh, 29;
  as performative, 134; politics, 139–140; and
  stigma and shame, 81; as umbrella term, 141;
  and unachievable queerness, 34–35, 167
Queer liberalism, 32, 96–96, 101
Queer studies, 9, 25, 56, 88, 139, 197n21; and
  the law, 90; and paranoid readings, 20; and
  queer theory, 167
Queer world-making, 6, 97

Raymond, Janice, 141, 187, 198n25, 205n18
Recognition: absence of as productive, 56–57;
  and agency, 97, 178, 183; and assimilation,
  94; intersubjective, 39, 42–43, 45; legal,
  16, 57, 99, 103; and legal agency, 24; limits
  of, 181; and misrecognition, 198n27; and
  norms, 167, 193–194; problematics of, 179
Rehabilitation Act of 1973, 64–65, 212n13
Reparative readings, 20, 25, 172, 201n69. *See
  also* Paranoid readings
Resistance: and hegemony, 41, 206n22; and
  hidden transcripts, 205n14; and power, 26;
  and queer studies, 25; spatiality of, 70–71.
  See also Hidden transcripts; Queer

ABOUT THE AUTHOR

Isaac West is Assistant Professor in the Departments of Communication Studies and Gender, Women's, and Sexuality Studies at the University of Iowa and serves on the Board of Directors for the Project on the Rhetoric of Inquiry.